A Family of Pioneers

The Evolution of a Wilderness Farm into a Modern Community on the Shore of Bay Lake

Albert L. Knieff

Front cover photo: This is a reproduction of one of Heinrich Knieff's watercolor paintings (1885) showing the home of Knieff's Indian neighbor, Kahwessie, and his family. The future Knieff home can be seen in the background, as Heinrich visualized that it would someday be, although it had not yet been completed at the time of his death.

Back cover photos:
Upper left: The author and his wife Judy with daughters Kirsten and baby Erin, as they celebrated the Knieff's Centennial in 1983.
Upper right: The Knieff home as it is today.
Lower left: "Old Man Depression," as he appeared, ready to be burned at the stake, in the summer of 1934.
Lower right: Author at the entrance to Knieff's Shore Acres.

ISBN: 0-9652032-0-4

Library of Congress Catalog Number: 96-94602

Prepress preparation by North Star Press of St. Cloud, Inc., St. Cloud, Minnesota.

Printed in the United States of America by Versa Press, Inc., East Peoria, Illinois.

Published by:

KSA Publishing
16750 Knieff Shore Drive, NE
Deerwood, Minnesota 56444-8028
Phone: (218) 678-2816

A Division of Knieff's Shore Acres

A special thanks to the family of Ed Keith, who spent his summers here during the early years of the resort. He was an accomplished photographer, and the picture albums he sent to us as gifts have supplied most of the pictures used in this book from that era. I would also like to acknowledge Mr. Charlie Topel, who, as a friend and fellow worker of my father's, took the early Montana pictures. All other photos are from the family albums.

Happy Birthday 1998
Love Adeline
Don & Anne
Emily
Hope you enjoy
the book!

A Family of Pioneers

Dedication

To my parents
who, by their love and the example they set for me,
as well as by their vivid stories of the past,
instilled in me the precepts
on which our little community is founded;

to my wife Judy,
whose help and constant encouragement
and suggestions kept me going;

to my two daughters,
Kirsten and Erin,
who will one day have to carry on the tradition;

and to all of you who have lived here
and played such an active roll in our development,

I most humbly dedicate these words.

Albert L. Knieff
July 4, 1996

The original pen and ink drawing from which the front cover picture was painted.

Forward

The fire in the kitchen stove casts a warm glow as I sit at the table in front of the big picture window and watch the huge flakes of snow gambol and tumble their way to the ground. All detail of the lake and its surrounding shoreline are fused, nearly obliterated by the dazzling, swirling whiteness as it casts a shroud of mystery over the muted landscape. It is a typical winter day in northern Minnesota, yet, as my eyes strive to pierce its depth, my mind is caught up in a peculiar reverie of long ago.

I see the land, not as it is now, but as it was in its primordial state. The great glaciers have withdrawn, leaving behind a rolling, pockmarked landscape of glacial drift. The huge Lake Agassiz, once filled with their meltwater, has receded, but the thousands of deeper depressions remain as our present-day lakes, while countless shallower depressions have succumbed to the forces of eutrophication to become bogs and swampland.

In my reverie I leave the cozy confines of my kitchen and stand, instead, in the forest of huge white and Norway pine that once occupied this spot. At ten degrees above zero, it is not cold by the usual standards of this area, and I am sheltered from the modest wind by the hill at my back. Not so the lofty pines, which whisper their joy at the slight breeze rustling their lofty boughs. A saucy red squirrel barks displeasure at my intrusion, his twitching tail punctuating each verbal blast. I have interrupted him as he dines upon a pine cone, while sitting on a low hanging branch.

Slowly I turn and make my way westward along the shore of the lake. Walking is easy here, for while there is over a foot of snow out on the lake, the giant green boughs above me have retained much of it as it fell, and what has sifted through is light, fluffy and undrifted. There is very little underbrush to thwart my passage because the green canopy above has stilled its growth. As I look out over the lake, the dead brown stalks of last summer's bull rushes bend under the weight of their snowy coats to form a tangled jungle. Only an occasional seed head remains upright to wave its defiance at the onslaught.

As I continue my walk, I become aware of a subtle change in the terrain. The sandy ridge along the lake remains, but the land behind it dips slightly below the level of the lake and assumes the character of a swamp. Here the pine give way to ash, alder, and hazelbrush, as though disdaining to wet their feet in the mire. If I look closely, I can see the outlines of cottontail rabbit trails in the tall grass and underbrush. I will skirt this marshy area by straying further from the lake, where higher ground supports a mixed stand of deciduous trees, primarily oak, maple, and basswood. This is the domain of the gray squirrel, evidenced by the well-worn entry holes into a hollow oak or basswood tree. Further along, I see the remains of a fallen giant oak, no doubt the victim of a summer storm or lightening strike.

Slowly, I awake from my reverie and realize that my vision has been prompted by a very real need to preserve the memories of this land as it was when my father first came to it as a two-year-old boy. I must tell again those stories that he delighted in telling, so that my daughters may know and cherish them as I have. Perhaps there will be others who will also recognize it as a part of their heritage.

But more than this, I must relive its evolution from my grandfather's original wilderness family farm of the nineteenth century, to the carefully knit little community of homes that it has become as we approach the twenty-first century. The transition has been gradual, progressing only fitfully over the years. Its course has followed the dictates of economic necessity, but always within those fundamental principles that had lead Grandfather Knieff to seek out his home in a land where he believed freedom, honor, and decency would prevail. Now, more that ever before, we must recognize the duty we have to cherish the land we live on as an inestimable gift from our Creator, given into our care, a heritage for our future generations.

Contents

A Family of Pioneers

This is a pen and ink sketch made by Heinrick in later years after the sawmill had arrived.
It depicts the same area as is described in the opening scene.

Chapter 1

Heinrich Fredrich Jacob Knieff

The patter of raindrops mingled with the creaking of the wagon wheels as the little caravan slowly made its way up the sandy trail to the crest of yet another hill. Occasionally distant echoes of thunder could still be heard as the late afternoon shower retreated to the east. Moses, the patient old ox, sore of foot from the long trek northward, heaved a sigh as though aware that the journey's end was nearly at hand. He stepped into the little opening at the top of the hill and came to a halt. Below them the family beheld a lake, its limpid surface only occasionally dimpled by the last remnants of the shower. The shore line twisted and turned as it receded into the distance, forming a variety of points and secluded bays, where white and yellow water lilies bloomed in profusion. From the right, a narrow, sharp-ridged point thrust its rock-tipped finger eastward, far out into the lake toward the large island that dominated the center of the bay. The shore line rose abruptly to form high rolling hills, which were crowned with towering white pines as for as far as the eye could see. Along the shore, and in the lower areas, oak, maple, and other hardwoods stretched their limbs to form a green-leafed bower. Occasionally a birch stood starkly white among its dark-skinned neighbors.

As the storm clouds gave way to a clear azure sky, the first rays of the reappearing sun mingled with the lingering mist to create a vivid rainbow that, when viewed from the top of the hill, formed a complete arc encircling the panorama before them.

After staring in awed silence for a few moments, Louise turned to her husband and said, "Henry, is this really Sis-e-bag-a-mah, the Lake of Many Bays, where we are to live?"

"Only a small part of it," he replied. "Our homestead is about two miles further on around the lake. What do you think of it?"

"Surely God in His Infinite Goodness could not have prepared a more beautiful welcome than this!"

So it was that Heinrich Frederic Jacob Knieff and his family arrived at Bay Lake in the late summer of 1883. Heinrich was tall for men of that era, though his broad and muscular shoulders belied his declining health. His heavy, dark, wavy hair, though receding from his forehead, fell to his shoulders and merged with his full beard to accentuate his high cheek bones and finely chiseled aquiline nose. But Heinrich's eyes were his most striking feature. Deeply set under his massive brow, they peered out from beneath his bushy eyebrows, steel grey and piercing, to invoke a vision of sternness and conviction. Even vicious dogs were said to have slunk away with their tails between their legs when favored by his fierce,

Heinrich Fredrich Jacob Knieff

unyielding stare. Yet this harsh demeanor belied a kind and gentle nature concealed within.

Louise Knieff

Louise, Heinrich's wife, was a small woman, whose long dark brown hair was pulled up in a bun on the top of her head. Her fragile body was sustained by a powerful inner spirit that never deserted her, in good times or in bad, and was manifested by her cheerful disposition and strong religious faith. With them were their three sons: Max, age ten; Oscar, who was six; and little Hugo, who was only two years old. Two older boys from Heinrich's first marriage, Edward and Johannes, were also with them. Arthur, the eight-year old, had been left behind with friends because of his delicate health, and would not rejoin the family until the following spring.

Why would a family with small children journey so far north into the relatively unknown wilderness to find a new home? We must search for the answer in Heinrich's past. His father, Klaus Heinrich Knieff, was born in Kroeplin, Germany, in 1762. Heinrich, the youngest of a second family, was born in Hamburg, Germany, in 1822. Six years later his father died, and at the age of fourteen, Heinrich was apprenticed to a tinsmith. After serving his four years as an apprentice, he traveled as a journeyman tinsmith through the Baltic countries to Turkey, Asia Minor, Jerusalem, and Rome. Heinrich was not of the Catholic faith, but he did visit the Vatican and was presented with a crucifix by Pope Gregory XVI. It became one of Heinrich's most cherished possessions. Leaving Rome, Heinrich proceeded to Alexandria, Egypt, where he boarded a Dutch vessel and headed homeward with a stopover in Spain.

When Heinrich arrived in Hamburg, he learned that his mother had died while he was away. With no home to return to, and a keen sense of adventure still in his heart, he shipped aboard a sailing vessel. Heinrich followed the life of the sea for over a year until, in 1845, he left the ship in New Orleans where he had a half sister. But work was scarce there, so he traveled on, plying his trade in Rochester, New York; Covington, Kentucky; and Cincinnati, Ohio. It was here, in 1853, that Heinrich met and married Doris Schlaffer. While living in Cincinnati, Heinrich became involved with a group of Germans, many of whom had fled from a period of political and religious unrest that pervaded Germany during the middle of the nineteenth century. They were to form the society of "American Turners," which was dedicated to the principles of "liberty against all oppression, justice against all exploitation, reason against all superstition, free speech, free press, and free assembly for discussion."

In 1856, Heinrich left Cincinnati with a group selected by the Turners and organized as the "German Land Association," to develop a new town out west in the Minnesota Territory. They traveled by steamboat down the Ohio River to its confluence with the Mississippi, then up the Mississippi to St. Paul. From there, they traveled by horse and wagon to their future home on the Minnesota River, which they named New Ulm. Their families would join them there the following spring.

Heinrich took a claim across the river from the new town where he built the first ferry across the Minnesota River in that area. After several years of operating the ferry, he sold it and moved into the village where he set up its first tin shop.

In the summer of 1862, Heinrich left his wife and their four small children to answer his adopted country's call. He headed for Fort Snelling where he enlisted in the Union Army on August 14th, and became a member of Company G of the Sixth Minnesota Infantry. He was still at the fort when the Sioux began their fateful uprising at New Ulm. Heinrich's wife, Doris, and the four children escaped to the fortified center of town, but their home and all of their belongings, including Heinrich's crucifix, were destroyed by fire. Later they were piled aboard a wagon and carried to St. Peter for safety. During the confusion of fire and smoke at the time of their departure, their youngest son, John, became separated from the rest of the family. Fortunately, the sharp eyes of one of the refugee women spotted the little lad running down the dusty road behind them and returned him to Doris.

Sketch made by Heinrich during the Indian campaign.

Meanwhile, Company G joined the forces of Colonel Henry Sibley and left Fort Snelling to put down the Indian uprising. It was with great relief that Heinrich discovered Doris and the children safely in St. Peter when the troops paused there for a brief rest.

The Indian campaign continued for nearly two years as the soldiers pursued the renegades through western Minnesota and the Dakotas, fighting major skirmishes at Birch Coulee and Wood Lake. It was during this time that Heinrich's natural talent as an artist became known. He was deployed as a scout to search out enemy positions and sketch them, as well as to make sketches of their own encampments and troop movements. Some of his sketches would later become a part of the permanent war records.

In June 1864, the Sixth Minnesota was finally sent south to play its part in the Civil War. Their first stop was at Camp Buford in Arkansas. It was an evil place, dirty, crowded and beset by pestilence. Heinrich was one of the fortunate 185 out of the original 900 men who survived the terrible four-month ordeal there, and remained physically fit for battle. Later he traveled to Memphis, which he described in a letter to his wife as "a very nice city [that] leaves Cincinnati way behind. If it just wasn't located so far south." He complained bitterly of the heat, which reached temperatures of 110 degrees in the shade, and concluded by saying, "Give me Minnesota, the paradise of the north. Give me 10,000 acres with niggers, mules, and cotton would I not take, even if made a present of, should I have to live here. Happy is the person who can live in Minnesota."

Heinrich, now Sergeant Knieff, was sent with his company to St. Louis in November 1864, and from there to Nashville, where they joined with other Minnesota regiments and went on to Alabama. There, they fought in the Mobile campaign under General Edward Canby. The campaign was concluded with the capture of Mobile. The surrender of the last of the Confederate armies, in May 1865, brought an end to the hostilities.

Sergeant Knieff was stationed in Montgomery, Alabama, until August 19, 1865, when he was mustered out of the service. After his discharge, he returned to Cincinnati where his family had been living. Together they returned to Heinrich's beloved Minnesota. They now made their home near the village of Long Lake on the shores of Crystal Bay, Lake Minnetonka. Heinrich, or Henry as he then preferred to be called, worked as a tinsmith in Minneapolis, commuting daily on the trolley that ran out from the city. On October 15, 1868, Doris gave birth to the last of their family, twin girls. But the ordeal was too great for her and Doris succumbed in the effort, leaving Henry with seven surviving children to be cared for by the eldest daughter, Carrie, a girl of fourteen.

Four years later, Henry left the children with friends of the family, and took a trip back to Nauvoo, Illinois. There he met Louise Wasserzieher. They were married in Minneapolis on October 12, 1872. Henry returned with his bride to the shores of Lake Minnetonka where their four sons were born.

In 1883 Henry decided that it was time to move again. He had traveled on foot over three continents, sailed the seven seas and fought in the great war between the states. Now he was tired, his health had been failing since his years in the service, and he felt crowded in by the rapidly growing metropolitan area. By 1871 the Northern Pacific railroad had started building westward from Duluth to Puget Sound, and speculation was rife about a new industrial center that would soon be built up on the north shore of Bay Lake, near the new railroad. The prospects for development were bright, free government land was available, and the opportunity to find a new and better life for his family, while he was yet able, stirred the adventure in his soul.

Chapter 2

The New Land

This was not the first trip north for Henry Knieff. Earlier in the summer he and his brother-in-law, Otto Wasserzieher, who had decided to join the Knieffs and bring his family north also, had made the journey into the new land to find suitable sites for their future homesteads.

In 1862, the Homestead Act was approved by Congress. It allowed a family to settle on unoccupied government land and claim 160 acres of it for their own. They were required to file a claim, build a home on the claim, live on it, and cultivate the land for a period of at least five years before a patent would be issued to them by the federal government. When the Northern Pacific Railroad was built, one of the inducements to its founders was that they would be given title to every odd-numbered section of land in a strip of land extending six miles on either side of the right of way. For that reason, only the even-numbered sections of land were available for homesteading in the northern part of Bay Lake township.

Henry chose his land in section two, along the north shore of Bay Lake. Although the lake was much smaller, its configuration reminded him of his old home on Lake Minnetonka. Here, too, he could look southward across a broad stretch of water and receive its cooling breezes in the heat of summer. To the north, a high hill and a heavy stand of timber would shelter him from the chilling winds of winter. Between the hill and lake, a level stretch of rich loam soil would provide an excellent garden site.

Otto chose his land in section six of Hazelton township of Aitkin County, which lies adjacent to Bay Lake township on the east, so the two farms would be separated by only a section of railroad land. Otto had been reared in the grape-growing country around Nauvoo, Illinois, where his family had a winery. His land was of a heavy clay soil, which would be excellent for raising grapes and fruit trees. The property was bounded on the south by Echo Lake, which was originally called Long Lake, then later changed from Echo Lake to Tame Fish Lake. Otto chose to build his home some distance back from the lake, on higher ground.

An air of excitement and expectation continued to grow as the Knieff family followed the meager cart track around the north shore of the lake. For the boys, each bend in the trail presented a new vision, a new concept of the extent and contour of the waters. Here new and mysterious bays constantly begged to be explored. For Henry and Louise, each step brought them closer to that new beginning about which they had dreamed for so long. Even old Moses appeared to quicken his pace, and the cow at the end of her tether behind the wagon lowed softly at the smell of fresh water.

They passed a newly built house set back from the lake on a gently curving point. The point commanded a broad view of the island and the long reaches of water on either side of it. This was the home of Dave Archibald, the brother of Robert Archibald, who was the first settler in the town of Deerwood. Dave had built his new

(4—404.)

THE UNITED STATES OF AMERICA,

To all to whom these presents shall come, Greeting:

Homestead Certificate No. 7404
APPLICATION 13063

Whereas There has been deposited in the General Land Office of the United States a Certificate of the Register of the Land Office at Saint Cloud, Minnesota, whereby it appears that, pursuant to the Act of Congress approved 20th May, 1862, "To secure Homesteads to actual Settlers on the Public Domain," and the acts supplemental thereto, the claim of Louise Knieff widow of Henry F. J. Knieff deceased has been established and duly consummated, in conformity to law, for the West half of the North East quarter and the Lots numbered one and two of Section two in Township forty five North of Range twenty eight West of the Fourth Principal Meridian in Minnesota containing one hundred and sixty one acres and twelve hundredths of an acre according to the Official Plat of the survey of the said Land, returned to the General Land Office by the Surveyor General:

Now know ye, That there is, therefore, granted by the United States unto the said Louise Knieff the tract of Land above described: TO HAVE AND TO HOLD the said tract of Land, with the appurtenances thereof, unto the said Louise Knieff and to her heirs and assigns forever.

In testimony whereof, I, Benjamin Harrison, President of the United States of America, have caused these letters to be made Patent, and the Seal of the General Land Office to be hereunto affixed.

Given under my hand, at the City of Washington, the fifteenth day of September, in the year of our Lord one thousand eight hundred and ninety one, and of the Independence of the United States the one hundred and sixteenth.

BY THE PRESIDENT: Benjamin Harrison
By Ellen Macfarland Asst, Secretary.
I. R. Connell, Recorder of the General Land Office.
ad interim

Recorded, Vol. 15, Page 401.

Copy of the Knieff homestead certificate filed in 1891 after Louise finished proving up the claim.

home two years before, becoming the first white settler in Bay Lake Township.

The trail finally left the shore of the lake and rose to higher ground. Beyond, a clearing came into view. Toward one side stood a small house and several outbuildings. This was the home of Nick Newgard, who had recently sold his home in Deerwood, and taken up the new homestead at Bay Lake. He had befriended Henry on his first trip north, and now welcomed him and his family with the true fellowship of the frontier. Nick's had been a lonely life, as his wife had died in 1878 after less than a year of marriage. Though quiet and retiring by nature, Nick was well pleased at the prospect of having new friends and neighbors.

It was decided that the Knieffs would stay temporarily in Nick's new ten-by-fourteen-foot log building, which he planned to use as a chicken coop in the spring. At least they would have some sort of roof over their heads until they could build a log "claim shanty" on their own property. Their meager belongings were soon unloaded from the wagon, and the little iron cook stove set up in their temporary home. Later, a table, some benches, and a double bed would have to be built. The boys would have to sleep on the floor. This meant that all of the following winter, table and benches would have to be carried out of doors at night to make room for their hay-filled pallets. The cow and the ox would be tethered at night and allowed to roam freely with Nick's cow during the day, as no one yet had the luxury of fences for their cattle. When the snow came, they would find shelter in Nick's barn. On their first trip north, Henry and Otto had cut slough grass from the meadow along Ripple River, or Mud River as it was then called, which connects Bay Lake with Echo Lake and eventually runs into the Mississippi River in Aitkin. This was the winter feed for their cattle.

The next morning dawned bright and warm, and it was with great excitement that the Knieff family set off down the trail to view, for the first time together, their new home. Little Hugo's short legs could not sustain their eager pace, so he rode the shoulders of older brother John, while Max and Oscar raced on ahead. The trail soon presented another glimpse of the lake, then dipped down around the edge of a small marsh overgrown with cattails and edged with alder brush, to reemerge at the water's edge. Here the little party stopped. Henry, with the first glisten of an ill-concealed tear in his eye and a catch in his throat, turned to his wife and said, "This will be our new land, Louisa, from that little point there on our right around to where the river leaves the lake, just beyond that other point there on the left. We will build our claim shanty up there," he added as he pointed across the trail from where they stood. "There is so much to be done, clearing and building, but it will be good, you'll see."

"Oh, I am sure that it will, Henry," she replied. "It is so beautiful, so peaceful. God grant that it will never change."

But even this quiet, unspoiled land had not always known peace. There was a time when savage cries of battle echoed across the waters and the beaches were bathed in blood. From time immemorial, the Dakota or Sioux Indians had roamed this land, from the endless prairies of southwestern Minnesota and the Dakotas, to the primeval deciduous forests of south central Minnesota, to the coniferous forests of the north, and to the shores of mighty Lake Superior. Their many clans had lived together in relative harmony, traveling with the seasons to hunt the deer and bison, to fish the lakes and streams, and to harvest the wild rice. They followed the wild bee to its hive for its honey, and tapped the maple tree for its sweet juice, which they evaporated to make syrup or sugar.

The development of white colonies on the East Coast however, soon led to traumatic cultural disruptions as far west as the Mississippi and Missouri River basins. The vast store of wealth in the form of fur-bearing animals brought the French Voyageurs and their English counterparts into the new land to supply the demand for furs on the European market. As the pressure of trapping diminished the ready supply of pelts in one area, the trappers moved ever westward. Fur trading companies sprang up, setting up trading posts where traps and supplies were traded for pelts. The Indians soon learned that there was a ready supply of the white man's trinkets, guns, and firewater available to them in exchange for furs. Advancing white settlements, and the resultant clearing of land, exerted pressure on the affected tribes to also move westward, in search of more abundant game and furs. These displaced tribes enjoyed the benefit of having already traded for the white man's muskets, and this gave them a distinct advantage of arms over the tribes that they in turn sought to displace. By the beginning of the eighteenth century, the Chippewa, more properly called Ojibway, tribes, and who called themselves "Anishinabe" or "the people," had secured firearms, and were beginning to push into the territory that had for so long been the home of the Sioux. Great battles ensued, which gradually forced the Sioux westward onto the great plains. The "Forty Sioux Villages" of Kathio at Mille Lacs Lake were captured in 1745, and the last Sioux stronghold in central Minnesota at Leech Lake was taken in 1748.

The point across the bay from the Knieff homestead was the site of one of the last of these battles. Here, the Chippewa discovered a Sioux encampment. The Indian custom was not to fight at night, because it was believed that a slain warrior's spirit would have difficulty finding its way to the Happy Hunting Ground without the light of the sun to guide it. So the Chippewa waited until the first rays of the morning sun glittered on the face of the water. Then with great stealth they crept up to the still-slumbering camp and set fire to the teepees. As the startled and dazed Sioux emerged from their burning lodges, they were met with a devastating hail of arrows and gunfire from the encircling Chippewas. The few Sioux who escaped the massacre fled from the area never to return, leaving only the bones of their fallen brothers and the memories of the battle of Battle Point.

Fortunately, the animosities that had frequently developed in the past between the Indians and the white settlers had now been largely forgotten, and firm friendships developed between members of the two races. One such friendship was that which was soon to develop between Kahwessie and the Knieffs. Kahwessie was a full-blooded Indian whose family was a part of the Chippewa tribe that lived along the western shore of Mille Lacs Lake. His story has been passed down in different versions by different people, but Henry, when he met Kahwessie on his first trip north, was given the following account: One evening Kahwessie was sitting around a campfire with some other young braves from his tribe when one of them passed around a bottle of the white man's firewater. When it came Kahwessie's turn to drink he refused, upon which one of the other braves picked up a stick whose end was smoldering in the fire and thrust it under Kahwessie's nose causing him to jerk back. Seeing this, the culpable teaser said, "Hmmm Squaw." Being referred to as a squaw, or woman, constituted the ultimate insult to a hot-blooded young warrior. A fight ensued in which Kahweesie stabbed the offender to death with his knife. Indian law decreed that the dead man's family could extract vengeance by killing Kahwessie, so he was forced to leave the village and live elsewhere. Thus he came to be living just across the river from the Knieff homestead with his wife and their son. The Knieffs always treated Kahwessie and his family with kindness and respect, and, in turn, Kahwessie taught them many things of great value about their newly adopted land.

Chapter 3

Building a Claim Shanty

Now the long and arduous task of hewing out a homestead began. Early each morning Henry and the older boys would harness faithful old Moses to the wagon, and together they would set off down the trail to work. Soon the rhythmic sound of their axes would fill the air with music, accented by the sound of falling trees.

Their first project was to make a clearing where the claim shanty would be built. As the trees were felled, those suitable for building were trimmed and skidded to the building site. The oak and maple were piled and allowed to dry for firewood. Brush and tree tops were piled to await an early snowfall when they could be safely burned. Stumps in the area east of the claim shanty, which had been designated as the future garden area, had to be grubbed out before the frost came. This meant digging around each stump so that the roots could be cut off at least a foot below the surface of the ground so as not to interfere with plowing. When this was completed, Moses would be hitched to the stump, and while he pulled, the boys would pry with long poles until the stump came free.

The work progressed steadily, but a new problem confronted Henry. The family had left Minnetonka with all of their worldly goods piled on the wagon and with a small sum of money they had managed to save while Henry was working in Minneapolis. Now they had to buy their winter supply of food—two hundred pounds of flour, one hundred pounds of sugar, a barrel of apples, and a pig to butcher. This would cut a sizable hole in their meager savings and would leave precious little for the essentials required to complete their claim shanty and outfit their little farm. Their only income was the $8.00 per month pension that Henry received as a Civil War veteran.

The decision was made—Henry walked the seventeen miles into Aitkin where he found a job working at his trade. The Krech's, long time friends of the family who had recently moved from Minneapolis, furnished him with a room during the week, but every Saturday evening he walked the seventeen miles home, to spend Sunday with his family.

The Knieff family's attention now turned to constructing the claim shanty. First, a hole was dug about ten feet long, eight feet wide and five feet deep. This was lined with rough hewn timbers to prevent the walls from caving in. It would serve as a root cellar for storing potatoes, carrots and other vegetables, and whatever they had put up in glass jars that had to be protected from freezing. Entrance would be gained through a trap door cut in the floor of the kitchen.

The foundation of the building was simply four long straight logs notched at the ends to overlap each other. The floor was constructed of smaller logs that had been flattened on three sides with an adze to make them fit reasonably tight together and form a comparatively flat surface. Next came the walls of carefully fitted and notched logs, which were chinked with a mixture of clay and hay to make them weather-tight. The steeply pitched roof was also made of poles, which were covered with hand-split wooden shingles or shakes.

By the time winter set in, the little log house had assumed its full stature, but the many finishing touches that would transform it from a crude log building to a livable home remained to be done. Enough was finished, however, to get them by before the approaching cold weather made this type of work too difficult. Then the boys turned their attention to the equally important task of clearing more land.

Giant white pines were scattered among the hardwoods that grew between the lake and the hill, while behind the hill, on the higher ground that was to become the large field, the growth was predominately pine. Clearing the land of these giants would be a long and arduous task that would not be completed for several years. The trunks of these trees were preserved as saw logs, as a colony of settlers was due to be established the following spring and it was rumored that they planned to set up a saw mill. The tops and stumps from these trees were piled high in the ever growing clearing, and when they were finally set on fire, their flames lit up the sky and could be seen for miles.

The long winter passed, and, when the lengthening days of early March brought warmer weather, the Knieff boys were eager to try their hands at making sugar from the numerous hard maple trees left standing near the claim shanty. Kahwessie taught them how to cut a diagonal slash through the bark of the tree and into the sapwood. A piece of birch bark was then folded to form a trough and inserted at the lower end of the cut to catch the sap and direct it into the pail below. The pail was a two foot section of pine log hollowed out to form a crude trough. Every night the sap was collected from the wooden troughs and carried up to the house where Louise would boil it down in large pans on the back of her kitchen stove until it was syrup. The Indian way had been to boil the sap in a large kettle hung over an open fire. In the days before iron kettles were available, they had used containers made from birch bark. These would not burn on the area that was covered on the inside by sap. By recurving the container inward at the top, the upper section of it would not come into contact with the fire and burn as the sap boiled away. The sap in the trees would not run until the temperature got into the forty-degree range in the daytime, nor would it continue to run if the nighttime temperature failed to go below freezing. These conditions generally prevail from the middle of March until the middle of April, and when they did prevail, a tree could be expected to produce several quarts of sap each day. The sap had to be boiled down at a ratio of about forty-to-one to produce syrup or sixty-to-one to produce hard sugar.

Time has added many sophistications to this ancient process. The wooden troughs gave way to open pails, which in turn were supplanted by covered buckets, plastic bags or in some instances complex networks of plastic hose which delivers the sap directly into large storage containers. The diagonal slash on the tree was replaced by the use of spiles or wooden spigots. These were made by hollowing out the soft pithy center of a short length of sumac bush about an inch in diameter. This stick was then cut half way through about two inches from one end of the stick, which was then reversed and a similar cut made on the opposite end and on the opposite side. By splitting the wood from the bottom of one cut to the bottom of the other cut, two spiles would be formed from a single length of sumac. The fully round end of each spile was then tapered to a given dimension, usually eleven sixteenths of an inch. A hole of that size was drilled about one and one-half inches deep into the tree and the spile driven firmly into it. The sap—the result of a bleeding process of the tree—would collect in the hole and follow the hollowed out trough of the spile to the end where it would drip into the container below. These home made spiles later gave way to molded metal or plastic spiles, which would support the collecting vessel by inserting the spile through a hole cut into the upper portion of the container.

A pair of homemade wooden spiles made from a single length of sumac.

The kitchen stove was replaced by outdoor fireplaces, then by more elaborate furnaces or "arches," which could boil one or two large flat pans of sap with a single fire, and finally, by huge evaporators housed in well-ventilated sheds that are capable of "taking off" a more or less continuous flow of finished syrup. The old method of testing the thickness of the syrup by watching it drip off the end of a spoon, or "sheeting," (in the same way that grandmother tested her homemade jelly), has been replaced by a hydrometer, or a candy maker's thermometer, to give uniformity to the finished product. These refinements have been dictated by an increase in the number of trees tapped, from the twenty or thirty trees used to supply syrup for an individual family, to hundreds, or even thousands of trees tapped in a single commercial operation.

Yet, through this evolution of modernization, the mysticism and excitement of the maple "run" remains. When the lengthening days of spring bring moderating temperatures, and the winters accumulation of snow softens in the woods, those of us blessed with a stand of hard maple still feel the quickening in our souls at the resurgence of life we are about to behold. We greet the raucous cawing of the returning crows with the reverence due the first harbingers of spring, and eagerly comply with the time-honored traditions of the sugar bush. After a long hard day of splitting and hauling wood, gathering sap and bottling syrup, we sit long into the night tending the fire under the boiling sap. Huge clouds of sweet-scented steam engulf us as we listen to the wavering chorus of frogs as they emerge rejoicing from their long winter's nap at the bottom of the near-by slough. Their song awakens in our hearts the happy reflections of those long-departed days that were the beginnings of our tradition. They sing, too, of the quiet serenity and satisfaction of that moment when we rest our aching bodies from the days exertions, and contemplate the rewards of our labors. It is also a song of the future, when each new generation in its time will experience this annual reawakening, and the resurgence of spring.

When the last of the snow has melted from the ground, the strengthening rays of the spring sun are absorbed deep into the earth, drawing the last of the frost out of the ground. The rapidly warming earth radiates its newfound heat back into the air, and the nighttime temperatures no longer dip below freezing. The sap remains high in the trees and the sapping season is over for another year.

Chapter 4

The Indian Neighbors

Before the maples had ceased their flow, another early spring phenomenon diverted the boys' attention. One balmy, quiet, starlit evening, the family noticed a flickering light bobbing along on the water east of the claim shanty. Intrigued, the older boys set off along the shore to chase the strange will-o-the-wisp. An hour later they returned, wet to the knees and full of excitement. Breathlessly they explained that they had followed the light to the mouth of the river where they spied Kahwessie in his canoe. He was holding a blazing pine knot torch in one hand and a crude spear in the other as he slowly drifted in the open water that had recently appeared between the shore and the ice sheet that still covered most of the bay. As they watched, Kahwessie suddenly thrust his spear into the shallow water and dropped his torch athwart the gunnels of his canoe to free his other hand for the ensuing struggle. As the spear was withdrawn from the water, the boys were thrilled to behold a giant fish impaled upon its barb-pointed head. With one deft motion Kahwessie flipped the violently flopping fish into the canoe and kicked it off the spear. Then with one sweep of his paddle he sent the canoe gliding silently in to the shore where the boys stood watching, unaware that their presence had been noticed. With a broad smile Kahwessie held his torch aloft to reveal ten or twelve still flopping fish on the floor of the canoe.

"Greetings, young neighbors" he said softly. "The spirit of the waters has been kind to me this night. Take a big fish. Your family will eat good tomorrow."

"Gee, thanks, Kahwessie. A fresh fish sure would taste good about now," said Max with a big grin. "I'm gettin' plumb tired of salt pork."

At this point the boys proudly displayed the ten-pound walleyed pike that Kahwessie had given them. "Ain't he a beauty, mother" said Max. "I sure wish we had a canoe, so we could spear our own fish. Daddy, could we make one for ourselves? Please!"

"Well son," replied his father, "making a canoe takes a lot of experience and know-how. The new mill will be setting up soon, and, when our logs are sawed, we will build a regular boat."

"But—"

"Enough now. Get those wet clothes off before you catch a cold."

This was not the first time that Kahwessie had presented the Knieffs with much needed and appreciated gifts of fish, venison, and other game. Louise always had some homemade bread or other "white man's" food to give him in return. This was a rare treat for the Indians, who would invariably tear the bread apart with their hands and greedily munch it down on the spot.

So while the boys got ready for bed, Louise got out her jar of yeast stock and "set" a batch of sponge for the next day's baking. This was an almost nightly chore for the little mother with the family of hungry growing boys to feed, for their diet was simple, and homemade bread played a major role at every meal.

The yeast stock was an essential in every home in those days. It was made by adding a small amount of yeast "starter" to a quantity of warm water, preferably that which was poured off after potatoes had been boiled in it. This "potato water" furnished nutrients to the yeast, which would multiply rapidly when kept warm. After saving out a portion for future stock, the rest was mixed with salt, sugar, melted lard, and enough flour to make a thin batter or "sponge." This sponge was covered with a cloth and placed on the rear of the stove, where it would stay warm overnight. Under these conditions, the yeast would grow prodigiously, and, by morning, the sponge would have nearly doubled in volume. It was then kneaded down and the balance of the flour added to form the dough, which was again allowed to rise until it had doubled in volume. Kneaded a second time, the dough was made into loaves and allowed to rise a third time before baking. This was indeed hard work for the little woman who weighed scarcely one hundred pounds and suffered from angina and palpitations of the heart. But it was done, as were all of her numerous household chores, with love and cheerfulness and never a word of complaint.

So it was not until late the following afternoon that Louise sent Max and Oscar over to Kahwessie's camp, or "farm" as he called it, with two loaves of bread, still hot from the oven.

The boys found Kahwessie sprawled out on the ground in front of his wigwam, a picture of contentment. Nearby his wife had built a framework of green saplings to hold the fish Kahwessie had speared the night before. The fish had been split in two vertically from head to tail, salted, and hung over the saplings with their tails dangling over a low smudgy fire from which the smoke billowed in profusion. Dried in this way, they would keep for an extended period without spoiling.

Kahwessie's son, Dummy, was busily engaged before the fire with a length of ironwood he had fashioned into a crude spear. He would thrust the sharp end into the coals until it began to char, then quickly withdraw it and scrape away the charred portion with a sharp rock. This process would be repeated until the wood was thoroughly dry and nearly as hard as steel.

The Indian's canoe was pulled up on the bank of the lake, its snow-white birch bark contrasting starkly with the black mixture of balsam pitch and charcoal that calked its many seams. The wigwam had a similar appearance, though its seams were not as heavily covered with pitch. It had been made by implanting slender saplings in the ground in the shape of a rectangle. The tops of the saplings were then bent inward and their tops lashed together to form a framework for the birch-bark covering.

Sounds from behind the wigwam indicated that Kahwessie's wife was bringing in more wood for the fire. The quiet of the scene was suddenly shattered by the Indian's two dogs, which rose yapping and barking to greet the young visitors. As the boys approached, Kahwessie rose quickly, grunted his thanks for their offering, and in no time at all the Indians were busily munching their prize.

Dummy could not verbally add his thanks to that of his parents. He had been born both deaf and mute. Thus his name was intended to be descriptive not derogatory. The sparkle in his black eyes revealed his appreciation and the native intelligence that lurked within. He was Arthur's age and was rapidly becoming a good friend with whom the boys would spend many happy days fishing, swimming and exploring the vast wilderness that surrounded them.

With the syrup season over, the Knieff family turned their full attention to adding the final touches to their claim shanty. Windows and doors had to be fitted, a chimney built, and numerous articles of furniture fashioned to go with the few pieces they had brought from Long Lake.

Henry's big surprise for Louise was a cabinet that he had found time to make while working in Aitkin. It was six feet high, three feet wide, and sixteen inches deep, with the upper and lower sets of shelves separated by two pull-out drawers. The doors enclosing the shelves were faced with metal on which Henry had inscribed patterns of tiny holes punched in with a sharply pointed awl. Simple and rustic by modern standards, Louise cherished this beautiful luxury in their primitive home. This same cabinet occupied a place of honor in the old "summer kitchen" of my childhood until 1948, when the new kitchen was built. It is now in the new basement serving as a cabinet for miscellaneous hardware. It has been painted repeatedly, and sometimes abused, but its symbolism lives on.

The garden, too, had to be prepared and planted. From then on, they would be almost entirely dependent on what they grew, together with their cow and few chickens. Potatoes were a major part of that first crop, along with sweet corn, which could be blanched and dried for winter use. Space also had to be saved for squash, carrots, onions, and rutabagas as well. Louise even started a few tomato plants on her kitchen window sill; these she set out with care when the weather warmed. She protected them with hot caps against the faint possibility of a late frost. In the fall there would be peas, beans, and tomatoes to can, as well as preserves and jams made from wild berries.

The big day finally came when the Knieff family could move onto their own land to live in their own home. While they faced a great deal of hard work if they were to eke out even a meager existence from this untamed land, the final leg of their journey was complete—they were home to stay at last.

The alder brush and willow trees originally screening their view of the lake had been cut out during the winter, and they could see a panoramic view of the bay that lay before them. Directly in front of them they could see the shore of Battle Point a quarter of a mile away. As their eyes followed its shoreline to the right, it continued westward for over a quarter of a mile, then bent back towards them to form the lily pad bay that separated them from Nick Newgard's property.

Past the point in front of them they could see the far shore, nearly a mile distant as it stretched far eastward before bending back toward them to form the northernmost bay of the lake. Their own shoreline, with its gradually sloping sandy bottom and thin layer of rich black silt, supported a growth of flat-leafed cane so dense that a boat could scarcely penetrate it. Beyond the cane in deeper water, bulrushes thrust their dark green shafts four feet above the water in thick profusion. Much of the shore of the bay was similarly shrouded with vegetation. However, a short distance down the shoreline to the east, the open water came in to meet the land. This was occasioned by a stretch of open sandy beach with no silt on the bottom to support weed growth. It was a natural landing site, and, because of its proximity to the mouth of the river, it had been used through the ages by the Indians as a layover camp when they traveled their regular water route from Mille Lacs Lake to Big Sandy Lake, which were the largest lakes in the area and served as headquarters for their various tribal activities.

This route took them from Mille Lacs Lake through Round Lake, Turtle Lake, Partridge Lake and across the length of Bay Lake to the head of Mud River (or Ripple River as it is now called), that left the lake at the eastern edge of the Knieff homestead. Following Mud River through Long Lake, Farm Island Lake and numerous other lakes in a northeasterly direction, it finally emptied into the Mississippi River at what is now Aitkin. At one point in its journey, the river makes a huge "oxbow" bend of nearly forty miles before returning to within a few hundred feet of itself on its way northward to Aitkin. From Aitkin, the Indians would travel up the Mississippi River to their final destination, usually Big Sandy Lake. These waterways necessarily entailed numerous portages between lakes as well as across occasional "oxbow" bends in the rivers, which saved miles of paddling.

In later years, Hugo took pride in pointing out several depressions that were still visible in the ground near this natural landing. They were the remains of long abandoned caches or storage pits that had been used by the Indians to store extra supplies while they continued their frequent journeys along this route. With white settlers so near, these caches were no longer in use when the Knieffs arrived. The Indians continued to use the water routes, however, and their canoes were a common sight as they crossed the lake in front of the Knieff home.

Bay Lake was also on the water route from Mille Lacs Lake through lakes Placid, Portage, Reno, and Serpent and on to the Mississippi. One branch of this route headed west to hit the river near the present site of the little town of Riverton. The other branch headed straight north from what is now Crosby, through Rabbit Lake and on to the river. Another route went west from Bay Lake to Crooked Lake, Nokey Lake and westward on the Nokisippi to eventually hit the Mississippi near Fort Ripley.

Chapter 5

The Growing Community

The spring of 1884 saw the arrival of Louise's brother, Otto Wasserzieher, and his family at their homestead on Echo Lake. This brought great joy to the Knieff family, for now they had "kinfolk" nearby with whom they could share the day-to-day experiences of developing a new land.

Otto was born in 1837, the eldest of a family of eleven children born to Eduard and Ottilia Wasserzieher. The family immigrated to the United States in 1849 where Anna, Ernest, and Josephine, the last of their children, were born. After spending five years in Stephensen County, Illinois, trying to wrest a living from the previously unbroken prairie sod, Eduard and his family moved to Nauvoo, Illinois, where they bought a home and started a vineyard, which proved to be a profitable venture.

The Wasserziehers were natural horticulturists. Back in Magdeburg, Germany, they had operated an outdoor cafe for which they had produced their own fancy fruits and vegetables. Here in America also, their fresh produce was in great demand. But as their vineyard matured and became productive, Eduard and his son Otto turned their attention to the fermentation of wine. Later they worked at developing new varieties of grapes and, as refrigerated shipping became available, more and more of their grapes were sent east for table use.

Otto Wasserzieher was a large, heavy-set man whose full beard had not yet begun to show the streak of grey that would one day distinguish it. His wife, Adele, was tall and slender, with a twinkle in her eye that bespoke of her love of people. With them were their three children; Paul, thirteen; Lillian, twelve; and the youngest, Edward, who was ten years old. For them too, the spirit of adventure and the unexplored possibilities of the new land urged them onward, like the fabled Lorelei of German folklore, whose singing could not be resisted.

With the willing assistance of the Knieffs, the Wasserziehers soon had their own clearing in the pine-studded forest and their own log home. Their cherished grape vines were planted and several varieties of apple and plum trees set out. As the two families worked together, and the cousins played together, a custom developed that would endure for many years. Each Sunday they would share their dinners together, at the Knieff's one Sunday and at the Wasserzieher's the next. These were fun-filled days of good fellowship, good food, and good conversation that drew the families ever closer together. Since

Otto and Adelia Wasserzieher with their son Edward pictured in the yard of their original homestead.

neither home was very large, and neither had room to seat everyone at the table simultaneously, the men and older boys always were served first. When they were finished, the women and smaller children took their turn. This practice was in accord with an Old World tradition regularly observed in the Wasserzieher home, even when no guests were present.

Commuting between the two homes presented a problem in logistics, particularly in the summer. In the winter, when the lakes were sheathed in ice, it was a simple matter to cross on the ice of one lake to the narrow strip of land that separated the two lakes, cross at that point and then follow along on the ice of the second lake to their destination. The trip was usually accomplished with a horse and sleigh or, in the case of the Knieffs, with old Moses furnishing the power. But even this mode of transportation afforded opportunities for misadventure.

On one such occasion, little Hugo slipped unobserved from the sleigh as it lurched up the steep embankment from the lake. Left alone in the deep snow by the side of the trail, he began to cry as he struggled vainly to regain his footing. As fate would have it, a family of Indians chanced to be following closely behind the Knieff family in their own sled. Spying the little boy lying in the snow crying, his stocking cap askew, they stopped their sled and lifted him to a seat between the two squaws who tried to comfort him. Seeing his long golden curls, which fell in profusion to his shoulders, they could not resist running their fingers through them, for they had never observed such blond hair before. Poor Hugo could only think of the stories he had heard of the Indian massacre at New Ulm, which was still a frequent topic of conversation, and of the Indian penchant for taking scalps. He naturally expected to feel the dreaded knife at any moment and he began howling at the top of his lungs. Fortunately the Indians soon overtook the Knieff sleigh, and Hugo was safely restored to his mother's bosom.

Summer presented a more complex problem in keeping the Sunday meal exchange because there was no road connecting the Knieff and Wasserzieher homesteads. Traveling by water was the logical solution, and both families soon had built themselves flat-bottomed boats. But the river portion of the trip proved to be difficult, especially after the spring freshet had run off and the water level had dropped. Then the sand bar at the mouth of the river would become vary shallow and little water escaped into the stream. No dredging had yet been done in the river channel, and its narrow, meandering path through the meadow, combined with the heavy weed growth, made rowing their boats nearly impossible. The channel was much better suited to the Indian's canoe and paddles. They soon worked out a simple solution. One family would row to the narrowest point of the land strip that separated the two lakes, beach their boat, and walk across to the opposite shore where the other family's boat would meet them and take them the rest of the way.

The boat proved to be a great asset to the Knieffs. They did not yet have a well, and so for several years their only source of water was from the lake. In the summer when the water near shore became warm and somewhat clouded with algae, one of the boys would row out into the deeper water of the bay to fetch cool, clear drinking water for the family.

And, of course, there was fishing. In those days, it was not thought of merely as sport and an occasional good meal. Fish and wild game provided a major share of the family diet. It was fortunate that fish were plentiful and easy to catch, because the available fishing tackle was simple in the extreme. It consisted of a length of heavy cotton line, a bucktail spinner or two, and a small assortment of hooks and sinkers. If none of these were available, a piece of grocery string tied to a willow stick, with a bent pin for a hook would suffice to catch a fine meal of sunfish. Hugo would one day catch an eleven-pound walleye while fishing in this manner. Trolling the bucktail spinner at the end of the hand-held line for a half mile or so would almost always produce a good meal of bass, northern pike (pickerel as they were then mistakenly called), or even a walleye or two.

One of the first trips they made in their new boat was down the lake to visit one of their new neighbor families, the Hunts, who had moved onto a homestead at the south end of the lake shortly after the Knieffs had arrived on theirs. It was a long row past Battle Point to the narrows formed by the big island, (later to be owned by the Lutheran Church), and the eastern shore where the Eraths would soon homestead, then diagonally across the next bay to the true narrows that separates the upper and lower lakes, and finally down the length of the next bay to a cove sheltered by two sharp points running out from the western shore. About three and a half miles by water, it would have been nearly six miles around the western shore of the lake along the ill-defined wagon track that served as a road. Old Moses was well pleased with the family's decision to take the water route. He got plenty of exercise without this foolishness, and besides, he probably wouldn't have enjoyed the visit anyway.

So the family rowed, taking turns at the long oars supported by unpinned open oarlocks, allowing the oars to be "feathered" or rotated with each stroke. This feathering greatly increased the efficiency of the stroke as well as reducing the danger of blisters forming on the hands as they continually slipped over the surface of oars that could not rotate. It was a beautiful trip, as each point they rounded presented a new view of pristine beauty unmarred by any sign of civilization, and a new concept of the vast proportions of this "Lake of Many Bays."

The arrival of the Knieffs brought first a look of incredulity from the Hunts at the unexpected company and a break in their daily routine. It was followed immediately by a warm smile of welcome as introductions were exchanged and the typical hospitality of the frontier extended. Thus began a friendship between the two families that has endured for over a hundred years and encompassed seven generations.

George Albert Hunt and his wife had recently arrived from Wisconsin accompanied by Mrs. Hunt's mother, Mrs. Mary Ford, and their son Wilber who was to become the latter day "Grandpa Hunt." Wilber served for many years as the "boiler engineer" for one of the local sawmills, but his abiding reputation was as an agronomist. His flowers and vegetables were admired throughout the neighborhood. The Hunts had arrived under a pall of grief, as two of their kin, the Coleman brothers, had recently been ambushed and slain while pursuing a pair of fugitives as law enforcement officers.

As the afternoon's lengthening shadows spread over the placid waters, the Knieffs began their long trek home, renewed in spirit, and enriched with their new-found friendships.

Chapter 6

Life on the Frontier

Now that their claim shanty was livable, their garden cleared and planted and a crude barn erected for Moses and the cow, the Knieff family turned its attention to preparing for their home of the future. Henry had long dreamed of this home. To begin with, it would have a large living room on the east end, and two bedrooms above it, accessed by an outside stairway on the north side. Adjoining the living room would be a smaller room that would serve as a combination dining room and kitchen with an attic or loft overhead. It would be fronted by an open porch, and on the west end, an enclosed entryway would also serve as a kitchen in the summertime. His vision called for this entry to be removed sometime in the future and replaced with another two-story addition. The house would be erected about a hundred yards east of the claim shanty, with its back up against the steep hill to the north which would protect it from the cold north wind of winter. The foundation would be built of rock and mortar with a shallow cellar dug under one end. Timbers of white oak and tamarack placed across the foundation would support the floor joists. Giant white pine trees cut to make the clearing for the house would also furnish the lumber to build it.

During this period, Henry's passion for painting did not wane. He found a spot down near Kahwessie's farm where he could get a comprehensive view of the entire bay by changing the perspective only slightly. Here he set up his easel and sketched with pen and ink. His sketches included the Indian camp, other Indians in their canoes, the ducks, deer, and other wild life, and even his home as it would some day appear! From these sketches he painted amended versions in finely detailed water colors. Even the squirrel peeking around the trunk of an old oak tree was so lifelike that its tail appears to twitch at the intrusion of the artist on its privacy. The little yellow home with the white picket fence and the chickens in the yard came alive to his loving touch, though he was not to live to see his dreams' final fruition. This piece of art occupies a place of honor in our home today and is a constant reminder for us of our heritage. Another of these pictures is displayed in the Crow Wing County Historical Society Museum in Brainerd. It shows the yellow house with the white picket fence, the chickens in the yard and the cow waiting patiently by the barn.

While Henry found time to paint, the boys also found a little spare time to learn from Kahwessie the finer points of trapping. Mud river was full of muskrat houses and afforded an excellent opportunity for making a little extra money, as the pelts could be sold for as much as ten cents each. Of course, there was also the possibility of taking a weasel, or even a mink, which would bring even higher prices. The remains of old beaver dams could be seen nearby, but these valuable furs had been trapped to the point of complete extinction in this area by white trappers, as well as by the Indians. It was not until the 1930's that Hugo saw the first beaver that he had ever seen in Bay Lake.

The reestablishment of beaver in this area may well be the result of a minor disaster. Perry Johnson, a teacher at the Crosby-Ironton High School, had bought some property a few miles north of Crosby on the Little Pine River, where he built a cabin which he would use for his summer retreat. The rapidly flowing little river gave him the idea of starting a fur farm which he would stock with several pairs of beaver. He enclosed an area encompassing a short stretch of the river with a heavy woven wire fence, and procured his "family" from a dealer in the south. The industrious little animals soon built a dam, and a house in the resulting pond. All appeared to be going well, until the following spring, when the freshet came and carried out the dam along with the fence. Alas, poor Perry's vision of wealth escaped along with the beaver who soon reestablished themselves in other waters. With no trapping season and few natural predators left, the prolific little animals could multiply with relative safety, and, no doubt did!

Kahwessie taught them the fine points of where and how to make their sets, and how to skin the animals so as to avoid damage to the fur. There was never a problem of anyone bothering their traps, although on occasion Kahwessie would warn them that it might be a good idea for them to take up their traps for a few days, as some "friends" would be traveling through who might have "sticky fingers."

Another chore that devolved to the younger boys in those early summers was getting the cows home in time for milking. As there were as yet no fences, the cattle were allowed to roam freely, in search of whatever browse they could find. The lead cow had a bell about her neck, and its tinkle would carry far in the quiet of the late afternoon. But sometimes the beasts would develop an unaccountable wanderlust, and travel far beyond the sound-carrying range of the little bell. Then the boys would have excellent opportunities to develop their skills as trackers. They would check with the nearest neighbors to see if the cows had been heard in that area, being ever watchful for tracks or other sign that they had come that way. Sometimes these sorties would take the boys for miles into the largely untracked wilderness that surrounded them. They might find themselves on the shore of Birch Lake, or on the back side of the Shirt Lakes, all of which were still one lake in those years before dredging had lowered the water level to its present state. They are now clearly defined as three distinct lakes.

The numbers of waterfowl that inhabited the area at that time were beyond description. At times, when all were aroused at once, their numbers would literally darken the sun as they arose from the water in flocks of tens of thousands. Partridge, rabbits and squirrels were also abundant, and to lend welcome variety to their diet, the boys would on occasion take the old muzzle-loading musket along on these trips. The largely undisturbed forest did not provide the richness of browse that they required, so while there were deer present, they were not as numerous as they are today.

Nothing can be more contrary than a cow, which on occasion led to downright frightening experiences. One such event was clearly recalled by my father, Hugo, in later years. The cows had been located near-by, on the shore of the lake, near Nick Newgard's. Only about a half mile from home by the trail, it should have been an easy chore to bring them in. But the cows had other ideas. They were on the water's edge when found, and they decided to follow the shoreline instead of the trail. This would triple the distance home. But worse, as they proceeded, they discovered an abundance of bull rushes which they found very much to their liking. As they moved along, feeding constantly, they got into deeper and deeper water, making it more and more difficult for the boys to keep them moving. Finally the boys, in desperation, began throwing stones at them to urge them onward. But alas, one well-aimed stone caught one of the cows on the base of her horn, and felled her as though poleaxed. Surely the day was lost! Fortunately, the fall into the cold water revived her, and she came charging out of the lake and made a beeline for home, with the other cattle following in her wake.

Chapter 7

Fourth of July 1885

The spring of 1885 brought a new feeling of optimism to the settlers around Bay Lake. The winter had not been too severe, and the return of warm weather meant that the newly cleared fields and gardens could be planted. The new colony was settling in on their property just west of Dave Archibald's, and work would soon begin on the new sawmill. A celebration was definitely in order, and the approaching Fourth of July was made-to-order for the occasion. There would be speeches and a picnic, with games for the children, and plenty of gossip for the adults.

Henry was asked to make one of the speeches, and the kindness of fate has preserved the original document for posterity. Its presence was discovered many years later when the old home was wired for electricity. As one of the wall outlets was being cut in, a piece of material was discovered blocking the hole from the inside. Only my mother's little hand had room to reach in and withdraw the little old purse, which had doubtless fallen down between the walls before the upstairs floor had been completed. In it was a carefully folded document written in longhand, signed and dated by Henry:

"Neighbors and Friends—

We gathered here today to celebrate a birthday, not of a King or Emperor, but of a Nation. It is one hundred and nine years ago that the founders of this Nation signed their names to the 'Declaration of Independence' and it should be with thankful heart we celebrate this day. Look around over the face of the earth, and try to find a freer and more prosperous nation, and you will look in vain. There was a dark stain left, it is true, but that was blotted out over twenty years ago, and now we celebrate this day in all truth as a free people. We are all equal before the law, the law that is made by ourself, and if the laws are not good we can blame no one else.

Therefore let us keep this day as a day of thanksgiving in joy and merriment and sincere gratitude that we are permitted to do so as citizens of this glorious nation.

Many of us have crossed the broad ocean to reap also the benefits that are offered to all, but let us also not forget, and make resolve that all differences of old worlds nationalities should be washed off by crossing the waters, that all should only and alone be Americans, from the north to the south, from ocean to ocean, whatever their language may be.

Also, let all of us as we are here assembled, remember that watchfulness of our freedom is the only safeguard to keep it, remember, in union is strength, let the union be broken and nothing but the name of this glorious Republic will be left.

See to it that the stars and stripes be honored everywhere.

That this be a protection to you where ever you go, that to be an American, be the armor against insult all over the world, and that our flag be a beacon light to all nations."

Bay Lake, Minnesota
July 4, 1885

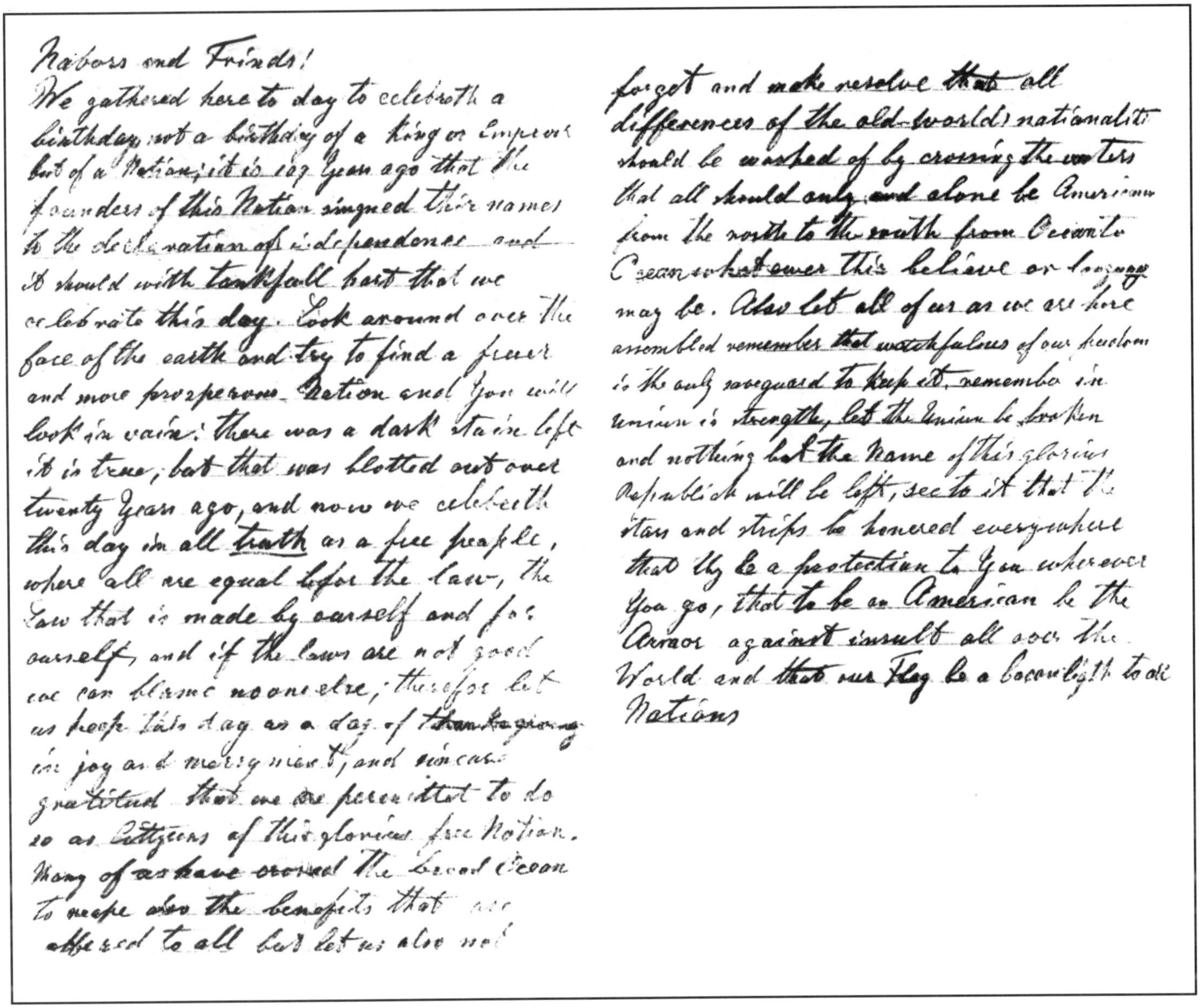

Nabors and Frinds!
We gathered here to day to celebrath a birthday not a birthday of a king or Emperor but of a Nation; it is 109 Year ago that the founders of this Nation singned their names to the declaration of independence and it should with tankfull hart that we celebrate this day. Look around over the face of the earth and try to find a freer and more prosperous Nation and You will look in vain; there was a dark staine left it is true, but that was blotted out over twenty Years ago, and now we celebrath this day in all truth as a free people, where all are equal befor the law, the Law that is made by ourself and for ourself, and if the laws are not good we can blame noone else; therefor let us keep this day as a day of thanksgiving in joy and merryment, and sincere gratitud that we are permitted to do so as Cittyzens of this glorious free Nation. Many of us have crossed The broad Ocean to reape also the benefits that are offered to all but let us also not forget and make resolve that all differences of the old world's nationalities should be washed of by crossing the waters that all should only and alone be American from the north to the south from Ocean to Ocean whatever their believe or language may be. Also let all of us as we are here assembled remember that watchfulness of our freedom is the only saveguard to keep it, remember in union is strength, let the Union be broken and nothing but the Name of this glorious Republick will be left, see to it that the stars and strips be honored everywhere that they be a protection to You wherever You go, that to be an American be the Armor against insult all over the World and that our Flag be a beaconligth to all Nations

The original prosperity speech written by Henry and given on July 4, 1885.

It was indeed a time of joy for the Knieff family. The seemingly hopeless venture of the past was beginning to show signs of a successful fruition in the not too distant future. True, life would not be easy and hardship would be ever present, particularly by our twentieth century standards. But the family was together, food was plentiful, if plain, and the pressures of an overcrowded society which had prompted their move northward were now behind them. Hard work was a way of life that brought with it a sense of satisfaction, fulfillment and pride that is all too often lacking in our present modern society. The boys were growing up and assuming an ever larger share of the responsibilities. Only little Hugo was exempt. He still led the carefree life of the very young, although even he was required to bring in kindling for his mother, or feed the chickens on occasion.

Henry, that stern old Dutchman, was viewed somewhat in awe by his neighbors. His steely blue grey eyes left no doubt as to the sternness of his character. The story was told of how he was warned about going up to a certain neighbor's house, as he had a vicious dog which would surely bite if given the opportunity. "No, I don't think so," replied Henry as he proceeded on. Sure enough, as he approached the house the dog came out, snarling and growling. Undaunted, Henry gave the beast a cold and steady stare, upon which the dog turned with his tail between his legs and slunk away.

Yet Hugo, in later years, recalled his father as a kind and loving man who, in spite of a sharp and fiery temper, had a soft and tender heart. He still remembered the two times that he had put his father to the test. Once, one of his older brothers was sent to the lake for water, just as the family was about to sit down for their evening meal. Hugo was expressly forbidden from going along but, in his own words "I simply forgot as soon as I was told, and followed my brother to the lake where I spotted a frog about to make his escape. I followed it in hot pursuit. The next thing I knew, there stood my father with a willow switch in his hand. He never said a word but I remember well how he tickled my bare legs all the way back up to the house."

Hugo's other problem was sitting still at the table. Being the youngest and often left out of the conversation, and being anxious to resume his play, he developed a habit of wriggling and squirming while he sat at the dinner table. One day his contortions caused a dish to fall to the floor. Henry bade him clean up the mess and remove his chair from the table. From that day forth, and for over a year, Hugo ate his meals while standing at the table. In telling me about it, he said, "I didn't think much about it — it was just the way I ate my meals from then on and seemed natural to me."

Kahwessie was not the only regular Indian visitor to the Knieff household. Another noteworthy guest was known only as Hank. He lived with his several Indian wives on what is now called Hank's Bay of Crooked Lake. He had been adopted by a white family as a child and given a formal education. He still retained a subscription to a newspaper and a magazine and kept himself well informed on current events. Hank enjoyed visiting with Henry because, while Henry did not have the formal education, he was widely traveled and had a keen interest in political affairs. Henry was mystified as to why Hank had not made more use of his education, and finally asked him. Hank replied "Because I like the life of a wild Indian better." Henry had great respect, and even empathy, with this reply.

Chapter 8

Early Schools

The spring of 1886 brought the long awaited "colony" to the shores of Bay Lake. It was formed as a cooperative association of German immigrants who visualized a rapidly developing community in the wilderness where they could ply their trades in a group effort. Among their party was Joseph Ruttger who was a machinist by trade and who would one day become more than a mere acquaintance of the Knieffs. The colony settled in section four, a mile and a half west of the Knieff homestead, except for Joe who chose his homestead on the island that the Knieffs had seen when they first approached their new home. The colony was soon hard at work setting up the steam-powered sawmill that they had brought with them.

The spring of 1886 was also an auspicious one for the Knieffs as they were about to start building their new home. Of course the everyday chores of daily living would have to take precedence. All winter they had been busy cutting and splitting their next year's supply of firewood. With a larger house to heat, the woodpile would have to grow correspondingly.

Another new wrinkle had also been added to their lives. With the arrival of the colony came an increased demand for some sort of school for the rapidly growing little community. As was the custom, an acre of land in each township was dedicated for a school. Bay Lake located theirs on the west edge of section three. This was as close to the center of the township as was feasible, because of the lake, and was also near the center of the population. Later on, three other schools would be located in Bay Lake township. Each family was required to donate a given amount of time, materials, or money, and construction was soon under way. A simple one-room building was erected, the necessary furniture built, and the school was ready to open. The first teacher was Miss Sophia Conzet, who would later be affectionately called "Aunt Sofie" Archibald. It was the duty of the older boys in school to take turns going in an hour early each morning to start the fire, so the building would be at least modestly warm when the younger children arrived. Discipline was no problem in those early days at Bay Lake. The older boys, who were often in their late teens, would be only too happy to assist the teacher if someone got out of hand.

In later years however, it was said that a situation arose in the town of Aitkin where a group of young men took over the school and terrorized the teachers—even the principals—who would resign after only a few months. Finally a young man was hired, though he was of modest stature and appeared mild mannered. Sure enough, the first day of his reign, the ring leader of the gang succeeded in raising enough havoc in class that he got himself sent up to the principal's office. It was the custom to set each new principal straight, in turn, so that their antics would not be seriously questioned in the future. The miscreant entered the office and proceeded to inform the principal of these limitations, and he backed his presentation with a show of force. This proved to be a sad miscalculation on his part, as he, forthwith, found himself flat on the floor with a badly bruised and aching jaw. Little had he known that he was going up against the former middleweight boxing champion of the U. S. Navy! Needless to say, the Aitkin school district no longer had a disciplinary problem.

In those days school was not held in the coldest months of the winter because the children were forced to walk great distances, sometimes several miles, in order to reach class. Even in spring and fall, classes were often curtailed for the bigger boys, as the necessities of the family farm were given precedence over schooling. Eighteen-year olds in grade school were the norm under these conditions, but the quality of the education that they received speaks well for their determination and effort.

Family pets played an important role in the lives of the early settlers, and the Knieff family was no different. Their first dog was a nondescript little fellow of varied ancestry that obviously included terrier lineage. He was well-suited to his name, Jip, for he was quick and feisty with a heart as big as nature would allow such a little animal. Both watchdog and companion, his sense of responsibility once led him to spend the night out in the field guarding a coat he had been told to watch. Not missed until the following morning, he was finally found still lying by the fallen coat. On another occasion, while taking a walk with two of the boys, he spied a hollow log with an enticing scent issuing from it. He dove into it headfirst, and there ensued a horrendous snarling and snapping and growling accompanied by a dreadful odor. Then out of the log came two skunks, their scent glands working overtime, followed by Jip with tears in his eyes and foam in his mouth. He was followed by two more skunks. Fortunately for Jip the remains of a snow drift lay near by. This he entered with his jaws spread wide and burrowed the length of it to rid his mouth of the dreadful excretion. This area of the woods was carefully avoided by the boys for several weeks, until the stench finally abated. Of course Jip's most useful function was in helping to bring in the cattle. Not only was his keen nose a big asset in locating them, but a few sharp "yips" from him at their heels quickly prompted them to make haste in their homeward way.

Cats, too, had their part to play on the farm by keeping the mice and other small rodents to a manageable minimum. When the Knieffs first came, it was said that every farmer had to keep his own tomcat because of the great distances that separated the farms. Be that as it may, the Knieffs had a breed that was quite apart from the usual run of farm cat. Called Brutus and Caesar and Timolese, they were huge by the standards of domestic felines, and they behaved accordingly. They loved to sleep behind the stove and bask in its warmth. At bedtime, when it was time for them to be put out of doors to go about their appointed business, they would object strenuously. That meant that one of the men would have to don heavy leather gloves to protect himself from fang and claw while the eviction was completed. There were very few rodents on the Knieff farm.

Hugo used to tell the story of how Brutus, as he advanced in years, had adopted a kitten that had been given to the Knieffs by one of the neighbors. Brutus kept the little animal scrupulously clean with his tongue and even suffered it to pretend to nurse on a tuft of hair on his belly. But then one day, as it grew older, Brutus discovered that it, too, was a male. So he ate it!

Chapter 9

Joy and Sorrow

As the days passed into months and the months into years, the pile of logs by the landing had continued to grow. Then the new sawmill two miles down the lake became operational, and it finally was time to roll the logs into the lake and float them down to the mill. This would have been a huge operation for the Knieffs to undertake by themselves, but, on the appointed day, all of the neighbors showed up with their boats and pike poles and whatever rope or chain that they had. Once the logs were all in the water they were herded into a tight group and tied together to form a loose raft. Then, with the constant pushing and tugging from all of the boats, the little procession slowly made its way around the point and down the bay to the sawmill where they were soon converted into lumber. Now it was time for Moses to haul the lumber back to the homestead where it was neatly piled with strips between each layer so that it could dry out over winter. In the spring it would be ready, and the building could begin.

"Uncle Joe" Ruttger was to play an important role in the lives of the Knieff family. He had quit his job in Minneapolis in the spring of 1886 and came north with a colony incorporated as the Pioneer Cooperative Company under the leadership of a Mr. Ranken. Joe was to become the millwright for their new sawmill. He did not, however, stay with the colony proper, but opted instead to stake his own homestead on the large island that lay but a short distance off shore from the colony property. He was an industrious, hard working man, and, although he had the full responsibility of setting up the sawmill and seeing that everything worked smoothly, he still found time to build a log home and clear a spot for a little garden.

Transportation was always something with which to reckon in those early days, but, for a man living alone on an island, it must have been even more precarious. During the winter, the problem was minimal as he had only to walk across the lake. At that time Joe did not have a horse to worry about. In the summer, a boat or canoe would serve very nicely, and an Indian canoe could easily be bought or bartered for. It was in the early spring and late fall that the real problem arose. By the end of March, the ice would begin going out of the lake. This was heralded by a gradually widening strip of water appearing between the more solid ice and the shore. As this process proceeded, the main body of ice became ever more "honey-combed" and unstable. At this time the only safe passage was afforded by using a boat to cross the strip of open water, and then pushing the boat ahead while walking across the ice, keeping it ever at hand to fall into should the ice break, and then reentering the boat again for crossing the strip of water on the far shore. In about three weeks the ice would finally leave the lake entirely, and the entire trip could be made in the boat.

A similar problem would evolve in the fall as the lake took on its winter mantle of ice. Then there was often a short period of time when the new ice would be too thin to support a man's weight, but too thick to allow a boat to be pushed or rowed through it. Skis were sometimes used to distribute a man's weight over a larger area to prevent the ice from breaking. This was dangerous in the extreme, as the thickness of the ice could vary from three inches to a half-inch or less in only a few feet, and a plunge into the ice water would prove fatal if the water were deep or shore could not be reached in two or three minutes.

Building the new home had been basically a family affair for the Knieffs, although several of the neighbors did stop by on occasion to lend a hand. Construction had proceeded without major incident and followed the same general pattern as the original claim shanty, but on a larger scale and with the substitution of sawed lumber for the rough logs. The large basswood tree that shades the front of the house today was only a three- or four-inch sapling at the time of the construction. Its top had accidently been broken off, and the plan was to cut it out of the way, but, somehow it got left to become the majestic matriarch of the landscape, which it now is, though it did suffer severe damage in the tornado of 1973.

The building of the home was also a valuable learning experience for the boys, and helped to develop their skills as carpenters, and their ability to improvise when the necessary tools or materials were not readily at hand. Little Arthur learned a valuable if painful lesson one day while watching his older brothers work. The nails used for the construction were of the old square-cut variety and came in fifty-pound wooden kegs. These were opened by setting the keg upright and breaking out the end with a hammer. This left the nails that had held the end in place protruding into the keg at a somewhat downward angle. Arthur spied one of these partially empty kegs and decided that it would make an ideal seat from which to view the proceedings. Alas, the longer he sat, the farther into the open end of the keg his skinny little bottom did slip until finally, when he attempted to stand up, he found his tender little posterior elegantly pinioned by those protruding nails! Needless to say, there was a period of pain and anguish for all the while the nails were being extracted.

Progress on the new house was slow. None of the lumber was planed, and its dimensions varied greatly. Aside from the floor joists,

The original Knieff home at Bay Lake taken in 1912 with Chester Powers standing on the porch.

which were two-by-ten or twelve inches, the rest of the frame was of two-by-fours. This meant that they were from two to two and one-half inches thick and from four to five inches in width. The walls were sheeted with one inch boards, which usually exceeded one inch in thickness. The random widths went up to twenty inches in some cases. It can be readily seen why such old houses have a distinct character but do not lend themselves readily to remodeling. The outside of the house was covered with tar paper and then with home-made shingles or shakes. The interior was first sheeted with one-inch boards, then covered with building paper and finally with wallboard. Keeping track of dimensions demonstrates why the walls ended up being eight inches or more thick, and why the old house has survived the elements for over a hundred years.

As winter approached, the outside of the house stood completed, but much was left to be done inside. Buying the square-shafted cut nails, the tar paper and wallboard, and buying the windows and doors and their frames had so depleted the family resources that finishing the building would have to wait for another year. Fortunately, the cost of sawing the lumber and procuring the other necessary supplies could be largely paid for by selling additional saw logs to the mill. With a large area yet to be cleared for a field, there would be no shortage of saw logs. There would be no shortage of work for the boys that winter either!

During those early years, the nearest doctor was in Brainerd, so medical care was primarily the responsibility of the family. When one of the boys ran a pitchfork into his hip while playing in a hay stack, a homemade salve consisting of carbolic acid, tallow, and pitch from a balsam tree successfully treated the wound and prevented infection. When one of the boys cut a toe off with his axe, Henry simply sewed it back on again, and with the aid of the salve, saved the toe, although it did come out a trifle crooked! Crude though they were, these simple remedies were effective, and the family remained in relatively good health.

Henry had long been in poor health. He was now sixty-six years old and still suffered from the malaria he had contracted while in the service. He also suffered from rheumatism. In a letter written to his daughter, Augusta, dated February 2, 1888, he wrote, "All the old fellows drop off one by one, and that reminds me that my longest road lays behind me also, but I am happy, yes indeed." The summer of 1888 saw a steadily worsening of his condition, till finally on the 26th of October he breathed his last and was laid to rest on the hillside behind the family farm. There he rested until the Bay Lake cemetery was organized and his remains moved there to the newly created family plot. A simple Civil War headstone marks his grave among the pines. His wife Louise and their four sons now lie nearby.

Although Henry had never actually moved into the new home, it was nearly enough completed that Louise and her family were in the process of making the move when Henry passed away. The new house would give them more room and would be easier to keep warm than the old claim shanty had been. In those early years, the upstairs was gained by an open stairway attached to the outside of the house. The upstairs was unfinished and consisted of a single room sixteen-by-twenty feet. The chimney for the heating stove below went through this room and afforded some measure of heat, and the cracks in the floor boards also contributed a little. This was the bedroom for the four boys, as well as storage for the entire family. Needless to say, there was little loitering done while getting ready for bed or getting up in the morning.

The winter of 1888 was notorious for its severity, but the Knieff family managed to survive with little ill effect. With the coming of spring came the planting of the garden, and so life went on for the Knieff family without their beloved Henry. Max, the eldest son, was now nearly sixteen and ready to assume the duties as head of the household. Arthur was nearly fourteen and Oskar would be thirteen in December. Hugo, the youngest at seven years, was growing rapidly and was ready to make his contribution. It was a fundamental necessity for those pioneer families that their children mature at an early age and share the responsibility for the family's welfare. The older half-brothers had already left home.

Louise suffered the loss of her husband most of all, though the daily chores of preparing the meals, washing and mending clothes, and knitting socks, mittens, and scarfs left her little time to mourn. But it was hard being the only adult as well as the only woman in the household. Relief came for her in the person of her younger unmarried sister, Josephine Wasserzieher. She had been living at home in Nauvoo, Illinois, and agreed to come north and help Louisa. What a transition this must have been, for her to leave the civilized landscape and relatively warm climate of Illinois for this outpost of northern civilization! Nor could she have guessed its consequences.

The colony of which Joe Ruttger had been a part had disbanded in 1887. Joe continued to live on the island though he had acquired a part of the company property on the mainland. It was only natural that he had developed a strong friendship for the Knieff family, and, when the attractive young relative moved into the Knieff home, his presence there became ever more frequent. During the following winter he was often seen early in the morning as he came around the point, heading for the Knieff's with his kerosene lantern in his hand. The whole family knew he was coming to court Josie and that it would be late in the evening before he left.

Josephine Wasserzieher and Joseph Ruttger were married in the front room of the Knieff home in 1890 and made their home on the island where their first son, Alex, was born in 1892. They moved from the island to their property on the mainland in 1894 prior to the birth of their second son, Max. The Ruttger home, located where the "Sis-e-bag-a-mah Trail" from Deerwood ended at Bay Lake, soon became the social hub of the community. There the neighbors met for a Sunday afternoon sing-a-longs, picnics, or simply to exchange the latest gossip. Joe and Josey were the perfect hosts, always ready to set an extra place at the table or to lend a hand to someone in need. This willingness to share no doubt prompted sportsmen, who had traveled the new railroad from Duluth tempted by Bay Lake's growing reputation for big and bountiful bass, to seek shelter in the Ruttger hay mow or to inveigle a home-cooked meal from the generous and good-hearted Josie. This practice soon lead to the establishment of the first resort in northern Minnesota.

In those times, the annual township meetings were often hotly disputed, and offers to step outside and settle some matter were not uncommon. Whether people were more contentious then or simply more willing to air their grievances in public, I do not know, but such disputes often led to long-standing enmities. History has long since forgotten the cause of the altercation that embroiled Joe Ruttger and Mr. A. N. Gray, who lived a short distance down the lake from Ruttgers. They simply would not speak or even recognize each other's presence.

Joseph and Josephine Ruttger

In late winter, the roads were deeply covered with a buildup of compacted snow. Driving under such conditions was hazardous even for a horse-drawn sleigh. On one such evening, as Joe was returning home, he came upon Mr. Gray. His sled piled high with wood had slipped off the road and overturned, spilling wood in every direction. Joe stopped his team and sprang from his sled. The wood fairly flew as the sled was pulled from under the mess, set back on the road and the wood carefully reloaded. Then Joe returned to his own sled and continued homeward. The only words spoken during the encounter were "Whoo" and "Getty-up"! Joe would not speak to Mr. Gray, neither would he leave a neighbor in distress without lending a helping hand. This was the spirit that prevailed in those early years.

During the last decade of the nineteenth

century, the little community continued to grow. The remaining vast stands of white and Norway pine were in great demand by the burgeoning lumber industry, and the woods rang to the tune of axe and saw. Rivers were dredged to facilitate driving logs down them to the lake and hence to the saw mills, which were in full operation. There was work for everyone who wanted to work and no need for government handouts. If illness or accident put a family in distress, the neighborhood was quick to respond; the community, as well as the individual, took pride in being self-sufficient.

This was the spirit of the times in which the Knieff boys were raised. They continued to live at home, working the farm and taking such odd jobs as they could find. When they were deemed old enough, they took winter jobs in one of the logging camps.

Louise continued to care for her boys until 1895, when her tired old heart finally gave up and she was laid to rest beside Henry in the family plot. Max was the first of her sons to marry. He bought a small parcel of land down near the colony property where his son and daughter were born. In 1904 he contracted diphtheria and succumbed to the dread disease. The following year, his brother Oskar came down with typhoid fever from drinking contaminated water while working in a logging camp. Hugo would often tell of receiving a letter from home, while he too was working in a logging camp, telling of Oskars illness but saying that he was then well on the road to recovery. That night Hugo dreamed that he was called home, and on arriving, he could see his brother's body laid out for burial in Ruttger's parlor. The next morning he did indeed receive a telegram from home informing him that Oskar was dead. On his arrival home, he found his brother just as he had pictured him in his dream.

Oskar's death was a severe blow for Hugo. The two of them had been the closest of all the brothers. They had shared a passion for boxing and had passed many happy hours sparring together and honing their skills. Being the most alike in physique as well as temperament, they had developed a bond that did not exist between

Crew from one of the local sawmills. Pictured left to right: front row: George McCalvy, Clarence Wheeler, Ira Torrey, Albert Miller, Varner, and Tom McCalvy; back row: Walter Waffensmith, Sam Varner, Bob Magham, John Christensen, Able Christensen, Abe Christensen, John Peterson, Frank Burglund, G. W. Hunt, Blumenischjen, and Dan Mack.

any of the other brothers. But, though life takes its toll, it must go on. The property had passed on to the four brothers, and now the remaining brothers, Arthur and Hugo, bought out the other interests and continued to operate the little farm as a joint venture. They would sorely miss Oskar's presence, as it was he who had born the brunt of the responsibility at home. Arthur was interested in obtaining his teaching credentials, and Hugo had inherited some of his father's wanderlust.

Chapter 10

The Trip West

In the spring of 1906, Hugo took what little money he had saved and headed west. The family home as he had known it was no longer the same, especially since Oskar's death. He had worked in the logging camps and on his half-brother Ed's farm near Marshall in the southwestern part of the state, but now it was time for the great adventure of his life. He had a half-sister living near Corvallis, Oregon, so this would be his initial destination. The long train ride west was far from boring for the young man with the inquiring mind and the active imagination. This seemingly endless expanse of gently rolling prairie through North Dakota and eastern Montana was a part of the Indian country where his father had begun his life as a soldier. It brought back those stories of the Indian war that Henry had so loved to tell. Hugo could visualize the Indian camps, the buffalo that once roamed the plains by the thousands, and the blue-clad soldiers with their banners streaming in the breeze as they rode across wild, boundless land with only an occasional jack rabbit or raptor soaring high above to lend emphasis to its solitude.

As the train journeyed westward, climbing steadily, rolling hills gave way to isolated buttes and rocky ridges with little patches of green nestled only in the river valleys. The foothills were relatively inconspicuous as the train approached the continental divide and gave little warning of the majesty that Hugo was about to behold. And then the summit was passed. The train started to gather speed as it began its long descent into the valley below, and the slow and meandering rivers of the eastern slope gave way to the rushing, tumbling torrents of the west. The rocky faces of the mountains were sheathed in glorious stands of conifers stretching their deep green boughs to the sky as though trying in vain to peek over the next summit.

Hugo had found a new love, and his heart went out to her song of mystery. He was totally captivated by the vastness, beauty, and solitude and, though he would travel far, and behold beauty in its many aspects, a part of his heart would ever remain within those beckoning hills. But for now, his journey was far from over and would carry him to distant shores before it would return him to his dream.

With a heavy heart Hugo saw the Main Range of the Rockies slip behind them to the east as the train entered the semi desert wasteland of eastern Washington. This was not the kind of country he enjoyed, but, fortunately, most of it was passed in the night. By early morning, the Cascade Range came into view. The train followed the Columbia River as it veered southward, then west again to the coast. When it finally arrived in Corvallis, Hugo left the train and continued on foot. When he reached their home, his sister Molly and her husband Jack Early, met him with open arms. Since Molly, who was his half-sister from his father's first marriage, had been raised in Minneapolis, and then moved west at an early age, they had never met before. Their conversation lasted well into the night as they became acquainted with each other. The Earlys had a little farm on the outskirts of town, although Jack was a fisherman and had been for most of his life. Being of Irish decent, his ready wit and lusty voice were well known throughout the area.

Hugo was struck by the beauty of western Oregon. He had arrived during their comparatively dry season, yet everything was lush and green. Flowers bloomed everywhere he looked, and he was particularly impressed with the great variety of fruit that grew in the area. There were peaches, pears, plums and, of course, apples of every description, as well as many varieties of grapes. Nuts were also a great favorite.

Hugo enjoyed his visit with the Earlys where he became a regular member of the family. He helped on the little farm and worked with Jack when he could. He learned to sail Jack's boat on the Alsea River and even became quite proficient at sailing upstream against both the wind and the tide. But his need for money and his urge to see more country finally prompted him to be on his way again. His experience in the logging camps of Minnesota made it only natural that he should turn to the huge fir and spruce forests of the coast range for employment. He was soon working as a cut-off man, whose duty it was to cut the fallen giants into twenty- or sometimes forty-foot lengths in preparation for their journey down the mountain to the sawmill in the valley below. This was accomplished by a two-man team, who made the cut with a twelve-foot-long saw with handles located at each end. A willingness to work and a natural sense of rhythm were required for this job. Each man pulled the saw toward himself in turn, and then followed the return stroke of his partner. Woe unto him who attempted to push or guide the saw on that return stroke, as this would result in the saw binding on the sides of the "kerf" or slot in which the saw was working, and greatly increase the energy required to pull the saw through the cut. If this happened, Hugo's partner would not be bashful in letting him know what he was doing wrong. These giant logs were often as much as eight feet or more in diameter and over a hundred feet long. No wonder such care was taken of the saw that it was always properly sharpened and never abused.

When Hugo had earned a reputation as a good cut-off man he was given a chance to prove himself as a faller. A tree selected to be cut was first notched by cutting out a wedge-shaped piece of trunk to determine the exact direction it would fall. The man responsible for this did nothing but notch trees. If a tree were to fall in even a slightly different direction than intended, it could well hang up in another tree. It would then be very difficult to get it the rest of the way down, and it would be extremely dangerous to anyone working in the area, for any change in conditions could bring it crashing the rest of the way down without warning. The notcher in Hugo's crew would often set a stake a hundred or more feet from the tree. His aim was such that the stake would always be driven into the ground by the trunk of tree when it fell.

The trees were usually cut off from eight to twelve feet above the ground. This was done because of the bowl or swelling at the base of the tree. To try to cut through this would greatly increase the distance to be cut, and would also make guiding its fall more difficult. It could also cause problems at the mill. To gain the height necessary to cut the tree this far above the ground, it was necessary for the wedger as well as the fallers, to use spring boards. These were strong, if somewhat limber boards about six inches wide, tapered down slightly and rounded at one end. On the face of this rounded end was secured a metal plate curved to fit the shape of the board. From the curved portion of the plate extended a sharply pointed ridge about three eighths of an inch high. To use the spring board, the faller would cut a notch into the tree about four or five feet above the ground and three or four inches deep into the tree. The top of the notch would go into the wood at a shallow downward angle while the bottom would be cut straight in. When the tip of the spring board was inserted into the notch, with the sharpened ridge pointing upward, the sharp ridge would bite into the tree and hold the board in place. The spring board would thus become a platform from which to work. The rounded tip of the board would allow the outward end of the board to swing several feet in either direction around the tree without unhooking, and thus give the worker a greater radius from which to work. A second board was usually put in above the first to gain enough height from which to work, and sometimes three boards were used. The loggers calked boots were necessary to keep him from slipping from his spring board as well as while on the ground.

The moment of truth would come for the fallers when the giant tree began its descent. They would have to jump well clear of the tree and its stump, for there was always the chance that the tree would kick back or slightly to one side as it left the stump. If this happened and they were in the way, they would be killed instantly. The worst that happened to Hugo was a sprained ankle when a tree did kick back and he missed his footing while getting out of the way.

The fallers were required to keep their saws sharp and with proper set. The set was obtained by bending the cutting teeth away from the center of the saw in alternate directions, so that the kerf would be slightly wider than the saw was thick to prevent the saw from binding. It was obtained by placing a piece of metal called a swage block against one side of the saw tooth and tapping the other side with a hammer. The swage block had a slight taper ground along the edge of one surface, allowing each tooth to take a uniform degree of bend.

Each logging camp had a blacksmith who, besides making and fitting horse shoes, was constantly called upon to repair broken chains and to make or repair skidding tongs and other hardware used in the camp. He had to have expert knowledge of metals and their properties. While they generally used a mild steel that would not be brittle, it was sometimes necessary to have a very hard face on a particular tool. Often on a Sunday, when the men were not busy, the blacksmith could be inveigled into making personal items for the men such as knife blades or belt buckles. On one such Sunday, Hugo went to the blacksmith and asked if he would make him a new swage block. The smithy smiled and threw a scrap of steel into his forge. In minutes the steel was cherry red. He grabbed it with his tongs and put it on the anvil where a few deft strokes of his hammer gave it the proper shape. He then watched it carefully as it cooled until it looked just right to his well-trained eye. He then threw it into a bucket of water and went about another project. In a few minutes he nodded to Hugo, who retrieved the swage from the water and studied it carefully. It was just what he wanted except that its face had a slight mar that he thought he would take off. The smithy handed him a file and grinned broadly as Hugo brought the file to the face of the swage. The file wouldn't touch the face of that swage, although it easily trued up all of the other surfaces. Hugo had learned about case hardening, which is obtained by controlling the way in which the nearly red-hot piece of metal is cooled.

Chapter 11

Salmon Fishing

Early the next spring, on one of his infrequent trips to town, Hugo learned that a salmon canning company was hiring a crew to go to their cannery located in Alaska between Ketchikan and Wrangell for the summer salmon run. The crew would be leaving from Seattle in about six weeks. This was an opportunity of which he had long dreamed. It would mean taking the company sailing boat up the coast to the cannery site and staying there while the salmon run lasted. He could not resist the temptation to join the expedition.

The trip northward was all that he had visualized it would be. They followed the inland waterway, a route sheltered from the swells of the open Pacific Ocean by a succession of islands located a few miles from the mainland. The scenery was almost unbelievable—the snow capped peaks in the distance with their heavily forested slopes gave way abruptly to a ruggedly rock-bound coastline and the azure blue of the sea. Nights were already very short by the time they were on their way, and soon would amount to little more than an hour of dusk before the sun reappeared in the east.

The cannery was located on the mainland at the head of a bay where it was well protected from the weather. A wooden pier jutted out into deep water and provided moorage for the trawler while it unloaded its catch of fish. The cannery itself was a large wooden building where the salmon were cleaned, put into cans, cooked, sealed and stored awaiting shipment. There was also a bunkhouse and a mess hall for the men. Here they would live and work until the run was over. Aside from the mail boat that dropped off mail once a week and the two or three Indian families who lived near by, they would see no one else until they returned to Seattle in the fall.

The crew was divided into those who manned the trawler, those who ran the cannery, and another group that fished from small two-man boats. Hugo was to be one of the latter group. However, on their arrival, it was discovered that they were one man short. This left Hugo without a fishing partner, and, since he could not work a boat alone, he could not fish. But since he had been hired on and they had no way of sending him back, they had to continue to pay him. He simply filled in and helped out where he could.

Hugo often found himself helping the camp cook, and they became good friends. There was always plenty of good food, although its variety was severely limited. Once a month they would get a side of fresh beef, but this would last only a few days for a crew of hungry men. Nor could it be kept for long without refrigeration. Naturally, there would not be enough choice steak to feed the entire crew, so, to avoid playing favorites, the meat was never cut into steaks. But if Hugo was in the mess hall when the meat was being cut, he and the cook would enjoy a good steak together. When the beef was gone, salt pork and fish would be the order of the day until the next month.

It became one of Hugo's favorite chores to provide fresh venison for the camp. Fortunately he had brought his .25-.35-caliber Savage rifle with him, and deer were plentiful in the salt marshes along the coast. These were the small coastal black-tails, to distinguish them from the white-tail deer of Minnesota, or the black-tailed mule deer of the Montana Rockies. A large one would seldom weigh more than 120 pounds. Hugo could easily dress one out and carry it back to the cannery on his back. He even learned to break the first joint of the front legs to form a toggle that he would then pass through the first joint of the rear legs, which had been opened between the bone and the tendon, and to form a sort of pack he could wear on his back without having to hold onto the deer. In this way he could continue hunting and would sometimes bring in two at once. Naturally this earned him quite a reputation as a hunter!

One day, while Hugo was standing on the end of the pier with his rifle in his hand, an Indian man came up to him and asked if he could see the rifle. The Indian lived nearby with his family and often did odd jobs around the cannery, so Hugo easily recognized him. The Indian looked the rifle over carefully then put it to his shoulder and sighted at a kelp weed pod bobbing in the waves several hundred feet away. "Nice rifle," said the Indian politely. "Can I try a shot?" "Sure," replied Hugo as he handed over a cartridge. The Indian adjusted the rear sight of the rifle to his satisfaction, slipped the cartridge into the chamber and smoothly squeezed off a shot. To Hugo's amazement the kelp pod fairly exploded! This was an extraordinarily difficult shot at a small and moving target. The Indian carefully returned the rear sight to its previous position, extracted the spent shell and handed the rifle back to Hugo. "Thank you," he said. "That is a good gun. Could I borrow it sometime to get some meat for my family?" Hugo nodded his assent as the Indian turned and walked away. A few days, later the Indian again approached Hugo and asked if he might borrow the rifle. Hugo brought out the rifle and also a box of shells. The Indian took the rifle but shook his head and held up one finger. "I only want one deer," he said. "Just give me one shell."

Several times that summer, the Indian borrowed the rifle and each time he would take only one shell. He never failed to bring back his deer. Later Hugo learned that the Indian had been a seal hunter. It was his job to stand in the bow of a small boat bobbing in the waves, and shoot the seal in a particular spot in its head, while it too bobbed about in the water. If the shot weren't properly placed, the seal would sink and be lost.

Sometimes Hugo did get to do some fishing, either from the end of the pier or from one of the small boats when it was not in use. Of all the beauties of his surroundings, the one that impressed him the deepest was the water itself. The water in Minnesota is quite clear, and one can often see into it for ten or twelve feet. Here the sea water was so nearly totally transparent that it was merely the lack of light at great depths that would limit visibility. The sea bottom with all its variety of rocks and weeds and sand was clearly visible at depths of up to a hundred feet or more. Its clarity combined with the slight magnification of its refractive index made passing over this submarine landscape an eerily exciting experience.

When fishing from the pier, small sharks were most often caught because they hung about to scavenge the discarded entrails of the salmon. Small bottom feeders such as cod or sole were also sometimes taken. One evening two of the off-duty crew took one of the small boats out into the bay to try for a larger sole or flounder in deep water. Their efforts were unexpectedly rewarded when a truly large flounder took the bait and was hauled into the boat. It lay there on the bottom of the little boat, its tail extending under one of the seats while its head protruded from beyond the next seat. It was an ugly looking creature, which swam with its body laying flat to the bottom while its head assumed a twist of nearly ninety degrees so that both of its eyes were on the upper exposed side of its body. It was truly a great prize as its hundred pounds of snow-white flesh was considered to be a culinary delicacy.

Suddenly the great fish began to flop, and, with the first impact from its mighty tail, it sent one of the seats soaring into the air. Soon the bottom boards of the boat began to give way under the pounding, and water began to rush into the boat. The tables were turned; the hunter became the hunted, and it was every man for himself. The two stunned and badly frightened fisherman had but one recourse. With one accord they flung the struggling denizen of the deep back into the water and bent every effort toward getting the foundering boat to shore.

Beautiful, peaceful, and serene as the surroundings appear to be, there seems always to be a danger ready to pounce on the unwary. Every man who lives or works on the coast has to be constantly aware of the change of the tide, which occurs four times daily. To neglect these times could place one in imminent peril. Consider the small fishing boat plying the peaceful waters behind one of the islands. The incoming tide is moving at about twelve miles an hour, the day is bright and sunny, and the modest fifteen-mile-an-hour on-shore breeze barely ripples the water. Slowly the boat leaves the shelter of one island and enters the unprotected strait between it and the next island. Suddenly the tide changes and begins flowing off shore. The wind, which had been moving with the water, is now moving against it. Instead of a three-mile-an-hour difference in their surface speeds, the difference is now twenty-seven miles an hour. Within minutes, the placid strait becomes a roiling heaving mass of five-foot waves as the accumulated mass of water from behind the islands and in the bays attempts to return to the sea through the narrow strait. This is called a rip-tide, and its fury can indeed rip a small boat to pieces if the fisherman fails to heed the warning of the hour.

Altogether it had been a rewarding summer for Hugo. He had made new friends and had learned a new way of life. But now it was time for him to return, and he was happy to be leaving, for his dream of Montana had not abated.

Chapter 12

Fire Guard

On his return from Alaska Hugo spent a few days with Jack and Molly, catching up with their current news and recounting some of his summer's adventures. But the call of Montana grew ever louder as he studied his maps and pondered the possibilities. His half brother John, who had never married, lived in Kalispell in the northwestern part of Montana. North and east of Kalispell lay Glacier National Park, which had been established in 1886. The park, extending all the way to the Canadian Border, was bounded on the west by the North Fork of the Flathead River. The Middle Fork of the Flathead forms the southern boundary of the park until it turns and heads far to the south along the western slope of the Continental Divide. The South Fork of the Flathead River lies west of the Middle Fork and is separated from it by a spur of mountains, as it parallels the Middle Fork from the south until they meet near Columbia Falls. South of Kalispell lies the very large Flathead Lake, and between it and the South Fork of the Flathead River lies Swan Lake and the Swan River Basin. John lived in a small house on the edge of town in the middle of this beautiful country. He made his living working on construction of various kinds including the railroads. So it was to John that Hugo first went in search of work.

John Knieff

In the early fall of 1907 Hugo returned to Montana, and the danger from forest fires was at its peak. The country had been without rain for over a month, and the mountains were tinder dry. Fires were all too frequent when this situation prevailed and, paradoxically, were most often started by lightning strikes high in the mountains. High cumulus clouds drifting through and around the peaks seemed to be supercharged with electricity, and, though they produced but little rain, they fairly crackled with thunder and lightning as they passed. When a ranger spotted a fire he would get to the nearest town as quickly as possible, assemble a crew with supplies and a pack train, and head for the fire. Of course they could not put the fire out, but they were often able to contain it and prevent its spread. Fires travel with the wind, and in the mountains this usually means up the mountain side. The heat created by the fire forms a powerful updraft, which carries the fire with it up the slope. When it reaches the top, the fire travels much more slowly as it is forced to travel downward against the natural updraft it is creating.

On reaching a fire, the crew would busy itself "cleaning up" by throwing any still-burning debris along the edge of the fire into the burned-over area, where a shift in the wind could not fan the embers into a new fire. The ranger in charge would always be on the lookout for an opportunity to start a "backfire." This was done by starting a small fire to burn an area toward which the main fire was heading. When the main fire reached the burned-over area, it would starve for fuel and die out. "Backfiring" was a very dangerous procedure demanding the greatest caution. The first requisite was a natural break or line where the spread of the new fire could be controlled. This might be a little side stream or ridge of rock, which would allow the fire to spread only in the desired direction. The greatest danger lay in a sudden change in the wind direction, which could allow the backfire to get out of control, or even worse, trap the fire fighters between the two fires.

Hugo had been with John only a few days when a call came out for more fire fighters. Any able-bodied man not actively employed could be impressed into service by a ranger. Hugo was more than willing to respond to the call. It was his opportunity to get right out into those beautiful mountains and receive wages besides. While most of the men complained vociferously about the endlessly long days of hard work with axe, saw, and shovel, the plainest food and the "privilege" of sleeping on the rocky ground with only a blanket, Hugo seemed to thrive on the challenge. When the rest of the men were released from duty, he was allowed to stay on and serve as a fire guard, assisting the rangers in their daily routine, ready to fight when the next fire broke out.

View of the South Fork of the Flathead River.

When the fire season was finally over in late October, Hugo returned to Kalispell where John was able to find occasional work for him. Toward the end of January, Hugo finally received his appointment as a permanent fire guard. After a short period of indoctrination, he was issued his "gear" and ordered to report to Ranger Bond at Bigfork. From there he was sent to the head of Swan Lake where he and another guard named Higgins were to assist Ranger Bond in building a log cabin for the new Ranger Station. The three men spent the month of February cutting, hauling and peeling logs and laying them up to form the walls of the cabin. The weather was often bad, with rain and snow, but the temperatures remained mild, and the work progressed with little interruption. The cabin was finished on February 27th, and on the 29th Hugo returned to Bigfork where he took his oath of office as a U.S. Forest Guard.

Hugo's next assignment was up near Coram, where the Forest Service was building a new road along the Flathead River through the Badrock Canyon. He often worked with the blasting crew, whose job it was to drill holes into the solid rock to receive the dynamite. The holes were several feet deep and spaced a foot or two apart along a line to be blasted. Drilling these holes was tediously slow hard work. Three men usually worked together on this job. One held the star drill in the hole and rotated it a few degrees after each strike of the hammer. The other two men alternately struck the head of the drill with a heavy, seven-pound hammer swung from over their heads with the full force of their body behind the blow. This required precision and rhythm, for a misplaced blow would spell disaster for the man holding the bit. When a line of these holes was charged and detonated in a progressive series of explosions, the face of the rock would fall away as neatly as though Thor had wielded his magic hammer.

During these days Hugo learned to respect the power of dynamite and to always treat it with caution. Double fuses were always used, as a misfire would mean working near a live charge and was extremely dangerous. Powder that had gotten wet could not be trusted. On one occasion over a hundred pounds of it got damp, and the problem arose as to how to dispose of it. They solved their problem by spreading it on the top of a large rock down near the river and firing a rifle at it from far above. The rock simply vanished! Yet if their firewood was damp and they needed kindling, they often used a stick of dynamite for this purpose. They simply cut it open, held a match to it, and it would burn with a steady controlled flame!

During this time, Hugo used his Sundays off to practice packing a horse using a diamond hitch, to practice running a compass line, and to estimate timber under the tutelage of Ranger Jack Clack, who had become a good friend. Toward the end of April, he went into Kalispell and took his final examination and became a full-fledged ranger. Work continued on the new road throughout the spring, although Hugo had frequent opportunities to go into the little town of Columbia Falls to get supplies and practice his packing skills.

On the 10th of July, Hugo went into town for supplies, and the next day picked up a string of pack horses and headed up the South Fork of the Flathead River. The rangers had lay-out camps established along the river at five- to ten-mile intervals all the way up to where it headed, over a hundred miles to the southeast at the lower end of what is now the Bob Marshall Wilderness. The first of these stations was at Hungry Horse, which is now the site of the Hungry Horse Dam. The dam is 504 feet high and creates a reservoir that extends over thirty miles to the south and east. Next came Riverside Park, where Hugo laid over a day waiting for Ranger Clack to join him. The following day they went to Coal Banks where they built a raft to cross the river with their provisions. They spent two weeks building a pasture fence at the Coal Banks station before moving on to Spotted Bear, the approximate midpoint of the river and the major up-stream station. From there they went up past Meadow Creek to Black Bear, where they spent ten days working on the pasture fence before returning to Spotted Bear, clearing the trail of windfalls on the way.

The following morning Hugo started up Spotted Bear River on patrol by himself for the first time. He found the going much more difficult here as there was no established trail to follow. By the middle of the afternoon he had made about five miles and decided that he would look for a good place to camp for the night. He soon discovered a beautiful little meadow that ran down to the river and was bordered on one side by a stand of lodge pole pine. An open limestone ridge ran down from the mountainside and out

Box canyon on the Southfork above Meadow Creek.

Spotted Bear River where it empties into the South Fork.

onto the upper edge of the meadow, giving it the appearance of isolation from all the wild country surrounding it. Small balsam trees grew along the edge of the pine and provided boughs from which he could thatch his bed. By "shingling," or lapping the boughs over each other twice, from opposite directions, a soft and springy pallet could be formed on which to lay his blanket. An extra layer of boughs at the head even provided the semblance of a pillow. His horse would be free to feed in the meadow while he tried his luck with his fly rod on the river.

Hugo chose a level spot not far from the river to make his camp. He unsaddled his horse, which promptly showed its appreciation by rolling gratefully in a nearby dusty patch. With his bough bed made and an evenings supply of dry pine and willow wood cut and piled, he next cast his fly upon the stream and soon had a brace of fine cutthroat trout for dinner. Cleaning them required little more that removing the entrails, as the scales were too fine to be noticed and even the heads had some choice bits of meat on them. Soon the scent of the smoke from his fire mingled with that of the pines and the smell of the fish as they broiled over the coals. His coffee contributed its aroma as it boiled merrily while the flour "bannock," or biscuit, was first browned on the bottom of the fry pan and then browned on the top by tipping the pan toward the fire. Hugo had even found time to pick a few handfuls of huckleberries that he had spotted near the edge of the meadow to make his dinner complete.

The evening dusk descended over the mountains as Hugo sat, pipe-in-hand by the flickering fire and listened to the night sounds as they intruded on the silence of the wilderness; the splash of a trout as it sought a belated dinner, the low murmur of a bird as it sought its roost, and the lonesome cry of a coyote from some far off ridge. It was time for him to contemplate the vastness and the grandeur of the mountains, and to recognize his total and utter aloneness with nature. The night was black and silent as he crawled under his blanket, though the stars shown with a brilliance unmatched in areas where civilization reigned.

Suddenly an unearthly scream pierced the silence as keenly as would a bolt of lightning pierce the blackness of a stormy night. Pure terror struck at Hugo's heart, and the hackles at the back of his neck rose as the screech echoed from the hills and hung upon the meadow like a pall. His horse, no less frightened than its master, came for solace in his presence and that of the still flickering remains of the evening's fire. Hugo rose and added more wood in a vain attempt to dispel the shroud of darkness that surrounded them. When the fire again blazed brightly, he lit his pipe and felt the slow return of reason overcome his fear. Since there was no woman about to rent the heart with her screams —What then? Hugo concluded that it was a lonely mountain lion searching for a mate, or simply voicing its concern over the strange scents wafted its way by the evening air. He returned to his bed, and though the screams were repeated two or three more times during the night, the terror did not return, nor would it ever again, although his horse remained by his side for the rest of the night. In the morning he found the puma's "sign" on the limestone ridge above his camp.

After breaking camp, Hugo continued on up stream for a couple of miles, where he left the river and climbed a mountain, then proceeded along a spur until he came to the ridge that divided the South Fork drainage from that of the Middle Fork. From here he could overlook the entire Spotted Bear basin, and no fire in his territory was likely to escape his scrutiny. This established his regimen for the rest of the fall. Up and down the Spotted Bear to the South Fork, and up and down the South Fork, ever on the watch for fires, and clearing trail whenever necessary.

On the evening of September 4th, Hugo spotted his first fire down stream from Spotted Bear on Sullivan Creek. The next morning he headed down to pick up additional fire-fighting tools. He camped at Beaver Creek that night and continued on early the next morning until he met his supervisor. The two returned to Beaver Creek, and the following morning they attempted to go to the fire by going up Sullivan Creek. There was no trail, so they had to follow the water, which was full of logs and drift wood. Finally they realized that they were in a box canyon from which they could not exit except by returning to the river. They spent that night in a heavy rain, but the next morning broke clear, and they were able to make their way to the fire by going up the north side of the creek for about eight miles. The fire was nearly out when they got to it, and a little trenching around some "hot spots" near the edge made all secure. About 150 to 200 acres of Douglas fir and larch had been destroyed. Such small fires were common, and did not represent a great loss.

On September 11th, Ranger Alan Calbick joined Hugo at the Spotted Bear Ranger Station. There was a log cabin there that needed a great deal of work and kept them busy between fire patrols. October proved to be a very wet month, so the fire danger was minimized. There were always trails that needed clearing, wood to be cut, fences to be repaired, additional cabin sites to be surveyed, and cabins built at the various camp sites along the river. Snow could come any time after the middle of October, so the horses had to be taken out before then. By Thanksgiving work along the South Fork was over for the year.

Chapter 13

Spotted Bear

Hugo went into Kalispell to spend Thanksgiving with his half brother John. On the following Sunday he started out for Swan Lake where he would spend the rest of the winter. His first chore was to purchase supplies in Bigfork and transport them to the Ranger Station at the head of Swan Lake. The foot of the lake was only about seven miles out of town and horses could be used that far. From there to the head of the lake was about ten miles by boat and still another mile of packing remained beyond there. The boat trip required a full day each way. Ranger Bond had his own cabin near the lake, some little distance from the Ranger Station, and many of their supplies were stored there until the station could be made fully usable. The logs had not yet been chinked, and other finishing touches still needed to be completed. When this was done, a pole bridge needed to be built across Spring Creek, and then the ever-present fence lines had to be cut. On December 21, Hugo went to Kalispell on leave and stayed there until January 2, 1909.

The month of January was very stormy, and at times the cold was severe—with the temperature reaching forty-five degrees below zero one morning. Fortunately, the severe cold did not remain for long at a time, but was interspersed with warmer periods. The snow, however, was persistent and accumulated in depths that made outdoor work very difficult. Hugo and Ranger Bond spent much of their time caring for the government horses, and cutting and preparing fence posts. In the spring the meadow would be fenced in, brushed, and burned, so that a crop of hay could be cut the following fall. Cutting firewood was another necessity, while occasional trips to Bigfork—for supplies or to make surveys—broke the monotony. They also made their own snowshoes, travel without them would be impossible! The snow became too deep for the horses and many of the fence posts that they had prepared were distributed along the fence line on foot.

Finally, toward the end of May, the fence was completed and the cabin area brushed out and made ready for the coming season. It was at about this time that Hugo's brother Arthur arrived from Minnesota and hired on as a forest guard. The two brothers worked most of June repairing the Swan Lake Ranger Station cabin. They also spent a few days with Ranger Clack looking for a route from Swan Lake across the mountain range to Spotted Bear on the South Fork. Hugo was then transferred back to the South Fork via Columbia Falls.

Hugo spent the summer of 1909 patrolling the South Fork from Hungry Horse to Spotted Bear and working on the trails to keep them in good shape. With well over forty miles of trail, there were often trees down over the trail or low spots to be repaired, many of which required a "corduroy," which consisted of a layer of logs laid down over the trail and covered with dirt. Various guards worked with Hugo, and when they traveled, there were usually two or three pack horses or mules with a rider at the head of the line and another bringing up the

Temporary layout camp, showing Hugo and his crew.

rear. While they carried their basic supplies with them, they usually depended on fresh fish or fowl in the form of Spruce Grouse or Fool Hens for their evening meal. All of the streams were well stocked by nature with native trout, or Cutthroat, which were easily caught. On arriving at a spot where they would stop for the night, one of the men would built up a fire and cut some boughs for their beds while the other would slip down to the stream and catch a few trout for their supper.

The Fool Hens, in particular, were extremely tame. As the men rode along the trail, a Fool Hen would often hop onto one of the packs and ride along for a while. If Hugo spotted one perched on a low branch near the trail, he would often reach out and tap it on its toes with his rifle barrel. The bird would then step up onto the barrel and ride along with him for a while. The men all carried long barreled revolvers too. If they were in the mood for "chicken," the man riding in the lead would shoot the heads off any birds that he saw, until they had enough for dinner. But if he should miss, he would have to trade places with his partner and let him do the shooting until he missed. The first time that Hugo tried this, he shot over his horse's head, which must have been painful to its ears. From then on the horse would usually spot the bird before Hugo did and would stop, drop its head and hold its breath, to form a steady platform for Hugo while he shot!

On October 22nd Hugo left from Coram to assist a Mr. Fitzwater on a timber survey project that he was beginning up along the Middle Fork of the Flathead River. Their job was to travel over a large tract of land and estimate the timber on it. It would not be finished until November 21st, and, during that time, the two of them would spend all but two or three nights on the trail. Often they would leave their horses and travel several miles back from the trail along long forgotten section lines to reestablish survey corners that had been marked years before with metal posts driven into the ground. These corner posts were in turn marked by a blaze on the trunk of a nearby tree,which was called a "witness tree." Mr. Fitzwater, over years of practice, had developed an ability to maintain direction and estimate distance, which fascinated Hugo. He would follow a heading along an imaginary line, until he estimated that he had gone a mile. Then he would stop and look for the witness tree. Even though he had been going over the roughest terrain, circling obstructions, and battling undergrowth, he could invariably spot it without having to move. He would point to a spot and say, "The corner should be right there." He was seldom more than a few feet off. At times, because of snow cover or other obstruction, the corner would be inaccessible. He would then have to go on for another mile to establish a corner. His only aids were a hand-held compass and a counter which he used to keep track of his paces.

Organizing a pack train.

While Fitzwater was running the line, Hugo would be taking notes on the type of timber, its age, and density. He would also note its general condition, whether it had suffered fire damage, or was under attack by insects. From these notes they could estimate the value of the timber in the corridor they were surveying. Fitzwater was instrumental in teaching Hugo a great deal about entomology as well as surveying.

Hugo returned to Hungry Horse Station on November 26th. He worked from then until Christmas on the new road they were building between there and Coram, as well as repairing some telephone lines and repairing and recaulking the cabin. On a Sunday when they were not busy, Hugo and one or two of the Forest Guards working with him would often do a little target practice. There was a natural "salt lick" near their cabin where the deer would come to lick a soft clay—apparently to satisfy their need for certain minerals. Over the years, the deer had literally eaten a good distance into the bank. This depression was a natural spot for the men to set up their targets of used cans or bottles. The deer did not seem to mind the noise and would on occasion actually come and use the lick while the men were firing at their target only a few feet away. Naturally, with the deer that plentiful and tame, it is no wonder that they ate venison whenever they wanted it.

A successful deer hunting trip.

Hugo and Charlie Topel with their elk.

On his return to duty in January 1910, after the Christmas holiday, Hugo worked with a crew building a new horse barn, wood shed, and ice house at Hungry Horse Ranger Station. Except for a two-week leave to assist with a survey between Swan Lake and Holland Lake in the later part of May, he would remain on the South Fork until the spring of 1911.

The winter of 1910-1911 was a memorable one for ranger Knieff. He and Ranger Hoke spent the entire winter at the Spotted Bear cabin, coming out only once for their annual Christmas leave. They were supposed to be building fences for the horses, but at that elevation the snow was too deep to accomplish anything of that nature. They had to take their horses down to Coram by the middle of October as there was no way that they could winter them that high in the mountains. That meant that their trip back in had to be made on snowshoes as well as their trip out and in again over the holidays and their trip out again in the spring. Each time meant four days of hiking on snowshoes over trails that were often obliterated by nearly eight feet of snow.

Cabin at Spotted Bear where Hugo and Hoke wintered.

Although they could not build the fences, they were by no means idle. After breakfast they would usually cut firewood until noon in order to maintain a comfortable supply ahead to cushion against those days too stormy to get out at all. After dinner they would usually go for a hike on their snowshoes. There was a herd of elk "yarded" down near the main river in a heavy stand of lodge pole pine. Because of the deep snow, even the elk with their long legs confined their travel to their established trails. If they were forced to leave them, they would soon founder and die. They fed off the lower hanging boughs until, by spring, the entire grove had been cleaned to a height of over eight feet. It was one of the rangers' favorite hikes to go down and watch the elk as they fed.

Hugo and Hoke (he must have had a first name, but it was never used) often crossed the Spotted Bear River on a large log that spanned it several miles above camp. As the snow continued to pack on the top of the log, it gradually built upward and outward to form a V-shaped cap on the top of the log. One day, as they were crossing with Hoke in the lead, this crust of snow gave way under Hugo and sent him splashing into the water below. Miles from camp and in the winter cold, this soaking could easily lead to hypothermia and death. Hoke heard the splash and turned to see Hugo struggling in the water. He continued on to shore and disappeared while Hugo fought to overcome the current and get to shore. When he succeeded, he found Hoke, sheltered behind a big rock, with a fire already blazing. Hugo stripped himself of his clothes, put on Hokes coat and got between the fire and the rock for warmth while Hoke wrung out the wet clothes and dried them over the fire. As all of the clothes were made of wool they did not absorb the water and were soon dried out. Within an hour the men were again on their way to camp suffering no ill effects. Had Hoke attempted to help Hugo get out of the water, one of them, and perhaps both, might well have perished. His decision had been made spontaneously and without consulting Hugo. Hugo, too, had accurately appraised the situation even as he struggled in the water. He knew what he would find when he reached shore though there had been no verbal communication between them during the entire incident. This type of mental interchange, often called e.s.p., becomes a near-daily occurrence for those who work together under the circumstances that these men shared. Riding down the trail together, separated by the pack animals so as to make talking difficult, their thoughts were free to wander far and wide. Yet when they stopped and came together they would frequently try to express the same thought to each other simultaneously. Fortunately Hugo's fall occurred on the Spotted Bear crossing, which was only a few feet above the water. The rangers frequently crossed the South Fork just above Bunker Creek on a log that was nearly twenty feet above the water where the river was confined to a narrow gorge and became a rushing torrent.

Supper was the big meal of the day for Hugo and Hoke. They had killed an elk and two deer that fall after the weather had become cool enough to keep the meat. They had plenty of dried beans, canned vegetables, flour, sugar, coffee, dried fruit, lard, and a slab of bacon to go along with their wild meat, although their diet did develop a certain sameness as the weeks went by. The long evenings were passed by making the necessary repairs on their clothing and tools, reading from one of the few books that they had with them, and of course playing the nightly set of cribbage games. After the long day in the cold fresh air of the mountains, sleeping aids were not necessary.

When spring arrived, and Hugo and Hoke came down out of the mountains, Hugo found that he had a decision to make. He had a good job with much responsibility, but his chance to progress was severally limited by his lack of formal education. He found himself taking orders from young men fresh out college—with a wealth of technical skill but no practical experience. He recalled the time he had been ordered to pack in a number of steel rods twenty feet long to be used on a new bridge under construction up in the mountains. Imagine the way those would bounce up and down on a pack saddle and how hard it would be on a horse or mule. Imagine too, how those flopping ends would continually catch on trees and brush as the trail continually twisted and turned. Hugo had scarcely gotten out of sight of the Ranger Station when he stopped, built a good fire, heated those rods in the middle and with the aid of a couple of near by trees bent them into elongated U's, which rode very nicely the rest of the way. He received no credit from the young engineer who received them on the job and was faced with the problem of straightening them again, however, although they were not actually damaged.

He also recalled the beauty of those mountains, and the smell of fresh-caught trout frying in a pan or broiling on a spit over the coals. He could still see that giant Cutthroat that he had caught up at the forks on Bunker Creek. It had measured twenty-two inches long with a girth of twenty-one inches. He remembered how

Old bridge over the Spotted Bear River. The rods mentioned in the story were probably used in building a bridge to replace this one.

puzzled he had been at the sound of apparent explosions up in the mountains during the fire season when no clouds or lightning were about, until he had had the privilege of watching the event as it occurred. He had been going to a fire that had started down near the river and was rapidly going up the mountain. It was "crowning," or burning in the tree tops far ahead of the ground fire that followed. Such fires could travel at over thirty miles an hour and were an awesome sight as they destroyed everything in their path, including the wildlife. The fire had split when it came to a sharp little draw, and was traveling on each side of the ravine as Hugo approached, leaving about thirty acres of unburned timber in the middle. Suddenly there was a terrific explosion and roar as the entire patch of timber burst into fire spontaneously from the accumulated heat of the surrounding fire.

He recalled those hunting trips that he had taken with Hoke or the Topal boys, when they had shot their winter's supply of elk and venison. He particularly remembered his first goat. It was not a happy experience, but it had taught him a lesson that he would never forget. They had spotted the goat high up on the mountain, and had spent nearly half a day working their way to a position above it before they moved around to get in position to shoot. It would be very leery of anything approaching from below but would pay little attention to anything from above. When the hunters came out on the lip of a ledge they spotted the goat lying on a tiny ledge far down the nearly vertical mountain side, its beautiful white fur gleaming in the afternoon sun. Without a thought, Hugo had fired nearly straight down at the goat at a point between the top of its shoulders. It died instantly, without so much as a kick of its legs. Only later did Hugo realize that there was no possible way to retrieve it. It had attained its perch by following a narrow ledge only six or eight inches wide at times, and at one point was interrupted by a gap of nearly eight feet. Fine for goats with their suction cup feet but not for man! When he eventually did get his goat, he made sure that it would be accessible before he shot it.

Much as Hugo had enjoyed his work and the mountains that he loved, there were still negative aspects to be considered. The work was hard and at times very dangerous. He recalled the time when he had spotted smoke well back

Hugo's Mountain Goat

from the river in what he thought was probably another fire district. But he could not be sure and his first mandate when he saw smoke was to find its exact location or determine definitely that it was out of his territory. So, although it was already nearly noon, he started up a mountain to get a better look at the fire, leaving his horse and gear below.

The mountain proved to be more difficult to climb than he had anticipated, and it was late afternoon before he could be sure that the fire was indeed out of his district. Another problem now presented itself. He had used the last of the water in his canteen some time earlier. Now he was beginning to really suffer from thirst. Ordinarily this would not be a problem, as every little ravine or canyon would have springs in it. Much to his chagrin, however, after exploring several possibilities, he realized that he was on a "dry mountain." The formation was such that there were no springs. If he attempted to go back to the river where he had left his horse and gear, it would be dark long before he got there. He was already feeling ill from dehydration and the heavy exertion of the long day's climb. In this condition he would probably never get to the bottom. His alternative was to go up to where he was sure there would be snow. Slowly he made his way upward as his head pounded with pain. Finally, as dusk began to descend, he reached the snow line. He put a handful of snow into his parched mouth and immediately realized that this was a mistake, as it began to make him even more ill. Fortunately he was able to start a little fire on which he could melt some snow in the little fry pan that he always carried. His thirst finally quenched, he slept till early morning when he melted enough snow to fill his canteen and headed down the mountain. He was thankful for a small bag of raisins that kept him going until he reached his horse late that afternoon.

Hugo also began to think of all the lonely hours. He would soon be thirty years old and what did he have to look forward to in the years to come? Arthur had returned to Minnesota and was trying to work the farm, but it was an uphill struggle. Much of what Hugo earned was sent east to buy fencing or whatever else was needed to keep the little farm going. Before reaching a decision, he decided to take a quick trip over to Oregon and visit Jack and Molly, whom he hadn't seen for nearly four years.

Chapter 14

The Bug Man

Hugo returned to Columbia Falls on the third of July, 1911, and reported to Supervisor Bremmer. He had decided that he would stay on in Montana but in a somewhat different capacity. He would be working for the U.S. Department of Agriculture as a timber inspector. His headquarters would still be in Columbia Falls, but he would be called on to work all over the state wherever there was timber. While he would be looking at all forms of damage to timber, he would be particularly interested in the Dendroctonus beetle, which was beginning to infest the state in alarming numbers. This beetle would bore into a tree to lay its eggs, and the larvae would continue their boring, leaving networks of tunnels until they finally pupated and emerged through the bark as adults. Heavy infestations could kill large stands of timber in relatively short periods of time. The only remedy was to find these infestations while they were still relatively small, and cut out the infected trees before the beetles could spread. It would be Hugo's job to identify infected areas and to mark individual trees for cutting where the infestation was just beginning and clear-cutting was not yet necessary.

Hugo enjoyed his new work because it kept him on the move and introduced him to different parts of the state. More importantly, it was a learning experience. He bought a microscope that he could carry with him and used it to study not only the wood-borers for which he was searching, but also other insects that excited his curiosity. On one occasion he was confronted by a huge tarantula spider with a body as large as a silver dollar and a total diameter of over four inches. When he tried to pass, it would spring at him and attempt to strike him about knee high. Hugo found a long thin splinter from a pine stump and attempted to skewer the spider on its point. The spider wanted no part of this, and the two were soon locked in mortal combat. When Hugo would thrust at the spider, it would leap and attempt to strike his hand or alight on his stick and follow it up to his hand. After several minutes of this thrust and parry, Hugo finally succeeded in impaling the spider on the end of his splinter and then transferring it to a specimen jar. Later he studied it at leisure under his microscope and identified its fangs and the poison sac attached to them. After returning to Minnesota he was able to examine a large native spider and identify similar parts on it, even though it was not generally thought to be poisonous.

Hugo spent a great deal of his time near Lame Deer, on the Cheyenne Indian Reservation in southeastern Montana. From there he worked east as far as Ekalaka, and on occasion even into North Dakota. There was an area of severe infestation on Lame Deer Creek, and during the summer of 1911 he marked over 5,500 individual trees to be cut. He had to see that a sawmill was brought in to process the timber, as well as being responsible for the hiring of Indians who would assist with the work. He also trained local foresters in identifying the Dendroctonus beetle, and the methods used for its control.

Hugo found the Cheyenne Indians easy to work with. While in some ways they were more backward than other tribes, they were honest and willing to work. While he worked on their reservation, he lived in a small cabin, which was never locked. The only thing ever taken from it was part of a loaf of bread. One of the adults explained that it must have been taken by a hungry child, who didn't know any better.

One of the experiences that Hugo liked to relate, in later years, was that of watching the Indians butcher. At that time the government provided the Indians with meat in the form of beef cattle, which were given to them two or three at a time. The Indians were allowed to do the butchering but were then required to turn the carcasses over to the Indian agent who doled out the meat to them as needed. The Indians were allowed to keep the head, hide, and the rest of the offal for themselves. Whole Indian families would involve themselves in the process. What blood could be caught in the process was drunk with relish. When the beast had been disemboweled, their first concern was the liver. This was laid out in such a manner that the bile was on top, in the center of a natural depression. The bile was then slashed open and strips of the warm liver were sliced off, dipped in the bile and eaten raw by all the participants. It was considered to be a great delicacy. The intestines were stripped of their contents and saved, as were the lungs and other internal organs. When the butchering was completed even the Indian dogs could find little to feed on from the remains.

In July 1912, Hugo had been working in the Ekalaka area. When he was finished, he decided to make the return trip to Lame Deer, which was well over a hundred miles, straight across country on horseback. His first night out he stayed at a cattle ranch where he witnessed a bit of the typical by-play that went on in the Old West. There was a young cowboy at the supper table, apparently a new hand, who was being ragged at unmercifully in an apparent attempt to spoil his meal. Finally he took his plate and left the table to the accompanying snickers of his tormentors. Moments later he returned, a portion of freshly deposited green cow pie on his plate, and proceeded with his meal. His harassment was never resumed.

The talk at the table turned to rattlesnakes and the danger from their bite. It seemed that the week before, one of the hands had killed a snake for its rattles. While he was in the process of removing them, the snake struck, apparently from a reflex, and bit the man on the wrist. He died that night.

Hugo left to continue his journey early the next morning, with the stories of rattlesnakes still fresh in his mind. As he followed cattle trails that went in his general direction he often had to cross coulees where the trail dipped down and the surrounding ground was even with his waist. He could easily envision a snake lying there in deadly ambush, and even his horse seemed to share his uneasy feelings. Later, Hugo did indeed kill a rattlesnake to take its rattles as a souvenir, but he took the precaution off cutting off its head before going after the rattles. The bloody stump where its head had been did no damage when it struck him on the arm!

After completing his work in the southeastern part of the state, Hugo returned to the mountains around Columbia Falls, the country he had come to know so well. While here, he became acquainted with an old trapper who used a pair of hounds to tree mountain lions so he could capture them alive and sell them to zoos. At times he would be gone for a few days and would ask Hugo to feed the hounds for him while he was away. On one such occasion the dogs were both gone when he went to feed them and were still gone on the following day. On the third day one of them returned, tired and hungry. Hugo fed it and it immediately left. The next morning the other hound made its appearance and was fed, only to leave when it was finished. This pattern continued until the trapper returned. He just smiled and asked Hugo to go with him to get the cat. Sure enough, the dogs had gone hunting on their own and had kept a lion up a tree until their master had returned. They had taken turns coming in for food, but the poor cat was getting mighty hungry!

In 1910 Hugo's brother Arthur had been called home to Minnesota. Their half sister Emma, who had been living in Washington, D.C. had lost her husband and was left with two young boys to raise. As she had nowhere else to go, she moved her family with all their belongings back to the farm at Bay Lake. Arthur would stay with them and help them while Hugo continued to work and send back what he could to help them out. In the spring of 1913, Hugo got word that Emma was terminally ill with cancer.

Arthur could no longer manage by himself, and Caroline, an older sister of Emma's, came to help out. This arrangement didn't work out very well, as "Aunt Carrie" was not used to dealing with two young boys and, moreover, she was anxious to get on with her own life. Hattie Reilly, a young niece of Emma's, who had helped her when her children were born and had also spent considerable time with her in Washington D.C., was again called upon to help. Hugo felt that it was now his duty to return home and help the rest of the family over this trying time.

Chapter 15

Hugo Comes Home

Hugo arrived home to a very different lifestyle than he had been accustomed. Emma was obviously in failing health and could do little to help with the daily chores. Hattie, her adored niece, cared for her and her two boys as well as doing the cooking and running the house in general, although milk separators and the like were still somewhat of a mystery to the slight, young "city girl." She had lost her own mother when she was only eight, and, although she did have a stepmother, her home was never again the same. She welcomed the chance to be with Emma, whom she loved as dearly as she had her own mother. She was also far better suited to cope with the boys than Carrie had been. She had the knack of understanding them and their needs during this difficult time, and of course, she already knew them very well.

Emma Powers

Hattie Reiley

The two boys were totally different. Robert, the elder of the two, had been adopted as a baby after Emma had lost three babies in infancy to an inherited breathing difficulty. Chester was born then, and he surprised everyone by surviving a similar respiratory problem. Robert was all boy and mischievous if not downright bad sometimes. Hattie recognized that he had special needs and was able to communicate with him in a way that the men never could. He would pout and growl when asked to do something for her, but when one day she pumped her own water instead of waiting for him, he came to her with tears in his eyes and said, "Don't you ever do that again, no matter how much I growl and complain."

Robert, sitting with his arm around Chester

Chester was the dreamer. When asked to do something, he would gladly agree, then drift off into a world of his own and totally forget what was expected of him. He often dreamed of flying and making wonderful discoveries up among the clouds. His father had been an inventor, and this urge to create was inborn in him.

Hugo's brother Arthur was the scholar in their family. He had taken normal training and had taught some school. He loved to read the

Arthur and Etta Knieff

works of the masters and did so at every opportunity he had. Shorter and stockier than Hugo, he had powerful arms and shoulders. His skill with a hoe and scythe were unexcelled. Now that Hugo had come home, he hoped that he would be able to return to his teaching.

The principal cash crop on the Knieff farm was rapidly becoming raspberries. Arthur had planted a large patch up in the field and every year he enlarged it a little. The old Cuthbert berries of that era required a great deal of work as they had to be "put down" in the fall and then "brought up" again in the spring to prevent winter kill. This job entailed tipping the canes over and holding them on the ground while a shovelful of dirt was put on them to hold them in that position. They were then covered with straw. In the spring they had to be carefully uncovered and returned to their normal upright position.

A big vegetable garden was of course a must, along with field corn for the stock and a hay field for winter feed. There were always three or four head of milk cows and a team of horses for which to provide pasture and feed. They always raised a pig for butchering in the fall, which provided them with their winter's supply of ham and bacon as well as lard, fresh pork and sausage. There was never an excuse for a farm family not to eat well.

Hugo's return meant that he could share Arthur's responsibilities and lighten his work load, but it also meant that they would have to do without the money that Hugo had been able to send home while he was working. The raspberry crop was good that year, and, when it came in, the whole family was pressed into service. Besides the regular farm work, picking and packing the berries took many hours every day. Then there was the seven-mile trip to Deerwood with the team and wagon every evening, to get the berries on the train so they would be in the markets the following morning while they were still fresh. The long return trek home and the care of the horses afterward meant that it would be nearly eleven o'clock before Hugo could get to bed. Five-thirty A.M. came mighty early in those days.

The raspberry season lasted for about a month, and, when it was over, life on the little farm could return to a more normal pace. Hattie had to learn to can the vegetables to feed them the following winter. There was a seemingly endless supply of pint- and quart-sized mason jars to be filled with sweet corn, tomatoes, peas, and both string and wax beans. There were dill pickles and bread-and-butter pickles to be made, as well as various kinds of relishes. Lugs of peaches, pears and plums were brought from town to be made into sauce and canned along with a generous supply of raspberries that continued to bear at a reduced rate after the main season was over. Canning was a hot and tiresome job over the kitchen range in the sultry August heat, but it brought the satisfaction of knowing that the family would be well fed in the long cold months to come. Later in the fall, gunny sacks of potatoes had to be stored in the root cellar, along with the carrots and rutabagas, which were covered with sand to keep them from drying out. Cabbages were piled against the wall along with a barrel of apples. Later, when the pork was added to the larder, and a bag of sugar and a couple hundred pounds of flour were brought out from town, the winter's supply would be complete. What other small groceries they might need, as well as dry goods and some hardware could be purchased from the little general store being operated by Arthur N. Gray at the point where the road from Deerwood first hit the lake near Ruttger's home.

Emma continued to fail throughout the summer, and, in the fall, surgery was tried as a last resort to stay the inroads of a malignant tumor. In a few short weeks she was gone after having extracted a promise from Hattie that she would "look after my boys."

Now was Arthur's chance to return to teaching, leaving Hugo and Hattie to care for the two boys. This arrangement was to continue until the boys had finished school.

But life was far from a total drudgery, in spite of the hard work. Simple pleasures were real pleasures in those days, and a two-mile walk to visit neighbors was as thoroughly enjoyed as are the electronic pastimes of the present. They may not have had a television, but their piano provided lively music for all to sing to, and their home-popped corn would easily hold its own against the microwaved variety, or any theaters have to offer today, for that matter.

When the freeze-up came a few days before Thanksgiving, the lake was transformed into a frozen mirror. How the ice would growl and complain as it froze, sending expansion cracks dancing across the surface from one shore to the other. When it had attained a thickness of at least three inches, it was deemed thick enough, and the skating could begin. Then the young people of the community would don their skates and congregate as if by magic in the cold crispness of the starry evening. Shouts of glee would soon arise as they skated singly or in pairs, while performing their graceful pirouettes upon the unblemished surface. On one occasion they all came together in a tight knot, and their combined weight caused the ice to sag toward the center threatening to send them all into the water. Fortunately, one of them became aware of the danger and gave the warning to disperse in time to avert a tragedy.

That winter the "boys" in the area discovered a new diversion. Louie Kinder, who lived with his mother across the bay from the Knieff home and would later become the judge of probate court in Brainerd, had acquired a chemistry set. He, along with Earl Archibald, John Christensen, and Hugo, spent a number of evenings performing the numerous experiments outlined in the instruction book. The Kinder kitchen would often reek with the ill-smelling effluvia emitted as a result of their efforts. One evening the trio was particularly gratified with their product, a vial of well-concentrated ammonia. Each in turn unstopped the vial and sniffed with the resultant appropriate grimace and teary eyes, to the delight of the spectators. As the vial completed its rounds, the family cat, who had been dozing peacefully on a chair by the fire, was aroused by their chortling and came to investigate the cause of their merriment. Now who could deny this unsolicited request to participate in their quest for knowledge? The vial was duely uncorked, and, as the stringent fumes arose from its neck, the unwary cat took a deep sniff. His transformation was immediate and complete. No longer the quiet lazy bystander, he became the life of the party! With a shriek of anguish, he leapt from the chair and raced with unbelievable speed in search of egress from this evil laboratory. He accelerated with each bound, as he began an orbit of the kitchen in vain search of escape. The floor could no longer contain his angular velocity, and his path rose up the walls as he continued his circuit of the kitchen. Curtains hung in shreds behind him, and the calendar fell in his wake.

The Kinder home on Battle Point

Earl Archibald, Hugo Knieff, John Christensen, and Louis Kinder

The sound of the ruckus brought Mrs. Kinder to the kitchen door—which flew open to her touch as the whirling dervish made its escape, narrowly missing her in the process. Before her spread the scene of destruction with the three miscreants literally bent double, convulsed with pangs of laughter at the havoc they had wrought. The cat and the kitchen soon recovered, but it was some time before the aspiring chemists were again allowed to assemble in her kitchen.

Of course there was work to be done in the winter as well. The supply of firewood had to be maintained, which meant that next winter's supply had to be cut, split and piled in ricks so that it would be thoroughly dry, before it could be burned the following year. This minimized the formation of creosote when it was burned, and thus reduced the danger of chimney fires, as well as making it much more efficient and easier to burn. Long hours out in the snow and subzero cold gave added meaning to the old adage, "He who cuts his own wood is twice warmed"! Red or white oak was the wood of choice for this purpose, because of its great heat content, and also because it was easily split. Hard maple and hickory were also good, but white elm was avoided because its twisted grain made splitting nearly impossible. Basswood and poplar made a good quick fire and were easily split, but their low caloric content and rapid burn-out made them best suited for the kitchen stove.

Another winter time ritual involved the putting up of ice to be used the following summer for the "ice box" of that era. Shortly after the New Year, when the ice in the lake had attained a thickness of about twenty inches, the men would be ready to begin this dreaded chore. If there had been a heavy accumulation of snow on the ice, an area had to be kept clear of snow for several weeks to allow the formation of good ice, and avoid the formation of "slush" ice caused by water being forced up through cracks in the ice and mixing with the snow.

Originally the ice was cut with a heavy, course-toothed ice saw, about five feet long, with a round wooden handle at one end set perpendicular to the blade. First, a hole had to be chiseled through the ice to start the saw, then two perpendicular channels were sawed and chiseled out to allow access for the saw in both directions. Blocks of ice measuring about sixteen by twenty-four inches could then be sawed and pulled from the lake with large ice tongs. These consisted of two curved pieces of metal with a loop for a handle on one end and a sharp point, like the barb on a fishhook, on the other. These were pinned together near the handle end, so that pulling on one handle would cause the hooked ends to come together, gripping the ice between them. The men wore metal ice grippers on their boots to prevent a slip and perhaps a very cold bath! These large blocks of ice, which weighed nearly 250 pounds, were skidded up onto a sled or "stone boat" and hauled to the ice house for packing.

The ice house was a room in an outbuilding that had no access except from the outside. Its doorway usually started two or three feet above the ground and extended up to the roof. In some cases it was simply a square enclosure of logs laid up to a height of about ten feet with no roof at all. Its earthen floor was covered

The old resort ice house

with sawdust to a depth of several inches, well packed and allowed to freeze down. Before the ice was brought in, the floor was covered with a layer of snow to prevent the ice from freezing too firmly to the floor. The ice blocks in each layer were packed as firmly together as possible, to within a foot of the walls. When the layer or tier of ice was completed, its surface was shaved off level and another inch of snow spread over it before the next tier was begun. Four or five tiers would usually fill it. When completed, the space between the ice and the walls was filled with sawdust, and the top was covered with at least a foot or more of the same. Packed in this way, it would keep well throughout the following summer. In the fall the sawdust would have to be removed in preparation for the next year's ice.

In later years, the old hand-saws gave way to circular saws driven with gasoline engines. The blades were set to cut to within five or six inches of the bottom of the ice. In this way a whole field of blocks could be cut, and later separated from each other with a long-handled chisel before being removed from the lake. A gang of four or five men would go from one home to the next, filling ice-houses during the ice harvest. The "lady of the house" was always well-prepared when the hungry crew came in for their noon meal, which was traditionally the largest meal of the day. If the workers would have carried a cold lunch, it would have been an insult to the family for whom they were working.

Chapter 16

The Good Times

Arthur had taught school up north in the little town of Ten Strike in the winter of 1915 and had acquired a wife in the process. He would later buy forty acres just a mile north of the Knieff's. Hugo bought out Arthur's interest in the original homestead, payment for which included grubbing out the hundreds of pine stumps that remained on what would become Arthur's field. Arthur would eventually move onto his little farm and spend his declining years raising raspberries and strawberries.

Robert finished his schooling in the little one-room schoolhouse in the spring of 1915. The next four winters he lived in town with relatives while attending high school. As soon as he graduated, he was off to make his way in the world. He eventually settled down to start a family of his own in California and became a police officer. He was killed in the line of duty when his motorcycle was hit by an intoxicated driver. He left a wife and two little girls.

This left Hugo, Hattie, Robert and Chester to run the family farm. Hugo could keep up with the work by himself until the berry picking season rolled around, when his fifteen acres of raspberries would require fifteen to twenty berry pickers to harvest the crop. This meant that he would have to provide room and board for them. Enter Albert Reiley, Hattie's father, who was a carpenter. He had remarried after Hattie's mother had passed away, but the new relationship did not go smoothly and had ended in divorce. Now at loose ends, he was more than happy to come up north and assist with the construction of a building that would serve as both work shop and dormitory for the pickers.

Albert was of Scotch and Irish descent and had been born and raised on Prince Edward Island. He and his brother Amos had emigrated to the United States when they were quite young and had settled in Minneapolis. Amos strongly resembled the Scottish side of the family, while Albert was as Irish as "Pattie's pig." Their Island homeland was, at that time, sharply divided between the Catholics and the Protestants. While the two factions got along well enough, boyish pranks and jibes between the two were a natural way of life. The Reileys were raised Protestant, despite the implication of their surname, and Albert loved to relate stories of the mischief he and his cohorts got into. On one occasion they broke up an evening prayer meeting of the

Albert and Augusta Reiley

Catholic ladies by inserting a greased piglet through an open window into their midst.

Albert never did relinquish his Irish wit and humor. The most dour of matrons would succumb to his twinkling eye and the sound of the lilting Irish tune he whistled as he worked. Even the crusty old Mrs. McCarvill, for whom he was working at the time, was forced to accede with a smile when he stole the fresh baked pie from her window ledge where it was cooling, in preparation for her expected guests, and held it ransom until she cut him a piece! The story even got out that he had her sit on the unfinished seat of the new privy he was building for her, so that he could trace the exact dimensions of the hole he needed to cut.

The project of building a combination shop and dormitory proceeded under Albert's direction. It would be a two-story building, with an open sleeping bay on each floor, as well as a screened porch wrapping around one end. The roof of the porch also served as a deck for the upper story. Measuring roughly twenty by thirty feet in size, it would easily sleep all of the berry pickers, with the girls upstairs and the boys down. When finished, its rough-board walls were covered outside with tarpaper. It was not a thing of beauty, but it served its purpose well, and would elicit many fond memories for the teenagers who would live there during the berry picking season. In those years it was known simply as "the shop" because of its utilization for that purpose during the off season.

The Shop—later called the "Black Mariah"—with Hugo's half sister, Carrie, standing in front of it.

Deerwood was the business center for the area. Being situated along the railroad, it was only natural that the Fruit Growers Association would have their offices there, along with their facilities for making berry boxes and crates. There was also a bank and two hotels, along with a livery stable, blacksmith shop, and several other small businesses.

The general store was run by Robert Coffin and was the natural assembly spot for those of the city fathers who had the time to idle on a

The Town of Deerwood in its early years

cold winter day. Old wooden chairs and benches arranged in close proximity to the wood-burning stove invited those who could to loiter a bit and swap a yarn or two as they luxuriated in the rich aromas of fresh ground coffee, pickled fish, apples, and onions and the ever-present cracker barrel. The heavier hardware and slower-moving items were kept in the unheated back room. Old Mr. Coffin was a willing party to the assemblages and often the butt of a good natured joke or story. On one occasion, on a bleak and dreary winter day, when a small group had assembled, one of them began sniffing, then said, "Bob, you don't have a dead mouse or something in here do you?" "No," he said, "I don't think so—I don't smell anything." One of the others piped up, "By golly, now that he mentions it, I think I smell something too. Could it be coming from the back room?" "Well," said the ever agreeable Mr. Coffin, "I don't think so—but we'll just go and see."

The back room was very dimly lit, so the old tin lantern that hung next to the door for just this purpose was lit, and Mr. Coffin began his search. At first he smelled nothing and let those who remained by the fire know it. But then he too, began to smell something. As he continued the search, the stench grew ever stronger. High and low he looked, with the awful aroma always just ahead. Finally, he returned to the main room, totally frustrated. Only then did one of the cronies speak up, "Say, Bob, did you check that lantern?" In disbelief, he examined the lantern. The stench was overpowering. He twisted and turned it, but saw nothing. Then he looked under the tin that shielded its top, and there it was. Someone had smeared Limburger cheese on the underside of the top. There had been no smell until the heat from the lantern had heated the cheese. From then on he had carried the source with him!

When the picking season finally began and the pickers arrived, no small part of Hugo's efforts were directed at seeing that they did indeed produce a reasonable number of crates of berries. First, they had to be roused out of bed, fed a good breakfast, and be in the patch ready to pick as soon as the dew was off the vines. They were paid two or three cents a box for a minimum of twenty boxes, after which they received a bonus of a penny a box. This psychology worked well as even the slowest of pickers would struggle diligently to reach this plateau, even if they never picked another box, while the good pickers could earn a fair day's pay. While Hattie and Hugo did pick berries too, one of them had to be on hand to check in the berries as the pickers brought them in and keep track of the number each had picked. The more imaginative pickers would sometimes try filling the bottoms of their boxes with grass, pebbles or similar debris to enhance their output. Care had to be taken to avoid even the appearance of favoritism in the assignment of rows, as the thicker the berries the faster they would pick. Clean picking was also essential and had to be enforced, since a ripe berry left unpicked one day would be over-ripe the next and could not be used, while an under-ripe berry would spoil the appearance of the entire box.

By three or four P.M. the patch had all been gone over, and while Hattie and Hugo finished packing the berries in the crates and loading the wagon for the trip to town, the pickers were free to go for a swim or indulge in their teenage games until supper was ready. A woman was engaged to do the cooking, as feeding such a crew was a full time job which included baking bread as well as cake or pies.

After the evening meal, the young people would often go for a walk or a boat ride but, after a long day in the hot sun they would soon be ready to settle down for the night. Bedtime, of course, was subject to numerous pranks; the

Berry pickers assembled by the berry house

pickers were always thinking up ways to bedevil each other. On one occasion, the boys discovered that the girls had been furnished with small porcelain "thunder mugs" for their convenience during the night, and an idea was born. Some sort of medicinal salts were procured that would foam up lavishly when introduced to water. A large bullfrog was caught on the shore of the lake, and, while the girls were safely distracted some distance from the shop, the two ingredients were secreted in one of the mugs with its cover in place. During the night one of the girls sought to avail herself of this convenience. The introduction of the moisture into the pot produced the desired results. Foam welled up in the pot, while the bullfrog awoke from his reveries and sought to escape from the unexpected deluge. The resultant screams brought pandemonium to the entire building. In the confusion, a pitcher of water was overturned in the upper bay, which immediately began to trickle down through the floor boards and onto the beds below. Who could blame the boys for thinking that it was something other than water? It took cooler heads nearly an hour to quell the near riot and restore peace to the troubled barracks. No wonder a collective sigh of relief was heard when the berry picking season ended for another year.

In the lull that followed the berry season and before the fall work began, a group of the young folks from the area decided on a boat excursion down the Mud River to Farm Island Lake. Robert and Chester were quite capable of taking care of the farm chores so Hattie and Hugo could both go. There was a total of five couples, including Earl Archibald, his sister Ethel, Louie Kinder, and Hattie's long-time friend, Lulu Stoppel, visiting from Minneapolis. The natural pairing had Earl with Hattie, Hugo with Lulu, and Louie with Ethel in the three boats needed for the journey.

All went reasonably well except that Louie, who was not very coordinated, continually attempted to compensate by teasing and cutting up with the girls. When asked to pass something, he would throw it or he would splash water with his oars to soak someone. The girls

The hardy group of voyagers on ther way to Spirit Island

finally decided that they had had enough, and, the next time they put to shore they all started chasing him. Badly outnumbered and outgunned, Louie made for the nearest tree and began to climb, pleading for mercy as he went. Sticks and other missiles followed and held him at bay until the girls finally relented and let him down, having extracted a promise that he would behave. Contrite, Louie sought to be on his best behavior, but the next time they went ashore he miscalculated again. As the bow of the boat ran up on the beach, Louie jumped out, and, as Ethel stood to follow him, he gave the boat a hefty tug to secure it more firmly on the shore. Naturally Ethel lost her balance and sat down again, but not in the boat. As the water was relatively deep, she went completely out of sight. She arose, coughing and sputtering from the river water inhaled in the process. Louie to the rescue. He hurriedly pulled her ashore, got her laid down and offered her—a drink of water!

Finally arriving at Farm Island, they proceeded out to the large island, appropriately named Spirit Island because it had long been used by the Indians as a burial site as well as for camping. They quickly set up their camp for the night. It consisted of two tents, one for the women and the other for the men. The sandy shoreline was a favorite place to hunt for artifacts such as arrowheads or pottery. While the women occupied themselves with this pursuit, the men went out and caught enough fish for their dinner. The evening was spent singing the hit tunes of the day, led by Ethel's beautiful soprano voice, and listening to Hugo's tales of the far west. As the shadows grew to darkness, enhanced by the flickering of the pine knots on the fire, the plaintive wail of a passing loon, and echoed by the far-off call of a whip-poor-will, there seemed to emanate the embodiment of those who had used this island through ageless time. The need for telling ghost stories around the campfire became imperative with such presences so strongly felt, while the occasional hoot of an owl lent emphasis to each chilling tale.

The following day dawned bright and clear with the scent of coffee and bacon sizzling in the pan soon mingling with that of the smoke from the fire and the pervading aroma of the pine-boughed canopy above. As the morning progressed, the wind came up ever stronger until the lake became so rough that they could not cross it to begin their homeward journey. Marooned on the island, they had to spend another night there and hope for calmer weather in the morning. They had food left, but the following morning promised to be one without coffee, until one of the men came up with the idea of scraping up the grounds from the previous days brew and reboiling them. The result was a rather anemic concoction that somewhat resembled coffee, and, while not the best, it did beat doing without. It was a tired and hungry group that arrived home that afternoon, with tales to tell that would liven up many a dreary winter evening in the future.

Chapter 17

War Years and Their Aftermath

The war that was to become known as World War I had begun in Europe in 1914. At first it had very little effect on the United States. People in far off Minnesota were, in fact, scarcely aware of it. But, as reports of the conflict became ever more graphic and the sinking of even unarmed vessels continued, a feeling of dread began to creep over the countryside. By the end of 1915, as relations between the United States and Germany became ever more perilous, President Wilson called upon the country to increase its preparedness. While he continued to work for a peaceful solution, it seemed that each combatant side was determined that the United States should play an active role in the war. In January of 1917, Germany began unrestricted submarine warfare against all commerce in the North Atlantic, and, on April 6th, President Wilson signed the declaration of war.

Now the full implication of war began to be felt even in northern Minnesota. American Red Cross chapters were formed at every little hamlet, and the women began to knit scarves, sweaters, and socks for the growing military need. The various groups vied with each other to see who could prepare the most bandages. Men began to sign up for the newly instituted draft, and rationing became a reality. Hugo, being thirty-six years old when the draft began, was one of the last to register, and was never called upon to serve in the army. But rationing came, and with it an extreme shortage of sugar. With no sugar to preserve them, the market for berries dropped to practically nothing. Slowly the realization came that he would have to plow up the berries and find a substitute crop to take their place. It was with a heavy heart that Hugo destroyed his berry patch, leaving only two short rows for the family use, and began preparing the land for the new crop.

Hugo's first venture into a new market took the form of planting potatoes to be used for seed. The war in Europe had produced huge food shortages, and the demand for seed potatoes appeared to be extremely high. Of course the initial seed would be expensive, and treating the seed afterwards would add to the cost, but a good harvest at the prevailing prices would bring a correspondingly high return. Unfortunately, many others had apparently seen the same possibility, and when the bumper crop of potatoes was harvested, the market became glutted, and there was very little chance to sell it. With no market, and no place to store the potatoes, Hugo had but one chance to recoup. He paid to have them all hauled into Deerwood and stored in a huge underground warehouse, with the hope that in the spring the market would improve. But it was not to be. In the spring he had to pay to have them hauled out of the warehouse and buried. So much for the potato farming era!

With the discovery of iron on the Cuyuna Range shortly after the turn of the century, small towns had sprung up wherever the ore was deemed suitable for mining. Crosby and Ironton were among the first of these mining towns, which also included Riverton, Cuyuna, Manganese, Trommald, and several smaller towns that did not endure. The height of the mining activity began around the end of the World War I, and brought with it a large influx of mining men and their families. This greatly increased the demand for fresh produce and provided an opportunity for Hugo to convert a portion of his fields to the raising of garden crops, particularly sweet corn, which he had no problem selling on the local market. It was a precarious livelihood, but, coupled with the sale of hay and firewood, and an occasional "odd job," it kept the little family going for several years.

The Fall of 1918 saw the onset of the great influenza epidemic that took so many lives across the country. Even northern Minnesota did not escape this terrible scourge, and nearly every family suffered its ravages. There were a fortunate few who were apparently immune to the dread disease, and it fell to them to go from house to house, caring for the sick and dying. Hattie was one of these. She had been terribly ill as a young girl, having suffered from a ruptured appendix. The doctors did not believe that they could successfully operate on her, and she was left to lay with peritonitis slowly destroying her internally. The size of her grotesquely bloated body was monitored daily, until finally, after several weeks of procrastination, the doctors told her father that she would soon die. They could operate, but that would surely kill her. The choice was his. Without hesitation he chose surgery. Long weeks of recuperation followed, but, in the end, she not only survived but seemed to have acquired a remarkable resistance to any infection.

Hattie was called upon to nurse Gilbert Gray while he lay dying, she nursed the Max Ruttger family while they were all ill, and, hardest of all for her, she nursed the Archibalds. Earl had gotten sick while working in a logging camp and had returned home where his sister Ethel cared for him until she, too, became infected. Hattie, being such a close friend of them both, took over their care, with the assurance from Ethel that, by the time Hattie came down with it, Ethel would be recovered enough to care for her. Alas, Ethel's flu took a virulent turn that very night, and by morning she was gone. Earl never forgave himself for bringing the dread disease home to his beloved sister.

There was great rejoicing across the country when the Armistice was finally signed on November 11, 1918, and the "doughboys" began marching home. Of course there were those who did not return, but the pall of sadness at their absence could not long darken the spirit of exhilaration that pervaded the nation. From the great ticker-tape parade on New York's Madison Avenue to the high-school marching bands across the land, the "boys" were welcomed home with open arms.

Even the little community of Bay Lake got into the act by putting on a gala banquet for the returning heros on the 28th of February 1919. The evening started with three different groups made up to represent American Indians, colonists from Massachusetts, and colonists from Virginia. Each group dressed appropriately for the Revolutionary War period, and each of these groups prepared and ate their own evening meals in a separate corner of the school house as a living vignette of Colonial America. The Indians cooked in a black kettle suspended over a tiny bonfire built on a sand box, and were headed by Earl Archibald, who made a convincing Indian with his sharply chiseled features, even though his eyes were blue. The Massachusetts group dined in typical New England fashion on baked beans and fish. Hugo Knieff and Hattie Reiley portrayed George and Martha Washington for the Virginians, who were the envy of all as they dined in style with all the amenities of the Old South.

After the first groups finished, the "Quakers" from Pennsylvania, who were played by Mrs. A. N. Gray, Mrs. W. A Fuller, Mrs. L. P. Hall, and Mrs. A. C. Christensen, and assisted by three "colored waiters" took over. They treated the 175 guests to a delicious dinner served by candlelight. The returning veterans honored at the dinner were: Ralph Hunt, Christ Brager, Arthur Johnson, Harry Nelson, and Albert Maghan.

Deerwood had started as a railroad town, but its proximity to the beautiful lake region soon brought well-to-do residents from Duluth and other larger communities to enjoy its recreational potential. Homes sprang up on Reno and Serpent Lakes, and the hotels in Deerwood did a thriving business during the summer months. From its modest beginnings at the Ruttger home at the turn of the century, the resort industry in Northern Minnesota continued to grow. With the war behind them and transportation improving, it was ready to boom.

The Knieffs began their involvement with tourism in the most modest way possible. While

Early road from Deerwood to Bay Lake. This was once called the "Sis-e-bag-a-mah Trail."

Site of the first campgrounds at KSA

Looking east from the campgrounds

the claim shanty had long since ceased to exist, the clearing between its former site and the lake, being relatively level and open with only a slight drop to the lake, made an ideal spot for camping. A family from Missouri, who were devoted to Minnesota fishing, had spotted it from the lake and made inquiry. Hugo, being hard pressed for money, agreed to rent the area for 50¢ per night and the "campgrounds" were born. This soon became a favorite spot for several families to enjoy their vacations, usually for a month at a time. Ed Kieth and his identical twin brother were among these first campers. After he was married, Ed continued to bring his family to Bay Lake for many years.

Hugo Knieff

Robert had finished high school in 1919, and Chester was staying in Deerwood with Arthur and his wife while attending school. There was really no reason for Hattie to stay on, so she went back to Minneapolis to work. But she was not happy there. She had become a part of the Bay Lake community and missed all her friends there. She no longer had relatives in Minneapolis, and she felt a stranger in the city of her birth. No wonder she found an excuse to return to Bay Lake in the summer of 1923 for an extended visit. Hugo had not been enjoying the life of a bachelor either and was happy to see her return. Once again they could enjoy together the simple social gatherings with their neighbors, the picnics, the sing-a-longs, and the quiet evenings of pleasant conversation. And they spent long hours contemplating the future. Hugo had spent too many lonesome evenings, both here and in Montana. Now he wanted a home and a wife, and he had realized while she was away that Hattie was the only one who could fulfill this need. Hattie had reservations, however. Although she now knew that she had come to love Hugo, she was keenly aware that there was a blood relationship between them, as her mother had been a half sister of Hugo's. She feared that it would be improper for them to marry. In the end, Hugo won out and they were married on November 2, 1923, in Mason City, Iowa.

Hattie Reiley Knieff

Chapter 18

Albert Luverne Knieff

While 1924 should have been the happiest year of Hattie's life, it was anything but. Indeed, it did start out very well. She was happily married and loved her husband dearly. Early in the spring she was elated to learn that she would be having a baby in the fall. What difference if money was hard to come by? They would work hard and spend carefully, and all would be well. Their first step in this direction was to rent their house out for two months that summer. This meant that they had to move out of the house and into the shop. It would make extra work moving many of their things and storing others. Hattie would dearly miss the little summer kitchen with all of its conveniences she was so used to, especially the pitcher pump right inside, that gave her all the water she needed without having to carry it.

It proved to be a particularly hot summer, and, as the new little life within her grew and the heat became more oppressive, she found it more and more difficult to cope with the daily chores of a farmer's wife. The separator, which had to be washed twice daily, was particularly vexing as it was heavy and awkward and hard for her to handle. She was, after all, thirty-eight years old, an advanced age to be carrying her first child. To compound her problems, severe storms that summer always seemed to come at night. Hattie had been badly scared as a little girl by the severe storms she experienced while living at Crystal Bay on Lake Minnetonka. Now the blinding flashes of lightning and the ensuing claps of thunder brought memories of those days of long ago. The shop building was within ten feet of the lake, and the howling wind and the waves pounding upon the shore seemed about ready to engulf the building, while the sound of near-by trees crashing to the ground sent her into near panic.

On the morning of August 20th Hattie received a telegram from Minneapolis with the awful news that her father was dead. He had fallen down a flight of stairs and smashed his head on a steel radiator, crushing his skull. He had died shortly thereafter. His body was returned to Deerwood and interred in the family plot in the Bay Lake Cemetery. The ordeal was too much for her in her weakened condition, and the beautiful little baby girl, who was to have been her pride and joy, came too soon and did not survive the birth. Hattie and Hugo were devastated at their loss and the thought of having children of their own now seemed remote indeed. The rest of the year passed in a blur of pain and resignation.

But life does go on, and they still had to find new ways to wrest a livelihood from the land. Since people had been so anxious to rent their house or even the shop building for summer vacations, Hugo decided to borrow more money and build three cabins on the lake shore east of the house. It was a bold venture that had not been tried in the area, but it did afford an opportunity for an annual cash income without materially effecting the farmland itself.

So after procuring a loan, and securing the services of a local carpenter, Oscar Melvic,

Hugo was ready, in the spring of 1925, to begin his new venture. Oscar was an old-time mechanic, tall and angular, and a man of few words. He didn't appear to move rapidly but rather with almost jerky motions, yet each was a model of efficiency. He had helped Hugo order the lumber, and, when it came, he sorted through it a bit and then began to saw. He sawed until he had piles of boards cut to various lengths and some with specific angles on one end or both. Hugo could only pray that he knew what he was doing.

Hugo had prepared the sites the previous fall and had poured concrete footings. When Oscar was satisfied with his pre-cut piles, he began to put it all together. In an unbelievably short time, he had the three cabins completed to Hugo's specifications and complete satisfaction. He even took an extra day or two to build three fourteen foot flat-bottomed wooden boats for the renters' use!

The first of the cabins had a single bedroom and a large living room, one corner of which would serve as a kitchen. A wood-burning cookstove would supply the heat in cold weather; in warm weather the cooking would be done on a kerosene stove. The large windows in the front and back of the cabin were screened and then covered with canvas-covered shutters opened with a rope-and-pulley combination from the inside. They were ideal for letting the breezes blow through the cabin on a hot summer day, but on cool, windy or rainy days they left something to be desired. Kerosene lamps furnished light when needed.

The second cabin was similar to the first except that it had only one large room, with the bed curtained off in one end. The third cabin was larger, with two bedrooms in the rear and a small kitchen between them. The front was all one big room.

"Oak" cabin at KSA

"Linden" cabin at KSA

In every case, the bathroom facilities were furnished at the end of a little trail that led out into the woods to a very small building with a single bench across one side in which two holes had been cut, hence the colloquial name, "two holer." These kinds of buildings were distinguished by crescent-shaped cut-outs on their doors. They were very primitive facilities; indeed that was a part of their charm.

The cabins were kept scrupulously clean, and fresh linen was furnished weekly to those who were staying for longer periods. Personal towels, however, were not furnished. Ice was replenished daily in the "ice box," and the garbage can emptied on a regular basis. Most important of all, the Knieffs were always friendly and helpful. This was not necessarily by design; it was simply their nature, and their guests responded in kind.

The idea caught on immediately, and, even that first year, the new cabins, along with the shop were kept occupied a large percent of the time. While the rental rates were extremely low, averaging only about $20.00 per week each, they did represent a steady annual cash income.

Before the summer was over, Hattie and Hugo had wonderful news, Hattie was again pregnant. It seemed too good to be true after their disappointment of the previous year. They were overjoyed, yet fearful, too, lest fate should again deny them their dream. But as summer turned to fall, and fall to winter, they took courage in Hattie's continued good health and made their plans and dreamed their dreams.

On the evening of January 12, 1926, Hattie knew her time had come. Hugo bundled her in to their old Dodge touring car and, with its isinglass side curtains flapping in the wind, they made the long, cold journey in to the Miners' Hospital in Crosby. There, on January 13, their son was born. It had been a long and difficult delivery, but when the nurse placed the well-formed baby in Hattie's arms, she knew the greatest joy she had ever known. And when their friends saw the baby they all remarked how very much he looked like his grandfather and practically insisted that he be named after him. So, somewhat reluctantly, Hattie agreed to name him Albert after his grandfather and Luverne after her brother. And that, my friends, is how I became Albert Luvern Knieff.

Albert and Hattie

Chapter 19

The Picture Changes—Early Memories

I did not inherit my father's ability to recall the minute details of my early life. I do know that, as a baby, I was somewhat sickly and a poor eater, and that my Mother, in her anxiety, took me to Brainerd to see a doctor who specialized in treating babies. He immediately diagnosed me as being tongue-tied, and, with a snip of his scissors, he freed my tongue, which has wiggled freely ever since! It also cured my eating problem. My failure to eat properly had contributed to a vitamin deficiency that he corrected by having my mother rub me all over with cod liver oil. I was apparently too young to care, but Mother would wrinkle up her nose in disgust every time she recalled the procedure.

The earliest established road around Bay Lake had followed the shoreline as closely as possible. Around our bay, it followed the shore within a few feet, and, of course, went between our house and the lake. There were but very few neighbors to use the road, and then only rarely, so it presented no problem. I do not know just when the road was moved back from the lake, but early on, perhaps by 1910, it was moved away from the lake as soon as it passed the swamp that skirts the river as it leaves the lake on the eastern edge of our property. It went north to the top of the high bank on the south side of Knieff Lake before it headed west again, and it did not come back to the shore of Bay Lake until it had passed the base of the large peninsula where Nick Newgard had originality homesteaded, now the Hall property. We continued to use the old road as our driveway until about 1929. I can still remember how frightened I was when Dad decided to move the driveway back from the lake to go behind the cabins he had built. There was heavy timber in that area, and he used dynamite to blast out the stumps. Of course, I was kept in the house while this was going on, but I can still remember the heavy BOOM and the ground shaking with every blast.

The resort business, as it was now called, was doing well, but four cabins simply did not bring enough income for the family livelihood. So Dad had another large two-bedroom cabin built east of the first three. To the west of our home, and beyond the shop, was our little family garden, and beyond it Dad, himself, built another cabin. This cabin had a small kitchen and a bedroom in the rear, and a living room with a dining area taking up the front half. It was unique in that it was built entirely of split logs, with each half log on the inside covering the joint between two half logs on the outside. I

"Log" cabin

can still visualize the huge pile of shavings that accumulated as Dad peeled the bark off all those logs with a draw knife. This cabin had no shutters in front. The large windows were divided into three sections, with the largest in the center consisting of a single pane of glass. On either side of it was a smaller, multi-paned section, that hinged outward to provide ventilation. Its crowning glory was a beautiful split rock fireplace on the inner wall between the bedroom and the living room. The other new cabin had a similar fireplace. They were built by Vern Taylor who had spent his life as a stone mason. His home, built entirely of stone, still stands alongside Highway 6 between Bay Lake and Deerwood. I remember that Dad paid Vern $25.00 each for building those fireplaces, and Vern split all of the rock that he used.

Rather than numbering the cabins, my Dad, the naturalist, opted to name them after trees, usually after a particular tree or group of trees that grew on the site of the cabin. The first of the cabins east of the house was under a huge spreading white elm tree and naturally became the Elm. Beyond it, under a large clump of basswood trees, was the large two-bedroom cabin, the Linden, which is the more common name in Germany. Next in line came the little Oak, which was guarded by a number of small oak trees. When the new cabin was built on that end, it was on the edge of the thick grove of maples (that would become our "sugar bush"), and quite naturally became the Maple.

"Maple" cabin

This system of naming became disrupted on the west end. First there was the shop, which remained just that until, in the late twenties, an artist, Mr. Fazel, and his wife from Topeka, Kansas, began taking that cabin for an extended period every summer. He did a lot of painting as well as fishing while he was here and made good use of the extra room. He began calling it the "Black Maria," and that is what it remained until it was torn down in the mid 1930s. The log cabin, naturally enough, remained just that, the Log Cabin.

Guest J. W. Fazel painting one of his favorite scenes on the road to Deerwood.

Another event, of perhaps the same year, is deeply imbedded in my mind. My mother became terribly sick. The surgery she had had as a girl had left her with adhesions throughout her abdomen. These had finally reached the point where the food simply could not pass and surgery was required. These procedures had not yet been perfected to their present state, and life hung in the balance for my mother for several days. The night of the surgery, Dad stayed in

Brainerd with Mother, and I was forced to stay with my Aunt Etta and Uncle Arthur on their little farm a mile north of our home. It was an awful night, my first away from my mother, and knowing full well the danger she faced. My mother was ever the fighter and ever the optimist, and I am sure these traits, along with her love for her family, brought her home safely.

Our early guests played a large role in my upbringing. First, I was told always to remember that they were guests in the good, old-fashioned sense. We were all to welcome them into our cabins as we would welcome friends invited into our home. This was usually very easy to do because it was the normal thing to do, and, after getting acquainted, I found them to be good people, just like we were. Being an only child, and living in the country, I had fewer opportunities to play with children of my own age than most youngsters do. So I spent a great deal of time with adults. I guess I must have been precocious, and I know I was spoiled rotten in some ways, but I was never allowed to forget my place or to be impudent. I learned how to converse with adults in a serious way, and it was the beginning of my habit of choosing older children as playmates.

It is interesting to compare the scene from our house, looking out over Bay Lake, as my father remembered seeing it in his youth, and as my grandfather painted it, with the scene as I remember seeing it as a youngster. Gone were the Indians gliding silently by in their birch-bark canoes. The huge pines were mostly gone too, and a few cabins had by then appeared, tucked in along the shore with small docks mooring a wooden fishing boat or two in front of each, where all had been wilderness before. Large areas of shoreline were still shrouded in dense patches of bull rushes, and a small patch still remained in front of the camp ground, although they had begun to recede. The first of the outboard motors were about to appear, but they would remain a novelty for some time yet. A sprinkle of little lights had begun to appear along the far shore where darkness once reigned, although electricity and yard lights would not make their appearance for several years.

Looking across the bay toward Battle Point in 1938

I am awed when I contemplate the quiet that must have ruled in 1883, especially a quiet summer evening broken only by the night sounds of the wild creatures. Even in my early youth, the murmur of voices carrying far across the water, a sudden peal of laughter or the sound of distant music were common. But, of course, the sound of highway traffic was seldom heard, and air traffic in the area was non-existent. Now, the stillness of the night is often shattered by the howl of high-powered outboard motors as they race from bay to bay. Even the traffic sounds from the highway two miles distant are usually discernible, while the drone of an airplane flying overhead is not uncommon. Yet by comparison, this home of ours is still a peaceful haven from the turmoil that surrounds us in our (so called "space age") of modern living.

In the fall of 1930, Dad got a job working on a drilling crew at the mines. I am sure that his experience with rock work in Montana helped him with this job, although he never spoke much about it. Dad's cousin, Edward Wasserzieher, his wife Hazel, and their two boys, Harlo and Kennith, lived in a large three-story house in Deerwood, which had originally been built as that community's hospital. It was decided that we should move into town and live with them for the winter. We could live on the second floor without crowding them, and it would be much more convenient for Mother, as Dad would be away at work all day. It also shortened his drive to work considerably.

My memory of that winter is sketchy, but some details stand out very clearly. The house seemed huge to me, three full stories above ground; I don't remember a basement, but I am sure that it had one. I seem to remember two separate stairways from the first to the second floor. This lead to my experience of nearly catching Santa Claus. When I was small, Christmas trees never appeared in our homes until Christmas Eve, when Santa himself delivered them. This particular Christmas seemed strange, being away from home and all, but decorations had appeared around the house, and a festive evening meal had been planned. I was just worried that Santa wouldn't be able to find us because we weren't really at home.

As evening approached on Christmas Eve, we were all gathered in Hazel's kitchen. Shadows were falling when Edward took his milk pail and went out to the little shed behind the house where he kept his cow. After a few minutes, there was a terrible commotion on the back stairs going up to our apartment. Dad tore down the hall toward the stairway with Hazel, Mother, Harlo, and I in hot pursuit. It was a scene of utter confusion, with kids and parents tripping over each other and blocking each other's way. When we got to the back door, Dad, who was in the lead, said that he had just caught a glimpse of a fat little man in a red suit disappearing around the corner of the house. About that time Edward came running in from the barn, wondering what all the confusion was about. We dashed up the stairs and into our living room, and there it was, the most beautiful Christmas tree that I had ever seen, with presents all around! How Santa had gotten into the house, with us all right there, without even letting us see him, I just couldn't figure out. I don't recall wondering why Santa didn't bring the Wasserzieher's tree and gifts until the next morning, but I do recall that among other gifts I got a little "pop gun," which Edward refused to allow me to "shoot" in his house.

In later years, Mother used to tell of her Christmases as a little girl, when Santa came for her and her brother. They would be confined to the kitchen for what seemed like hours while her father carried on a lively two-way conversation with the jolly little elf. They were very poor then, and even a new dress for an old doll, a hand-knit scarf, or an orange were greatly appreciated gifts.

It wasn't uncommon for people who lived in small towns like Deerwood, to keep a cow or two right there on their lots to ensure an ample supply of good fresh milk and cream. Edward's cow was memorable to me because of the way he solved one of those nagging little problems faced by everyone who ever had to sit on a wee little stool with a pail between his knees and milk a cow. It seems that this is always the appropriate time for the cow to decide that her tail needed swishing. I know from later experience that the whack of a cow's tail, often wet or dirty, across one's face is not a pleasant experience. Edward's solution was to nail the tail to the wall! Actually he only tied a hank of the hair of the cow's tail to a nail driven into the wall. The cow didn't seem to mind too much, and Edward's face remained clean and unbruised.

The city water in Deerwood was good, but quite ironically, I remember that it left yellow stains on things and that Mother didn't like the coffee made from it. To solve this problem, Dad would carry a container with him to work each morning, and bring home the softest, best tasting water you ever saw. It was pumped right out of the iron mine!

The following spring Dad and our neighbor, Wallace Hunt, who was a carpenter, got a job building a real log cabin on little Bird Island, around the corner from Battle Point. The huge logs were hauled out to the island over the winter ice and were all ready when the weather warmed sufficiently in the spring for work to begin. Naturally, Dad would talk about the cabin when he came home at night, and I became very anxious to go out and see it. Finally Dad agreed that the next day I could pack a lunch and go along with him to work. When I got there, I found that Wallace had also brought his oldest son, Gilbert, who was exactly one month older than I. The two of us had the time of our young lives that day. There were so many games to be played and so much getting acquainted to be done that the day fairly sped by. We watched the loons that had a nest nearby, and marveled at how their baby rode on its mother's back. We even went swimming on that glorious sand beach without our clothes on! We had never really known each other before, but from that day we have remained the best of friends.

Chapter 20

Growing Up

Mother and Dad spent considerable time searching for a name for their new business. They finally decided on "Knieff's Shore Acres," and so it remains to this day. How well I still remember the names of some of those early guests who came to our resort. There were the Springers, who first came as campers before any of the cabins were built, the Lanes, and the Richies, of whom I will speak later. Many of them were from Iowa and Kansas and Missouri. They came north as much to escape the heat, as for the wonderful fishing we had then.

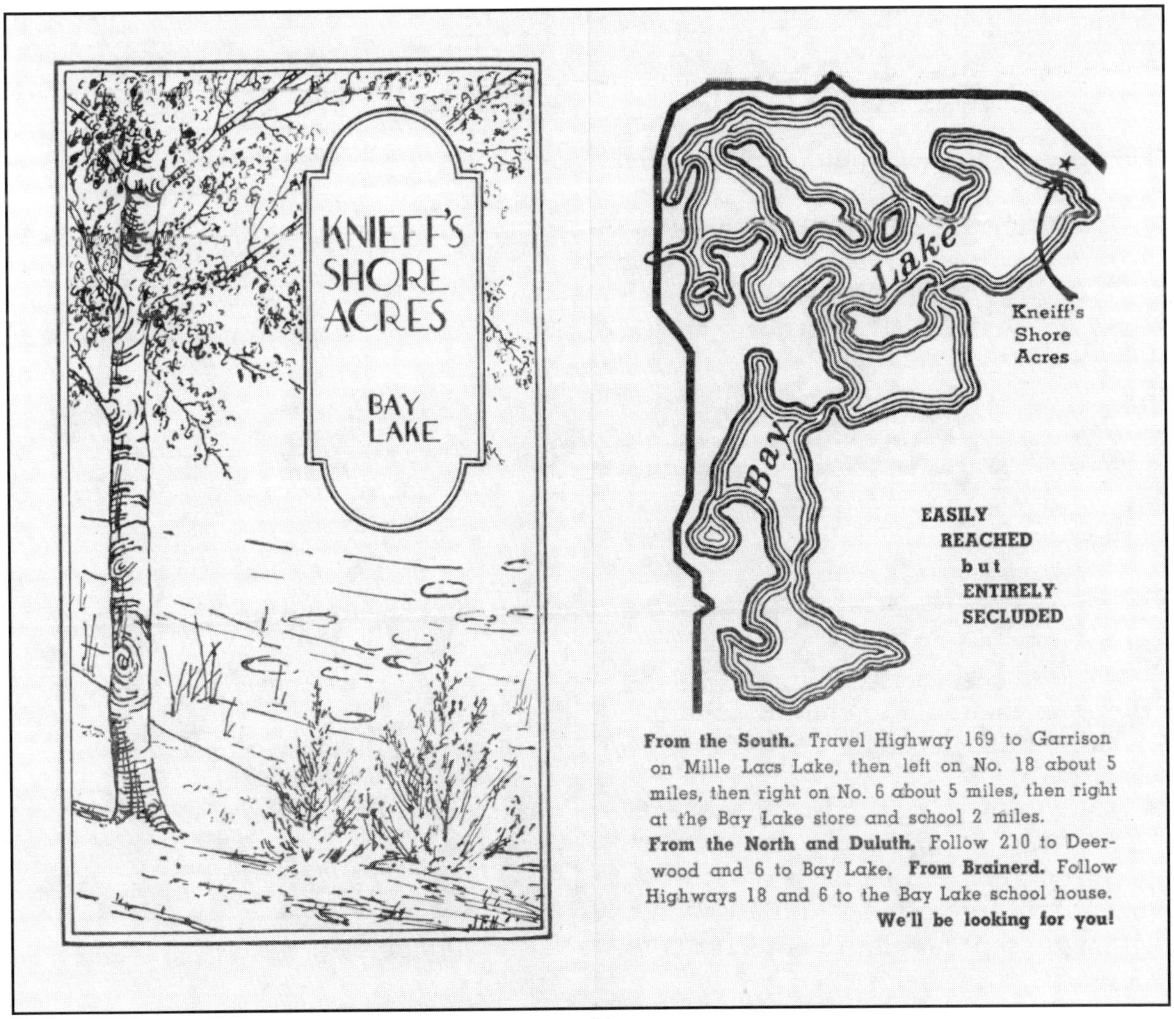

Kneiff's SHORE ACRES

LOCATION. Shore Acres is located 117 miles from Minneapolis, 23 miles from Brainerd, and 7 miles from Deerwood. A good general store, golf course and other amusements are within two miles of the resort. The roads are excellent in all kinds of weather.

MAIL AND TELEPHONE. The mail is delivered daily by rural carrier. A telephone connects Shore Acres with the outside.

BAY LAKE. This is one of the most beautiful lakes in Minnesota. The water is clear and most of the shore is sandy. The shoreline is very irregular and true to its name, the lake has many bays and islands.

OTHER LAKES. There are numerous other lakes in the vicinity of Bay Lake that are easy of access from Shore Acres.

BATHING. This is an ideal lake for bathing. The shore is sandy and has a gradual slope. The experienced swimmer and an amateur will both find the depth and kind of water that he likes best.

FISHING. Fishing is good in Bay Lake. Bass, crappie, pike and sunfish are the kinds usually taken. The many bays and islands make this a very interesting lake to fish. Rushes, weed beds, lily pads and deep holes are in abundance.

COTTAGES. We have cottages to rent at prices from $15 to $30 per week, with special prices by the month or by the season. These cottages are furnished — all that our guests need to furnish is towels. All are equipped with innerspring mattresses. The rental price in all cases includes a boat, ice, wood, electric lights and Pyrotax gas for cooking. All cabins have sinks and drains.

A TRAILER CAMP GROUNDS and BOATS. In addition to the cottages we have good electric lighted camp grounds for those who prefer this kind of vacation. Our prices for the camp grounds are 50 cents per day or $3.00 per week. Boats, $1.00 per day.

For further information write to . .

MR. and MRS. H. E. KNEIFF

R. F. D. No. 1 Deerwood, Minn.

Tel. 65-F-111

This and the picture on page 71 show the original Knieff's Shore Acres brochure.

The Alvin Springer Family in their camp

Bob, Dick, and Ed Keith with a nice catch of bass

I especially remember the Keiths. Ed first came in 1925 with his identical twin brother. They camped that year and fished a great deal. Ed was particularly interested in photography, and that winter he sent an album of pictures to my parents that he had taken of the camp and of Bay Lake. That little album, bound with natural Birch bark covers, is one of my most prized possessions. Ed continued to spend his vacations here with his wife and their two sons, Bob and Dick, and their little Boston bull dog terrier. He was then a professor of journalism at Kansas State College at Manhattan, Kansas. His interest in photography never waned, and his position in the college gave him the opportunity to use the finest of equipment, including a Lieca camera and several very expensive lenses. He sometimes used Kodachrome color film, which at that time he had to develop himself, and several of these pictures are still proudly displayed in our home. In 1938 he sent us another photo album that includes many pictures of our resort, our family and our pets, and remains to this day, a valuable historical record of those early years.

Pets have always played an important role in our family. My mother used to like to tell about the old white tomcat they had when I was born. He was an affectionate old tom but an excellent mouser nonetheless. When Mother brought me home from the hospital, she was quite concerned about the cat. There were always stories about cats smothering newborn infants by "sucking" the baby's breath. That part was probably no more than an old wives tale, but, of course, a cat could simply lay on the baby's face and smother it. At any rate, my mother was cautious and put the cat outdoors. The next morning, the cat came in and went unnoticed for a short while. When Mother thought of the cat, she hurried to my crib and found that the cat had indeed been there. He had left a dead mouse for me on my blanket and then left.

Mother really loved that old cat (called only "White Cat," I think), and, when a couple of years later, he failed to return from one of his frequent nightly excursions, she truly mourned his loss and blamed it on someone's untended trap. That did happen to another cat I remember. He was gone for several days, and, when he returned home, it was evident that one of his front feet had been in a trap. It had turned black and was as hard as stone, probably frozen. I can still hear him coming across the floor with it, pad—pad—pad—thump! He used to use it to knock on the door when he wanted in. The paw finally dropped off, but the cat lived out a normal lifespan.

The first pets I remember were, the above mentioned "Whiskers," and "Buddy," the dog. They were constant companions of mine when I was little, at that first "running around by myself" stage. Mother might have worried about me all the time, with the lake so near, but she knew that Buddy would not let me get into any serious trouble. She had only to look up and spot one of them, and I would surely be nearby. I hope that Whiskers enjoyed being dressed up in old bonnets and being lugged around with his tummy over a little boy's arm, his feet nearly dragging on the ground.

The author at age five with Whiskers and Buddy

My mother used to tell of another pet that they had when Chester was a boy. He came home one spring day with a baby woodchuck he had found up in the field. Mom was always a soft touch for a baby animal, and naturally she could not deny this poor little creature. Being a baby, it needed milk, and she had no nipple small enough for it to use. It didn't seem to be able to lap it up either, as a kitten or puppy would, though it would eagerly suck up milk from her finger tip. Finally she hit upon a solution. She cut the entire top out of a sardine can and put a little milk in it. The baby woodchuck still could not drink until she laid him right down on his tummy in the milk; then he drank just fine.

From then on he did very well, and in no time he had three little "escape" holes dug under the back porch and, I presume, his own personal den as well. Mother got to calling him her Little Nuisance because he was forever reaching up and grabbing her skirts as she went by. When Dad came down from the barn with the milk, the little pest would set up a terrible fuss until he had some in his dish. Usually they gave him some of the skim milk as it came out of the separator, with a big head of foam on the top. Needless to say, he was foam from head to tail before he got through drinking. One day he simply couldn't wait for the milk to be separated, but chinned himself up on the edge of a full pail and promptly fell in!

When winter came, he retired to his den and was not seen again until spring. He emerged a full-grown woodchuck, but just as friendly and full of mischief as ever, only now he was big enough to really bother Mom when he wanted to play. One day Mom headed out to the strawberry patch to pick some berries, and her Little Nuisance just wouldn't leave her alone. So she picked him up and walked down by the lake with him, set him on a stump and said, "now you stay there until you can behave." He never did come back to the house, although they saw him from time to time that summer, until he finally disappeared for good that fall.

Although they were several years older than I, I used to play with the Keith boys quite a bit. We would go swimming, and, when we stepped on a live clam, we would dig it out of the sand and save it for fishing. The meat was quite tough, and when it was cut up into little pieces it would stay on a hook pretty well. It made good sunfish bait and was much easier to get than angleworms. I am sure that our folks got tired of picking the bones out of little sunfish we caught, but they ate them anyway. The clams might have been edible for humans too, but their odor did not encourage this experiment.

We also liked to explore in the woods in back of the cabins. On one such occasion we found ourselves far from the cabin and its facilities when Bob had a rather urgent call from mother nature. The obvious solution was for Bob to drop his britches and satisfy these demands on the spot, using what leaves or other debris was available for the cleansing afterward. For the next few days Bob would periodically have to go back to the cabin where his mother would administer to his discomfort by rubbing calamine lotion on the area that had been inflicted with poison ivy when he wiped himself. It was a very embarrassing experience for Bob but an effective learning experience for us all. I have been fortunate in regard to poison ivy. I pull it out by the roots whenever I find any in the yard around the cabins and have suffered only a very rare blister between my fingers as a result. Of course, I do wash my hands as soon after pulling it as is convenient.

In the fall of 1931, I began the first grade in the little one-room school house located just north of Ruttgers where our road met the state highway. It was a long two-mile walk for a little boy who would not be six until January. Of course Dad drove me down, at least for the first few days, and also in colder weather. I usually walked home, however. When it was very cold, I simply did not go.

I am glad that I had the opportunity to experience the little country school house that has played such a prominent role in our nation's history. I can still visualize going up those cement steps and into the cloak room that stretched across the front of the building, then into the school room proper. Just inside the door to the right was a window, with a water cooler by it. Almost the entire left side of the room was continuous windows. Straight ahead was the teacher's desk, and in the corner between her desk and the windows was a huge, round, wood-burning stove with a steel safety shield enclosing it. Between the stove and the desk was a door that led to the unheated back shed, where the wood was stored along with whatever other props and supplies not required for daily use. The balance of the front of the room and the right side were chalk boards. A large globe was suspended from the ceiling on a pulley arrangement, so that it could be pulled up out of the way when not in use. High on the wall behind the teacher's desk was the clock, with its pendulum slowly swinging. Our country's flag stood on its staff in the right hand corner, and the area above the chalk boards was enhanced with several pictures, including portraits of George Washington and Herbert Hoover. The seats were arranged in rows facing the front, with the smallest ones for the first or second grade next to the windows, and progressively larger seats in succeeding rows to the right. Of course, there was a piano, too, but for the life of me I cannot picture it in that room, perhaps because music was not one of my talents.

Our teacher's name was Mamie Guire. She was a little slip of a girl, probably not much older than some of her students. Mamie got along with her teaching surprisingly well, in no small measure because of the excellent cooperation she received from the older students. Lois Adolovich was the oldest girl in school, and she was constantly helping us, the "little kids" with our school work or when we had physical problems. The older boys helped to enforce discipline whenever necessary, which fortunately was not often. Our present-day teachers would be overawed by the prospect of teaching a room full of thirty or more children ranging in age from five to perhaps fifteen years old and representing most, if not all, of the first eight grades.

Little remains in my memory of that first year of formal education. But of course, there are incidents that stand out sharp and clear. There was the first grader who, on his first day, was terrified of school. No sooner had the door closed on the outside world and the students taken their seats than he sprang from his seat, out of the door and down the road toward home, as fast as his little legs could take him, with his big brothers in hot pursuit. Later, shortly after recess, we noticed a growing puddle of yellow under his seat. He apparently had been too shy to use the segregated facilities that stood out behind the school house. On another occasion one of the older boys had been playing too hard on the merry-go-round at recess. After returning to class, he suddenly turned away from his desk and engulfed me with his entire breakfast of oatmeal mush! I am eternally grateful to Lois Adolovich, who came to my rescue and helped to clean me up.

The Christmas pageant was one of the high points of the year. Everyone in the school participated, some portraying the Christmas characters, some reading those well-known lines, and all joining in with the traditional Christmas carols. A curtain made up of bed sheets, or whatever, was suspended across the middle of the room to separate the cast from the audience, which was composed mostly of the parents. When it was over, Santa made his appearance with treats for the kids. Of course we all knew that he had to be the "real McCoy," but in retrospect there was only one person in our little community who had the well-rounded stature to fulfill this important roll. Thank you, Gordon Gray!

Alongside the school grounds was Ruttger's big red barn, with its hay mow above and the tack room on one end of the lower level. What an ideal place for the "secret society" to hold its illicit meetings during the lunch hour and to practice those secret rites of childhood, which I am sure included smoking then, as it no doubt still does. I remember being introduced to one of its clandestine meetings, although I never frequented it on a regular basis.

The long trek home after school must not be overlooked. The road from the school followed the shore of the lake until it reached the Hall property, as mentioned earlier. At the end of the Ruttger property was a small tract owned by Edward Wasserzieher. There were stored the remains of the steamboat that he had built for himself in earlier times, when there was no bridge to foil its passage from Bay Lake to Echo Lake, and the freshly dredged river afforded ample draft. How proudly it must have sailed those pristine waters!

Once past the golf coarse, the road was bounded on the north by heavy woods with faint traces of old trails leading into them. How vividly I recall the afternoon when some of my older "friends" with whom I usually walked volunteered to show me a short-cut through those woods on one of those trails. Naturally, they all disappeared as soon as we were well out of sight of anything familiar and the trail had nearly disappeared. The whole detour was hardly a quarter of a mile long, but I was a thoroughly frightened little boy before I found my way back to the road and home. I know that my mother was extremely angry at the perpetrators when I arrived home, considerably later than usual and still crying, more now from anger than from fear.

The following spring Dad build a tiny one-room cabin behind our house. A niece of his and her husband, Frank and Mertle Buss, were to stay there and help with the resort, as it was getting to be too much for Mother to handle by herself, and Dad could use a little help too. They came from the farming country down near Marshall, and were looking for something that was a little less strenuous than what they had been doing. Mertle was a friendly and generous soul, who made the best lemon-flavored sugar cookies that I have ever eaten. Poor Frank, he had the misfortune of being kicked in the knee by our

Edward Wasserzieher at the wheel of his homemade steamboat with his parents, Otto and Adelia, and another lady, possibly Mrs. Voit.

cow, while he was milking. It broke a blood vessel or something, and he hobbled around for the rest of the summer. I doubt if he ever recovered completely.

Chapter 21

Old Man Depression

In 1933 our Bay Lake School district decided that it was no longer practical to hold school for so few students, while the Deerwood School could easily absorb us into their school without crowding. So, for the next six years the Bay Lake children went to school in Deerwood. Since I had missed so many days of school the year before and had not turned six until January, it was decided that I should start over again in first grade in the new school. Perhaps this was the best thing for me, as I was now in the proper age group and school was easy for me from then on.

I remember that first day of school. I was to catch the bus up at Fuller's driveway, which was a little over a quarter of a mile from home. It left a little after seven in the morning. I got to the end of our driveway in time to see it drive away, and Dad had to take me into Deerwood. The high-school students also rode the same bus, and, in order to get them to Crosby in time for their classes, we had to leave early. That meant a half-hour wait before school began. In the evening, we had to wait another half hour before the bus came from Crosby to take us home. I missed the bus again! I can't blame the driver, Emery, for leaving me. I hadn't ridden in the morning, and it was his first day, too. I rode that school bus for a total of eleven years, and I don't remember ever missing the bus again.

Those long bus rides, and the long waits both before and after school made for awfully long days, especially for a six-year old. But they also served to weld us into a tight little group. We were the Bay-Lakers, and we stood out as such throughout our school years. Of course, bussing was new then. Today, most of the children ride a school bus and the stigma is gone.

The long school day did not, however, excuse me from my chores. At first I had only to carry in the kindling that Dad had split, then I could listen to "Jack Armstrong, the All American Boy" or some other favorite on our battery-powered radio. Later, the kitchen stove wood also became my responsibility, and finally, the "heater" wood, which was stored in a huge woodbox on our front porch; pumping water, emptying the "slop" pail, and other chores, were gradually added to the list. These chores established a work ethic in us, but they were also played a necessary role in the operation of the family unit.

Oh, what a grand day it was when school was finally out for the summer, usually just before Memorial Day. Each class would take their collective lunches down to the Deerwood Tourist Park, or some other exotic place, where we could romp and play all day, bragging of the wonderful adventures we would have over summer vacation. Then we were handed our final report cards for the year, free at last. I still thrill to the memory of the exhilaration that I felt.

Of course, I soon learned that no small part of this freedom was merely a figment of my imagination. Spring work around a resort is exhaustive, and I soon found myself playing an ever larger part in its completion. Not that my parents crowded me to overwork, far from it. But

I discovered that I had pride. Raking leaves was a huge chore I found that I could do, even when only seven or eight years old. The yard looked so fresh and clean after the debris of fall and winter was swept away that I actually found myself enjoying it, at least up to a point. I found that I was proud to be able to help my parents.

Caring for the boats that were furnished with each cabin was also a spring chore. Our original boats were all flat bottomed, but there were problems with them. It was hard to prevent them from leaking, and a dropped anchor would usually spring one of the bottom boards and start them leaking again. Of course they didn't row as well as the newer strip boats, which were built with rounding bottoms and were actually more stable. By the mid 1930s, our conversion to the round-bottomed variety was complete. Still, they all had to be scraped and painted both inside and out each spring before they could be put into the water. Even then they would leak until they had been anchored out in deep water and allowed to soak up moisture for about a week. This had to be completed before the 15th of May when the fishing season opened.

Docks had to be ready too. Each cabin had its own dock because the cabins were so well-spaced along the shore that in only one or two cases could they share a single dock. In that case, the docks had to be longer in order to accommodate an extra boat, should one of the parties require an extra one or bring one of their own. At that time the docks were made of two parallel ten inch planks supported on each end by brackets, which were in turn fastened to wooden poles driven into the lake bottom. Each dock had at least two sections. They all had to be removed each fall or the winter ice would demolish them.

Of course the cabins had to be cleaned and made ready too. This often included repainting the floors and making numerous small repairs, as well as taking all of the mattresses outdoors for beating and airing. Once the cleaning was completed, it was time for the annual trip to Brainerd for supplies. Every cabin was found to be short of something or other: new brooms, replacement dishes, fry pans, fly swatters—the list was endless. It seemed that Mother was always making new curtains for at least one of the cabins, but of course she did this earlier, while it was still too cold to work in the cabins.

By 1935 Dad realized that he had to increase his income to keep going. The only way to accomplish this was to build more cabins. Once again, faithful Fred Swanke and his Deerwood Bank came to the rescue. This time four cabins were added: the Birch, which was built between the Log Cabin and the campgrounds, the Lilac, where the old garden spot had been, then the Willow and Spruce on the far east end beyond the Maple. The Lilac was small, with a separate kitchen and the bed curtained off from the rest of the living room. The other three were identical, with two bedrooms on one end, and the kitchen behind the living room dining room combination.

The new cabins build west of the house

This year also saw the demise of the old Black Maria. Mother always complained that it smelled of old wood, tar paper, and bats. Perhaps it did, but on those rare occasions when I had a chance to sleep up in its old sleeping bay, I thought of it as a wonderful aroma and a natural part of its charm. How I loved to hear the raindrops falling on the roof boards directly over my head, as I snuggled in that old cot that engulfed me in hammock-shaped proportions! Now it no longer served its purpose, and it had to come down. It was replaced by the little cabin from back of the house, which was no longer needed there, as Mother had hired a girl to live with us for the summer and help out. This would be the pattern every summer until I was seventeen. It meant that I would sleep on a cot on our front porch. This was not all bad. When I was old enough to have my own activities in the evening, I could sneak in without being heard, or at least so I thought. I would come in as quietly as possible, lay very still for a few minutes, then start bouncing around and making noise. Mom would call down to me, “Albert, is that you just getting home?” I would answer, “No, I've been here for quite a while.” I don't doubt that she quickly caught on to this subterfuge, but she never let on to me if she did. The drawback was that it sure got light terribly early in a porch with solid windows on three sides and facing south!

One of my first paying jobs was to deliver the daily newspaper to the cabins. I bought them for three cents and sold them for a nickel. On Sundays I made big money—I paid seven cents and sold for a dime. In this way I earned my first bicycle, with more than a little help from Dad, I am sure. My other responsibilities continued to grow too. Most of our guests had reservations in advance, especially during the peak of the season, and in that way we remained full most of the time. But on occasion someone would drive in without one, and, if I was alone and we had a cabin open, I would show it, and try to rent it. My was I proud then!

It was as a fishing guide that I probably enjoyed myself the most. From the time I was six or so, I fished sunfish with the sons of some of the guests. In a couple of years, Dad started taking me bass fishing with him. He had only recently started casting with a rod and reel himself, and he was eager to teach me. He was in his fifties by then, and this was the best way to bridge the age gap and develop the comradery that is so essential between a father and his son. By the time I was ten, I had graduated to bass fishing with the guests. Dad had taken me to most of the small, seldom-fished lakes in the area, where nice strings of big bass were easiest to catch. Of course I knew the north end of Bay Lake like I knew my own yard. Whether it was 4:00 A.M. or 4:00 P.M., I was always ready to go fishing.

One of my favorite fishing companions was Bill Hagen. He was a disabled World War I veteran who spent his summers here for many years. He camped with his wife, Clara, using an old umbrella tent as a dressing room and storage room, but sleeping in his old Chevrolet car. He made this possible by somehow altering the seat backs so that they would fold down backwards, allowing them to put their bed across both seats. For a kitchen, they went in style. Dad had built a ten-by-twelve-foot tin-roofed shelter in the camp grounds, which they adopted as their own. One end had an old cookstove with burned-out grates and some sort of an oven. With a picnic table set inside and a little cupboard nailed up next to the stove, their kitchen was complete. On cold, windy days, a tarp hung from nails driven into the vertical supports were a big help.

Bill Hagen resting in his "summer home"

In the summer of 1934, at the height of the Great Depression, Bill got an inspiration. He came across an old water-soaked log one day while walking along the beach. With a little help he pulled it out of the lake and set it upright on the bank near the campground landing. With a little blue and red paint he gave the log a face, adding a red ball for a nose and tinfoil for teeth. Some dry grass from along the shore made whiskers, while seaweed made the hair and a five gallon pail the hat. Next came some poles for arms and legs and an old towel for a jacket. Some old gloves made hands and a bread wrapper a bow tie, while jar caps served as buttons. One hand held a whisky bottle and the other a hobo's kettle. Bill had created “Old Man Depression.” A good sized bonfire was laid at its base.

Gleefully Bill went up and down the shore, announcing that on the following evening the “Old Man” would be burned at the stake. Of course I had to contribute a couple of left over fire crackers to add a little life to the party. That same day our cow and her calf got out of their pasture and wandered along the lakeshore until they came to the lillypad bay west of the campground. There the calf proceeded to get mired in the muddy bottom, and started bawling. Bill heard the commotion and went to the rescue. The calf only struggled deeper into the mire. So Bill went to Dad for help, and with the aid of a rope and a couple of volunteers they managed to

Old Man Depression

haul the calf out. Mr. Fazel, being informed of this, made preparations.

The next evening everyone from the resort was on hand to witness the cremation. At the height of the ceremony, Bill was presented with a garbage can cover on which Mr. Fazel had painted "HERO" in honor of Bill's part in the previous days rescue. The celebration went off so well that "Old Man Depression" was burned twice more before the summer was over.

During those years, Mom and Dad operated a little store on our front porch. They sold a few staple canned goods and some of the necessities like sugar, flour, salt, pepper, and the like. There was also pop and candy bars, and on Sundays, homemade ice cream. Milk, cream, eggs, home-churned butter, and homemade cottage cheese were also available, as well as fresh vegetables from our garden. This store was really a defensive measure. My folks had found that when someone drove in who was just shopping around, they might well want the cabin, but, if they had to drive out to find groceries, they would often go to a store further north and then decide to just keep going. If we had the essentials right here, they would settle down, and we would not lose the rental.

Chapter 22

Water Levels and Weather Patterns

One of the advantages of living on the old family homestead is the historical record of the property as it is passed down through the generations. My grandfather came here in 1883, but the record of the environment that he moved onto was far older than that. The old and rotting beaver dams gave evidence that these industrious little animals had plied their trade here over the ages. Civilization was just beginning to gain a foothold in the unbroken wilderness, yet the beaver had been gone for many years, wiped out by the early fur traders and the Native Americans who found in their pelts the key to the White Man's wealth. Over the millennia, their dams had created and enlarged the wetlands, which serve to charge the giant aquifer that furnishes water to a large portion of what was to become the breadbasket of our nation. This record was plainly visible, but the understanding of its implications would have to wait another hundred years to develop.

The natural regulation of the water levels also played a major role in this process. Snow melt in the spring produced a heavy run-off that filled the lakes and wetlands to overflowing. Rivers ran wild and free until the lake levels began to drop. Then a natural sand bar would form at the mouths of the streams and hold the lakes at their "normal" levels until the hot days of summer, when heightened evaporation would cause them to drop. If heavy rains came, the sand bars, which stretched wide across the mouths of the streams, would once again be inundated and the excess water would quickly run off. Normally the low water at freeze up would allow the winter ice, which expands through a succession of temperature changes throughout the winter, to push up and replenish the sand bars at the mouths of the streams and prepare themselves for another cycle the following year. This pressure ridge continues to build where there is no river to continually cut it back, and is usually plainly visible around our lakes.

When civilization came to this lake country, the rivers presented a natural highway for travel and transportation. Logging was the first big business, and floating logs down the river was the most logical way to move them. But the sandbars were in the way, blocking the mouths of the rivers and contributing to heavier weed growth downstream. So the rivers and sand bars were dredged, and the logs moved freely in the river. Naturally, the "normal" water level in the lakes was also lowered. The logging industry soon faded as the giant pine forests were cut until only a few scattered trees were left. The dredged-out streams remained, however, keeping the water levels low. Then came the severe droughts of the early thirties, and the owners of the summer homes and cabins beginning to spring up in remarkable numbers along the lakeshore, were left with mixed emotions. Those who had property on deep shores were pleased. Now they had a little beach to walk and conditions were perfect. Those on shallower shores, however, were irate. As the water receded, it left ever-widening expanses of old lake bottom, still soft and moist and covered with lake moss and weeds. It stank! Abnormally warm lake water caused a giant fish kill; they washed ashore, and they stank! Many of the docks could scarcely reach the waters edge, and mooring boats was impossible. For some on the lake, it was a smelly situation all around.

Beach in front of KSA during the mid-1930 drought years

Finally the Minnesota Department of Natural Resources became alarmed and began constructing dams to artificially control the water levels. In the early nineteen twenties, a bridge had been built over the river as it exits Bay Lake. The original road had crossed on the sandbar. When the dam was built in the nineteen thirties, it was placed down stream from the bridge. Its central section had a fixed height nominally set at 1.60 feet. I am not sure to what the reference was made. Above this fixed height, there were accommodations for stop logs up to a 3.0 setting, which was the top of the gauge and nearly the top of the dam. The overall width of the opening was perhaps ten feet including the center pier. Earthen abutments swept back to the roadway on either side. Unfortunately, the bridge span was too narrow to allow adequate run-off during times of high water. Most of the natural drop between Bay Lake and Tame Fish Lake, as Echo Lake is now called, occurs right at the mouth of the river. Consequently, during high water, the bridge held back more water than the dam, and a pronounced drop could be seen in the water as it passed under the bridge. Later the DNR attempted to correct this problem by replacing the earthen abutments with wooden weirs set permanently at 1.80 feet and discontinuing the use of stop logs completely. This was largely ineffective. The bridge was still an effective dam during periods of excessively high water.

In the summer of 1951, we had "the rain-of-the-century." One afternoon the heavens opened up, and we had six inches of rain in about three hours. When it let up, our docks were floating. We had long since abandoned the plank-and-driven-post type of docks, for sectional docks with attached legs which set on the lake bottom. The inner end of one section sat on the outer end of the preceding section, which made them much easier to put in, but also subject to floating in high water. I pulled the first section further up on the bank and reset each section in turn, and they appeared to be stable once more. That night it rained again—hard, and again I had to reset the docks. After a day's respite, it rained more. In a four-day period, we had nineteen inches of rain! I finally had to remove two or more sections entirely from each dock in order to get them to hold.

Now the situation was reversed. Those who were located on low ground found themselves tying their boats to their front steps, while those on deep shores had hardly room for a dock at all. Fortunately, Bay Lake has a relatively stable water level, and it only rose a little over two feet. Other lakes in the area rose much more. Hamlet Lake is a good case in point. During the drought years, there was an island with some good-sized trees on it that could be seen from Highway 6. After the rain, the island was covered by over six feet of water. Some trees along the shore stood in up to ten feet of water.

While the dam had the removable stop logs, my father had the job of reading the gauge once a week and recording the readings in a log. He could only alter the setting, however, on authority from the DNR. When he was not feeling well, I would take over this job for him. In this way I became very much aware of the water levels. To this day, the people who bought their property during the drought years think that the conditions then were normal, and those who bought right after the big rain think that the extreme high water was normal. Currently, the water is being held a little higher than I think it should be. It results in more erosion along the shores and tends to increase the rate of eutrophication.

It is also interesting to recall our weather pattern over the years. 1888 has been known ever since as being the most severe on record. My Dad used to talk of it, of the terrible snows and extreme cold. 1917 was also a winter to remember. Dad used to tell of how he walked to Deerwood to get the mail on snowshoes. He followed along where he knew the road to be, but only the top of an occasional telephone pole was visible. He also told of having to crawl out from under the eaves of the back porch on his stomach because of the snow drifts.

I remember in my youth, how the snow used to drift out from the top of the hill in back of our house until it formed a regular cliff that reached nearly to the bottom of the hill. Our driveways would often drift full overnight, and many are the hours that I spent shoveling so that we could get the car out. Of course our modern plows throw the snow much better and don't leave such a ditch-like path to catch more snow. But in recent years we have received far less snow. Another factor must be the underbrush. In those early years, when the land was freshly cut over, there was little ground cover, and the snow could travel freely until some natural obstruction caused it to fall in huge drifts. Much of the land in this area is now covered with brush or planted with trees that break this pattern.

This snow pattern is not unlike our temperature patterns. It seems that when our weather service quotes the records, they were usually set many years ago. I remember that terribly hot summers of the 1930s, when the newspapers kept a daily record of how many had succumbed to the severe heat. Of course, most of us now live in air-conditioned comfort, although many have not succumbed to its use here at the lake. The cold is no longer such a problem either, because of our new insulating fabrics and the improved structure and heating facilities of our homes. One cold winter in the mid-thirties will remain forever etched in my memory. For a period of about six weeks, the temperature never got above zero, and within that period there were ten straight days when the temperature never rose higher than twenty degrees below zero. Dad had his cows in a little barn back behind the hill, about three hundred yards from the house. When he got up in the morning it would still be pitch black outside. Dressed in the heavy woolen clothes of the era, he would don his heavy wool mackinaw, put on a skull cap made from the top of one of Mother's stockings to cover his ears and neck, then his heavy wool cap. Then off he would go to milk, with the milk pail in one hand and the little kerosene lantern in the other. One such morning, with the wind blowing a gale, the thermometer read forty-nine degrees below zero. Oh, what he would have given for one of our new-fangled snowmobile suits then!

Chapter 23

Characters

I believe that spending my adolescent years growing up on the family resort was just about the best thing that could have happened to me. It gave me the opportunity to meet people from all walks of life and taught me to get along with nearly everyone. One exception springs to my mind, one of less than a handful. The first record that I have of the Van Winkles is from 1936, when they registered in the Log Cabin, but I am sure that they came a year or two before that. He was a chemistry professor from the college at Manhattan, Kansas, who, with his wife and two sons, came nearly every year until the late 1940s. The first time that they drove up, we had two cabins vacant and Dad showed both to the Van Winkles. They were about to take the larger one, when another car showed up and wanted the Log Cabin, which they had decided against. Immediately, Mr. Van Winkle changed his mind, and the other party was forced to change also.

It was obvious from the beginning that theirs was a somewhat different family structure. Mr. Van Winkel, known to all of us as "Rip," but *never* to his face, of course, was the consummate autocrat. He chose the cabin (the Log was really too small for their family), he picked out their menu from our meager little stock of supplies, and he paid all of the bills. I doubt if his wife was allowed to carry money. Every decision, both large and small, was his alone to make. His younger son, Jim, was a year or two older than I, and we got along quite well. The older boy, I believe his name was Phil, was very quiet and best remembered for a severe case of acne. The boys were ordered about from daylight to dusk but they never allowed a sign of rebellion to show, at least not in Rip's presence. The older boy would sneak off to the little building with the half moon above the door and read by the hour. Jim was allowed some time for play and occasionally to go swimming with me.

I remember the first time Rip took his sons fishing. Great were the preparations. The boys had to be fitted with life jackets. The boat had to be equipped with a second anchor, tied at the stern, so that the boat could not swing about in the breeze. I remember being held responsible for this item. Fishing poles were made ready and angleworms dug from our garden. Finally the great moment arrived with each son in his allocated seat, one in the stern and one in the bow. Rip rowed the boat straight out from the cabin about 150 feet into perhaps five feet of water, the bow anchor was lowered, the boat pulled back to take up the slack, and the second anchor lowered. And that was how they fished. I was glad that I wasn't fishing with them!

After taking a cabin for a few years, The Van Winkles showed up pulling a "travel trailer" that he had made, and of which he was very proud. Actually it was more like one of the folding tent trailers we see today. Built on a wooden chassis, each side folded down to make a full-sized bed. The top and the two "bedrooms" were canvas covered. The center was the combination kitchen and living room, with built-in cupboards and, wonder of wonders, a panel that lifted out of the floor to access a bathtub! It was truly quite a remarkable contraption, although we all got a snicker out of watching him try to open one of the drawers to demonstrate its function. It simply wouldn't come, and he got into quite a snit until his wife demonstrated that it had to be lifted up a little bit first before it could slide forward. This help from his wife did not improve his disposition.

"Rip" Van Winkle's homemade folding tent trailer

Those first years with the Van Winkles weren't really so bad, mostly just amusing. Of course, Rip was always ready to let us know if something didn't please him, but on the whole his demands were innocuous. As I grew older, my duties at the resort increased, and I took an ever more active role in its operation. Among other things, I began servicing the ice boxes. We had a wheelbarrow with a flat bed on it, which would allow me to load eight good sized pieces of ice at a time, probably four hundred pounds or more. It had a steel-rimmed wheel that tended to cut into the ground if it was soft, and made going up the incline from the ice house to the driveway an experience. Dad was always getting after me for taking such a big load, but in this way I could service all the boxes in two trips. One morning, just as I had gotten to the road, the load began to tip. I set my arm to stop it, but the strain on the wooded handle was too great, and it snapped off, spilling the ice all over. Just then Dad came by and proceeded to remind me of his admonitions about taking big loads. As I was taking this lecture, none too happily I might add, Rip came along and said, "You broke your wheelbarrow. You were trying to carry too much ice!" I don't think that Dad appreciated that remark. I know that it made me so angry that I could only walk away and look for something with which to make a temporary repair. I did not return until I was sure that Rip was gone.

When I got out of the service, the Van Winkles were still coming, although Jim had been lost in the war, and I believe that Phil had been institutionalized. Rip was worse than ever. His neighbors down in the campground were rudely awakened early one morning with an extended series of loud bangs. It seems Rip's wife didn't want to go fishing with him that morning, so he was throwing fist-sized rocks into the front of his aluminum boat to compensate for her weight. This was to make the boat ride level in the water. A few days later, he heard someone shooting a twenty-two rifle up in our sand pit. He came up to the house in a rage, telling my mom that he already had enough holes in his head and didn't need any more, and that she was to see that the shooting stopped immediately. Poor Mom was still shaking when I came in. She hadn't known that I had given someone permission to shoot into the sand bank, and that it was perfectly safe.

Another time we were about to go water skiing. My boat was tied at the main dock in front of the house, so we would start from there. I preferred slaloming on one ski, and the easiest way to start was to step off the end of the dock onto the ski just as the boat took up the slack in the line. I went into the house to change into my trunks, and when I came out I saw Rip sitting and talking to my folks. As I headed for the dock, Rip sprang from his chair and approached me with fire in his eye. "You can't go on that dock! I have my minnow trap set at the end of it so keep off!" Needless to say, this didn't change our plans one bit.

The final straw came the next year. We were just about to sit down to supper when we saw Rip and his wife drive in and head for the trailer park. I didn't pay any attention, as I was sure he would go down and get hooked up and then come back to register in. We were nicely into our meal when Rip came storming up shouting, "You have a leak in your water line down in the park." I said "Okay, I'll come down as soon as I finish supper." "I said come right now, the whole park is flooding!" So I got up from the table and went down to the park to see what was going on. Rip had driven over one of the water risers with his trailer! Again Rip came up to me and said, "You have to fix this right now!" I just said, "Okay," went back to the house where I had a valve that shut off the entire camp, shut it, and finished my supper. Then I drove over to our plumber's place to get what I would need to repair the pipe. By the time I got back to the park I hadn't cooled off a bit. I made the repair, then told Rip that I would turn the water back on, and that I would expect him to be leaving in the morning. That was the last time that I ever spoke to Rip. It was the first time that I had ever exerted my authority in this way, but both of my parents were secretly glad that I had done so. Mom did say how sorry she was for Mrs. Van Winkle though. Rip left in the morning, and later we learned that he and his wife had both been killed in an automobile accident.

There were others who tried my patience at times, but without ever really provoking anger. And there were those who are indelibly etched in my mind for other reasons. One in particular comes to my mind, though I cannot, for the life of me, recall his name. I"ll just have to call him "Mr. Mork." The first time that I met Mr. Mork, I had the feeling that I world not soon forget that gentleman. He was not a large man, nor did any of his features stand out particularly. The stench of the stogy that seemed to grow from between his teeth was certainly identifying, but it was his speech that I remember most. Not just his Hoosier drawl, which was pleasant enough to listen to, but the stories themselves. I don't know just how to say this except to come right out with it—he was a natural-born liar. Not your everyday garden-variety liar either. I mean you could talk to him for an hour and probably never get one completely true statement out of him. Don't get me wrong; he wasn't mean or vicious or anything like that. He simply couldn't keep his stories straight. For example, he loved to talk about his ill health. One day he told me how he had had a bout with cancer, and how they had removed one of his lungs, the operation apparently being very successful. But then the next winter he had caught a bad cold which eventually turned into double pneumonia!

Mr. Mork had another obsession, and that was fishing. He could fish every morning and evening and talk about fishing the rest of the time. He was anxious to catch a really big fish, and was continually after me to guide him to one. Now I have been around these lakes all of my life, and I do know some pretty good spots, but I just couldn't see myself listening to his line of bull for four or five hours at a time. I certainly had better things to do than that. Then one morning I had an inspiration, so I thought, *let him corner me.* Sure enough, he wanted me to take him fishing. I said, "Well, Mr. Mork, I surely would like to, but I just can't get away. But I know just the man for you. He has a couple of cabins over on Crooked Lake, and he likes nothing better than to guide someone like you. He keeps boats on several little private lakes in the area, and he could get you a trophy if anyone could." Mr. Mork gobbled that bait just like a big bass going after a nice green frog. So I told him how to find Floyd Warren, one of our local characters, then I sat back and waited with great anticipation.

The next day about noon, as I was just about to sit down to eat my lunch, I saw Mork drive up and stop in front of the house, and I knew the fat was in the fire. I walked down to the car and said, "Well, did you find old Floyd?"

Mork's face was simply livid! He said, "My God, man, where did you send me?"

I said, " Wasn't he home?"

"Oh, he was home all right, and I talked with him for over an hour. In all that time he never told me one true thing! I have never in my life heard such a liar. When I asked him if there were any big northerns in Crooked Lake, he told me there were plenty of twenty-pounders but that the biggest he had caught was a forty-eight pounder. Then he told me about all the other big fish he had caught. He told me about fishing in the winter when there was three feet of ice on the lake, and he caught a fish so big that he couldn't get it up through the hole in the ice. So he reached down with his arm, grabbed that fish in the eyes, and then had to wait for over an hour for someone to come along and chop the hole bigger, so he could pull the fish out!

"I listened to those lies for as long as I could stand it. Then I decided that the next thing that he told me, I would call him on. So I asked if Crooked was a deep lake, and he told me that there was ninety feet of water right at the end of his dock, but that the water was so clear that you could see the sand on the bottom. Then I asked him if there were big crappies in the lake, and he said, 'Sure.' When I asked how big he said, 'Three pounds,' and that's when I called him a liar!

"Well, sir, he didn't say a word. He just grabbed me by the arm and led me up to his cabin. There, just inside the back door, was an old ice box. He opened the lid and took out three of the biggest crappies I have ever seen in my life! I said, 'Man, those sure are the biggest crappies that I have ever seen, but you are still a liar—no crappie could weigh that much!' Well sir, he just set his old kitchen scales on the table, put those three crappies on it, and there it was—nine pounds! Here I had listened to that son-of-a-buck lie to me for nearly three hours, and then I'd called him a liar the first time that he told the truth all day!"

Of course I knew all along what Mork was going to get from old Floyd, but I am still not entirely sure which of them was the biggest liar. Oh, yes, Mork and Floyd did eventually go fishing together, but I never did see any big strings of fish.

The most vivid of all my memories, however, are of all the wonderful, and lasting friendships that I have made through the years.

Chapter 24

Summer Friends

As I sit here at my machine, recalling those early years and the many friends that we made, I am prompted to introduce a few who have made a particularly noteworthy contribution. You have met Bill and Clare Hagen briefly. Bill first came in the 1920s as a bachelor. He was such a friendly and outgoing person that my parents couldn't help befriending him. He had pernicious anemia and had rented the little Oak cabin for a month in an effort to improve his health. He left before his month was up, saying that he would be back in plenty of time to clean up the cabin before the next party was to arrive. I think he was lonesome; a distant relative had arrived from Sweden, and he was anxious to spend some time with her. At any rate, he did not return on time, and Mom had to go in and pack up his things so that she could clean. Mom said that she had never seen such a mess. Suitcases and boxes were piled under the bed. She could find no dishes in the cupboard; they were all dirty and hidden under some wood in the woodbox! The floor was filthy, and he had used the curtains as hand towels.

Mom ultimately forgave him when he returned with his new bride, Claire, the cousin from Sweden. She was very nice and spoke English quite well, although we did get quite a kick out of her Swedish accent. But it was especially Bill who seemed to take to me. My morning ritual, after I had eaten breakfast, was to walk down to the camp ground where Bill would just be fixing his. He would fry me a piece of bacon and an egg, make me some toast, and we would eat breakfast together, while we discussed the plans for the day.

We set up a little tennis court on the lawn in front of what is now our boat-launching site, and he taught me the rudiments of the game. We had another thing going, too. Bill had started out calling me "Private," in memory of his army days no doubt. When I did something that particularly pleased him he would give me a promotion. I was Corporal, then Sergeant, and so on up the line. My promotions came rapidly, and, when Bill ran out of convenient ranks for me, he dubbed me "Prince," and there I remained. Bill, of course, was always "His Lowness." When Claire would send Bill down to our little store for something she needed to make dinner, he would come with his hands alongside his eyes to act as blinders, so that he would not be tempted to stop and talk to someone. If he did, his trip could easily take an hour.

Sometimes we would walk back to Knieff Lake, the little lake on the back of our property named after Grandfather Henry. There we had a boat, and we would go bass fishing. We used cane poles then, and slowly rowed along the shore with our bobbers dragging behind. Frogs were our bait of choice, so, before we could fish, we had to catch frogs. We had some very nice catches of bass too. I remember one time in particular when a man from one of the cabins went with us to what we called Little Shirt Lake. It is Arbor Lake now. I was doing the rowing, and we had caught several nice bass, when Bill had a powerful bite. Around and around the boat Bill went, his cane pole bent in an awesome arc, while the other man and I ducked to keep out of the way. Suddenly the line snapped; the fish was gone. In deep dejection, Bill said, "Let me row now, Prince. I have no more line, and there is not enough left to fish with. Even my bobber is gone." We offered to go in, but Bill said, "No," and continued rowing. About this time I noticed a bobber across the lake and suggested that we could at least retrieve that much. As we drew near, the bobber commenced to retreat, The fish was still there! I again took the oars and maneuvered the boat, while Bill crouched poised, ready to grab the line. Finally he had the line in his grasp, and gently raised the fish to the surface. Meanwhile, our companion had searched his tackle box and come up with a gaff hook. Suddenly the giant jaw broke the surface, the gaff slid under it, and the eight-pound northern pike lay flopping in the boat. Bill tied his line back together, and we fished for a while longer. But Bill was in a hurry to get home, and before nightfall, everyone in the resort had heard the story of the miraculous catch.

Bill Hagen holding his "miracle" northern with our fishing companion in the middle and Albert the guide on the far right

The Renquists first came in 1934, and stayed in the Elm cabin next to the house. Their son Donald was only three at the time. One afternoon Mr. Renquist decided to go to Mille Lacs to try for some walleyes. Shortly, a little storm blew up, and Mom spotted Mrs. Renquist sitting on the steps of the cabin, her baby in her arms, crying lest her husband would not come back. Mom went down to comfort her, and soon her husband returned, and all was well. The Renquists continued to return year after year, and, to this day, two of their granddaughters and their families rent three of our cabins by the season, continuing a sixty-year friendship with us and our beautiful Bay Lake.

When I was about twelve, Bill and Marge Getsch stayed in the same little Oak Cabin on their honeymoon that Bill Hagen had once occupied. The first night that they were there, Mom, having learned that they were newlyweds, baked them a pie and sent me down with it. Bill was particularly thrilled with the pie; I don't think that Marge was such a good cook yet. With a little encouragement, Bill talked me into staying and playing a few games of cribbage with him. The cribbage was repeated on other evenings as well, and Mom thought that it was terrible that I should so occupy the groom on his honeymoon. Apparently Marge didn't mind, for the Getsches came for many years, and every Christmas we would receive a card with their growing family pictured on it.

The Rowes came from Duluth. They had turned south at Aitkin and inquired for a cabin at the first resort they came to on Farm Island Lake. The operator could not accommodate them, so, rather than trying to place them at one of the neighboring resorts, he sent them to Bay Lake. We happened to be the first resort that they encountered; they became fast friends and continued to come for many years. They had two sons, Nat, or Bud as we called him, and Jack. Bud and I became particularly close. When I was going to school in Duluth in 1947, my two roommates and I were invited to several delicious dinners at the Rowes. That spring Bud took me trout fishing for the first time. He knew the North Shore at sixteen like few others will ever know it. He spent many of his winter weekends with his little white dog, Pal, up along the shore, backpacking and trapping and developing his love of the wilderness. We drove up the shore to Schroeder, then cut inland past Cramer to where we hit the Dumbbell Lake trail. Here we parked, put on our packs, and headed off for the upper reaches of the Manitou River where we made camp. The stream is quite small there and easily fished. I started upstream, and, almost as soon as I got my bait in the water, I had a little trout on the line. After a few minutes of catching and releasing these little seven- and eight-inchers, Bud called to see how I was doing. When I told him, he said, "Hey, those are nice trout for this stream! Don't throw those back, or we won't eat tonight."

We had all the trout we could eat, and packed out a few for me to take home with me the next day as well. The bear didn't give us any trouble, although we had seen one several times on the way in. When we came upon a little field, there was the bear pouncing on field mice. Pal took after that bear in a hurry, and we didn't see it again. That trip probably changed my whole life, for I developed a love for trout fishing and camping that is as strong today as it was forty years ago. Dr. Nathanial Rowe now owns a lovely cabin on the Au Sable River in Michigan. He has gained international renown among his peers for his studies in oral pathology, and his travels have taken him all over the world. In 1978 I had the great pleasure of joining Bud and his youngest son, John, on a trip to the Flathead River country in Montana, of which he had heard so much from my Dad while he was a boy. I have also joined the same pair on one of their extended trips canoeing in the Boundary Waters that we both love so well.

The Neels came our way a little later on, from Grand Junction, Iowa. They also spent their vacations with us for a number of years, and their younger son, Bob, and I did a lot of fishing together. He had cousins from What Cheer, Iowa, who also spent time here, and Bob, Ronnie, and I did a bit of the night life together during those years. They both owned cabins on the west shore of the lake later on, but times change, the cabins have been sold, and we gradually lose touch.

Bob Kalsted, his wife, Joyce, and Steve Souder are among the many who once stayed with us and now own their own cabins here on the lake. The list goes on, and, to those I have omitted, I can only plead lack of space, for their memories linger on!

Chapter 25

Local Friends

By the fall of 1938, the facilities of the Deerwood school system were becoming overcrowded, and the Bay Lake district No. 11 was asked to seek other arrangements. Riverton, which is four miles beyond Ironton, had a beautiful big school, originally equipped to include high school, and too few students to justify keeping it open. Arrangements were made for the grade-school children from Bay Lake to ride their bus to the high school in Crosby, then transfer to the Riverton bus after it had dropped its load of high school students off, and ride back to school in Riverton. The arrangement worked very well except that it made for an inordinate amount of bus riding for the children—about sixteen miles one way from where I got the bus. Actually, the hours away from home were shortened a bit if anything, about nine hours in my case.

That same fall, Clarence Kalberg and his wife and family came to spend the winter in one of our cabins. His brother, Ed, was a close friend of Bill Hagen, and in that way we were well acquainted with the family. Clarence had two daughters, Margaret (Muggs), who was about my age, and Francis, who was a bit older. It was fun to have someone my age nearby in the winter. Clarence had to move out of the cities because of his health. He was an auto mechanic, and years of working around running motors with improper ventilation had left him with severe carbon monoxide poisoning. He could feel its effects when he walked behind an idling car, even outdoors.

The following spring Clarence helped us make maple syrup. He loved being out in the woods, and I think he must have spent eighteen hours a day by that sap pan. In those days, we gathered our sap in wooden barrels loaded on a trailer pulled by our old Ford car. It was this spring that I learned to drive, with Clarence a willing and able instructor. Backing a trailer in an S-curve down through a mud hole and aligning it with another series of barrels is no mean feat, believe me. No, I didn't learn to do it all that year!

While we were not too busy with the syrup, just out tending the furnace, Clarence also taught me a little about competitive rifle shooting. He had been a member of the Minneapolis Rifle Team for a number of years, where he shot with some of the best shooters in the world. I had carried and shot my little twenty-two since I was about eight, but lining up a seventeen-pound match rifle, equipped with a twenty-power scope and a sling, was a whole new experience. I would later take up the sport myself, and eventually earn my "master" classification, but I would never be in his league.

Dad had had a heart attack in the summer of 1937 and had to be careful what he did. He had tried hiring a young single man the year before, but there really wasn't enough to keep a man busy full time without constant supervision, and the one he chose had proved to be not very reliable. With World War II heating up in Europe, gas rationing became a real threat. So Dad built a store building, with living quarters in it, up on the edge of our field near the junction of county roads 10 and 14. The Kalbergs, who still needed a place to stay, agreed to live there and manage the store and gas pumps. Mrs. Kalberg would do a little home baking, while Clarence would have time to service our ice boxes and haul our garbage. Clarence had purchased some property on Clearwater Lake, and he worked at building a log home there when he had free time.

Clarence Kalberg was easy going and soft spoken, with more than a trace of Scandinavian brogue and the instincts of a true naturalist. His legendary skill as a marksman lent itself well to his love of hunting. He also loved to fish, most often with a fly rod from his canoe. He always bent down the barbs on his hooks to enable him to release fish more easily if he didn't wish to eat them, and he never used a gaff hook or net to land a fish. Yet he once landed a fifteen-pound northern while fishing in this manner. No wonder that through the years Clarence became a sort of idol for me. I truly hated to see the Kalbergs leave here and settle on their own place when their log home was finished.

I must not leave this period in my life without more mention of the Fuller families. Frank Fuller, the oldest of four boys, lived with his family on the west end of Knieff Lake. His oldest daughter, Merle, was married to Alex Ruttger, the oldest of Joe's boys. His youngest son, Davis, was two or three years older than I. His proximity made him one of my most frequent playmates, especially in the winter. We had ski trails going all over in the woods between his house and mine, and really enjoyed them, sometimes with picnics in the snow around a blazing fire. One day we even shot a squirrel and roasted it, but it didn't get very well done and we had forgotten the salt, so it wasn't very good. We didn't try it again. I remember skiing along the cliffs of snow that overhung the hill behind the house. Too close to the edge and the crest would break off, leaving us in a heap at the bottom of the hill.

In the summer we would go on fishing trips or take expeditions down Mud River. One time we went up Coffee Creek into Coffee Lake. On the way back, when the creek became too narrow to row, we were just gliding with the current, with one of the oars trailing in the water while Davis, from the front of the boat, would push off from the bank with the other oar, when necessary. Of course we were both standing. Suddenly the upper end of the oar that was trailing in the water caught on a snag. The boat stopped suddenly, and I, just as suddenly, sat down. Unfortunately I missed the boat! Coffee Lake is well named, it has the darkest water that I have ever seen. The paddle end of a snow white oar will totally disappear from sight when dipped over a foot under its surface. I can still see those brown bubbles over my head as I sank. I don't remember whether I could swim at the time or not, I only remember Davis standing in the front of the boat and laughing so hard that he could not help me back into the boat. I guess that I showed him that I could vault into the boat if I really had to.

Emery Fuller was the youngest of the Fuller boys. He was married to Marjorie, who was a niece of Dave Archibald, and my mother's best friend. They had two children, Walter and Lois, who were just a little bit older than I, and they operated a small American Plan resort, which included all meals for their guests. It was located southwest of Ruttgers, across from Indian Point. In the summer, we were all so busy that we rarely saw our neighbors, but when fall came we made up for lost time. Scarcely a week would go by without our families seeing each other. Sometimes Mother would call Marjorie and ask her what they were doing that day, and if they would like to come down for dinner. Marjorie might say, "Oh dear, I just started some bread." Mom would say, "Just knead it down and bring it along. You can bake it here." And that's just what she would do. Our folks played a lot of bridge in those days, and, when I was a baby, I know that I spent considerable time in one of Marjorie's dresser drawers. When we grew older, their kids and I played games by the hour, "hide the thimble" being one of our favorites.

I have mentioned that Emery drove the school bus. He was a good driver, and he kept pretty good control over the kids. I can still remember looking in the rear-view mirror and seeing his eyes on us when the bus got a little noisy. Drivers had a little more latitude in those days, and, if someone got too far out of line, off the bus he went! Our bus had bench seats that ran along either side, from the driver to the rear end, with girls occupying one side and boys the other. Smaller seats, with backs, and set perpendicular to the benches, occupied the middle. It made a wonderful opportunity for the "big kids" to torment the little ones. If an older boy was caught misbehaving, he would end up riding in front on the girls' side for a week or so.

Emery's skill as a driver was really put to the test in the spring of the year, when the side roads, including the one that ran from Ruttgers down our way, would have nearly bottomless mud holes in them. Having to drive those spots twenty times a week, he knew them perfectly and practically never got stuck, although he often had to stop and help others in the evening when they were at their worst.

Albert Miller Jr. was a class ahead of me, but less than a year older. He was the worst tease that we had on the bus, or in school either for that matter. He loved to snatch a hat from someone, or poke him, and when the victim turned around, Jr. would point to a nearby innocent and then sit back and enjoy the ensuing scuffle. Of course this did not always work, and Jr. himself would sometimes become embroiled. He and Clarence Sanders would go at it now and again, with the outcome never in doubt. Jr. would hit Clarence in the nose, then go into a clinch with him. Clarence would drape himself over Jr. and bleed until a truce could be arrived at, then both would go their bloody ways. For some reason Jr. and I got along very well. He would try me now and again, but I would always answer in kind without getting angry, and that would end it. We had many long and serious discussions on those tedious bus rides that I fully enjoyed, and I believe that he did too.

Chapter 26

The Resort Matures

The resort business was a growing industry in the 1930s. At first, any little cabin that offered some sort of place to sleep and an access to a lake could be rented. Fishing soirees for men only soon turned into family vacations, and typically mom wanted a little more comfort and convenience. Our first step toward modernization came in 1933 when Dad purchased a used Kohler electric generator and put electricity in the cabins. This was before the days of R.E.A., and the only other way he could have gotten power would have been to pay for the construction of power lines from Ruttgers, which was the nearest approach that Minnesota Power and Light made to us. The cost of this would have been prohibitive.

How I remember that old "light" plant, and how great it was to have electricity in the house and not have to read by the light of a kerosene lamp, or even a gasoline fueled "gas lamp." The plant did have its drawbacks, however. It started on demand, which meant that whenever someone turned on a light, the engine would start. It was installed in our root cellar, with its exhaust piped up through the vent hole in the ceiling. Whenever a light was turned on, the raucous sound of its exhaust would fill the air. This was perfectly acceptable in the evening, but when it lasted past midnight it became more than just annoying. I remember more than one occasion when Dad went out and threw the switch on the power and left some "night owl" in darkness.

Another drawback was keeping it running. It became a daily chore for Dad to take out the spark plugs and clean them or clean the fuel filter or something. But it was a major improvement, and we enjoyed it until the R.E.A. arrived a couple of years later.

In 1935, when Dad decided to build the new cabins, he also made a major step toward modernization. Up until this time, the cabins had depended primarily on kerosene stoves for cooking. They were smelly, hard to keep clean, and in constant need of wick trimming and the like. A bottled-propane gas company had just started up in Crosby, and Dad decided to put gas-burning hot plates in all of the cabins. The cabins on each end were linked together and fed by a single setup of hundred-pound cylinders. The women loved the new stoves, although some expressed concern about the dangers of burning gas.

When we finally went on line with R.E.A. the door was opened for running water. Until this time water had been furnished by shallow wells, with sand points driven fifteen to twenty feet into the ground. This water supply was available nearly anywhere on the property, and the wells were spotted along for the convenience of the cabins. Now a deep well would have to be drilled, but this was in line with the ever increasing restrictions placed on public facilities.

Having running water piped into the cabins meant that we had to install sinks with drain systems. These were simple in the extreme, but quite effective. A pipe through the kitchen wall brought cold water to the single faucet mounted over the porcelain-lined steel sink. The sink drained through a goose neck, through the floor, and into a fifty-gallon drum, with its bottom cut out, holes punched in its sides, and buried alongside of the cabin. Wouldn't the inspectors have fun with such an arrangement today! Actually, with only "gray" water going out, they did no more harm to the environment than throwing the water on the ground—probably less.

In the early 1940s Dad sold two pieces of property. The first was a hundred-foot lot on the lake abutting on the highway. One of our guests had become enamored of the cabin that they were using and wanted to build one just like it, only two feet longer and two feet wider; he wanted to be on our shore, but in his own cabin. Dad finally acceded to his wishes and sold him the hundred feet at twenty dollars per foot, with the provision that should he ever wish to sell it, he would give us the first chance to buy it back. How very thankful I am for that stipulation! When the man did die, in the late 1940s, his wife honored the agreement, and we were able to repurchase the property at a fair price. Today our shoreline is valued at $500.00 per foot for tax purposes!

The second sale was of the forty acres that adjoined our property on the north and encompassed most of Knieff Lake. The road that had formerly followed above the lake had been rebuilt during the 1930s and now followed along the line between the two parcels of land, thus creating viable lakeshore property along Knieff Lake. Ed Ruttger bought the property, platted it, and soon had the lots sold. I knew that Dad needed the money to complete the improvements he was making, but I have regretted the loss of that property ever since.

Knieff Lake is such a pretty little lake, with huge white and Norway pines along the shore, and, when I was little, it had some of the best fishing to be found anywhere. Besides big bass, northerns, and walleyes, it had huge sunfish, and crappies that commonly weighed over two pounds. The largest that Dad ever weighed from there was two and three-quarters pounds, so you see, Floyd Warren may have been telling the truth, at least that once! But the public became aware of this, access was gained through other property, the fish sorely depleted, and its mystique somehow destroyed. I believe that this was, in a large part, the reason that Dad sold.

A great tourist attraction to this area in the 1930s and 1940s were the AK-SAR-BEN GARDENS. It had been a summer home owned by the Vogt family from Omaha, Nebraska. Mrs. Vogt had been a Wasserzieher, and so was a relative. Her two sons, Bud and Hugo, kept the home after she died and took great pride in making it as beautiful as they knew how. Hugo was the "stone man." He made stone pathways, arches, fish ponds, a wishing well, and even a stone castle, complete with a moat. Little streams fed the waterfalls and emptied into the fish ponds, well stocked with gold fish.

Bud was the "flower man." The entire area was a profusion of color, featuring practically every variety of flower that would grow here. Dahlias were his chief pride however, and he consistently won ribbons with his at the Minnesota state fair. He also did the house work, which included baking. Every Saturday morning he would bake bread, and often pies, to display to the public. He put out the prettiest loaf of bread that you ever saw.

Their chief claim to fame, however, were the fish. They had a moderately deep shore in front of the house, which made it ideal for feeding the fish which came to enjoy the shade from their dock. At first it was only sunfish, but soon bass also became aware of the free handouts. A crust of bread held at the surface of the water would disappear into the hungry mouths of hundreds of sunfish. A little green frog held two or three feet above the water would soon bring a four- or five-pound bass careening out of the water to take it from one's fingers, if he had the courage to keep them there. An added attraction was a cow bell that hung near the water's edge. If you were to ring the bell on a calm morning before anyone had been there, you would see a series of wakes coming from up and down the shoreline, as hundreds of fish answered their call to breakfast.

When people heard of this beautiful spot, and the "tame" fish, which would eat out of one's hand, they were intrigued, and came to see for themselves. In time, their numbers increased to the point where the Vogts had to either keep them all out or charge admission and make a business of it. They had a sister who lived not far from there who would make ice cream and sell it, along with candy and pop, from a little concession stand located near the entrance. Ak-sar-ben (which is simply Nebraska spelled backwards) and the tame fish soon became known throughout the entire upper Midwest. Eventually, even the name of the lake was changed to "Tame Fish."

In the early winter of 1943, Dad, who had recovered somewhat from his heart problem, went to work out in Hanford, Washington, building an atomic power station. Mother and I got along very well, and, in the spring when the snow began to melt and the birdsongs changed to those of courtship, I got itchy fingers to tap our maple trees. We had a fine pile of slab wood near the furnace, although it was still in eight-foot lengths, and the rest of the equipment was all ready to go. I knew of a neighbor boy, Willard, one of the Bickfords, who would like to help me. I figured that with his help after school, I could go to school in the mornings when most of my important classes were, then drive home and work in the sugar bush until ten o'clock or so in the evening. With Mother's rather grudging consent, I began tapping. I don't believe that I have ever worked so hard in all my life. I would get up by six o'clock to get the fire started in the furnace, then saw wood into the proper lengths so that Mom would have plenty ready for her to use while I was in school. Then a quick breakfast and a change of clothes, another firing of the furnace, and I was off to school for my three morning classes. Mom kept the furnace fired up for me while I was in school. She also had to add sap to the back pan every half hour or so. One morning she tried to empty some pails that hadn't been emptied after a snow fall and, in trying to cross a little ravine that was filled with snow, she sank in over her waist and nearly got trapped there. Fortunately she was able to roll and get herself out, but she nearly froze, as there was quite deep water under the snow.

At noon I hurried home, ate a bite, and began gathering sap, for I had about three hundred trees tapped. My friend Willard arrived shortly after four, and we would gather until nearly dark. Only then could we finish off the batch of syrup. We didn't take it quite all of the way to syrup, however, as in those years we reheated it and bottled it in the house. When that batch was finished, often after dark, I would put the pan right back on and start another batch, then fire it until midnight. Hopefully, I would have found a place somewhere in that schedule to eat supper.

Naturally, the trees did not run this well every day. When it turned cold for a day or two I could relax a bit. Fortunately the Easter vacation came during the peak of the run and gave me a ten-day "vacation" just when I needed it the most. We canned over ninety gallons of syrup that year.

Chapter 27

The War Years

The summer of 1943 was one of discontent for me. Dad was home from Washington, but he could not really do all of the hard work around the resort. This I did gladly, but I was now seventeen and subject to the draft in January. I knew that I wouldn't be able to finish my last year of high school, and I didn't want to go just part of a year and then have to leave. At the end of August I went to Minneapolis to look for a job, hoping to earn a little money before I was called. It was not to be. I was too near to my eighteenth birthday. No one would hire me. Frustrated, I called home to explain my problem. Fortunately the Keiths were visiting with my parents when I called. Mr. Keith suggested that I go over to the University of Minnesota and inquire about beginning college on a test basis. That way, I could get in at least one quarter before I was called. It seemed far-fetched to me, but I had taken extra credits during my first two years of senior high and lacked only two more to graduate, so I decided to give it a shot.

I went over to the campus the next morning, was interviewed, and told to come back in about ten days for my testing. When I returned, I was given about four days of testing, much of it on social development. When it was over, I learned that I had passed and that I could enter the Institute of Technology. What a break! I had not had solid geometry, which was a prerequisite for I.T., and normally I would have had to go into S.L.A., but because I was entering on a test basis, this requirement was waived. I.T. was the school for engineering, which was my goal.

My college career began while I was only seventeen, a high school "drop out," and with very little money saved. My first chore after registering was to find a place to live. I settled on the student co-op club, where the meals were inexpensive and I could do janitorial work for an hour or two a night in exchange for my room rent. Fortunately it was right on campus and within easy walking distance of all my classes. I was assigned a study room on the second floor, where we also kept our belongings, and which I would share with another freshman. We all slept in a large dormitory room on the third floor.

Next came job hunting, and here I really lucked out. I was hired to work at the mines experimental building from eight to twelve, five nights a week for sixty cents an hour. The going wage on campus was fifty cents. The university was engaged in a continuing study of the feasibility of digesting low-grade iron ore with sulfuric acid to transform it into a usable form of taconite. The fumes were so strong that I had to wear two pairs of pants, and throw the outer pair away every two weeks or so, and add a new pair underneath. But the nature of our work did allow me some time for homework. I also talked my way into another job, that of managing a concession booth under the stands on Saturdays when there was a home football game. This paid a whopping seventy-two cents per hour and was usually good for seven hours or more.

I am nearly six feet, and had always considered myself moderately tall. My roommate was six two, which is common enough, but when I went to see the student head of the co-op, I found him to be six-foot-six, and I could just feel myself shrinking. Imagine how I felt when I reported for work and found my working partner to be six-foot-eleven! Strange how our perception of ourselves, and of life in general, changes through such minor experiences.

My studies progressed fairly well, considering the seventeen-credit load that I was carrying and the number of hours that I worked. I finished the quarter with B's and C's, thanks in no small measure to some excellent teachers that I had had in high school. Lack of sleep took its toll, as it usually does for college students. I got home from work by twelve-thirty and could usually have been in bed by one or one-thirty. But here the perversity of human nature comes into play. Our club was comprised of students from every field of endeavor and from freshmen to post grads. This made for some wonderful "bull sessions" that went on into the wee hours nearly every night. I simply could not resist them, and they probably contributed as much to my education as the classroom did. Trouble was, if I wanted breakfast at the club I would have to finish it by eight o'clock, and I couldn't afford to eat out. I was finished with classes no later than three-thirty, and often by noon, so I had time to study if I could stay awake. I would sit cross-wise on my chair or hang my head out of the window, but all too often my only recourse was to involve myself in a card game. I dared not sleep or I would miss dinner.

Dad had again gone out to Hanford to work, and poor Mom could not stand to remain home with little to do but worry about the two of us. So she came down to the cities and found a job for herself helping a widowed lady, Mrs. Pete, who ran a boarding home for girls. It was in "Dinkytown" and only five or six blocks from the club, so I could easily walk over to see her when I had the time. Mrs. Pete was a wonderful lady, and without her help I doubt that Mom could have endured the break-up of our home.

The author as a G-I during basic taining.

Mom and I spent the Christmas holidays up north with Hazel Wasserzieher and her boys. Thank God for relatives and friends! On January 13, I had to report to Fort Snelling to volunteer for induction into the military if I wanted to get into the branch of service of my choice. I had tried to enroll in the ROTC and the NROTC, but had failed them both because of bad teeth and a sinus condition. Now my choice was the Army Air Corps where I still had an outside chance for pilot training. I passed the physical exam required before I could be accepted in the military, and also a literacy test that I was required to take because I had not graduated form high school, never mind that I was enrolled at the university at the time. This was my introduction to military logic. I was told to go home and wait to be called, that it would probably be a couple of months. Mom had told me to come back to Mrs. Pete's when I got through with my exam, and when I got there I found that she and Mrs. Pete had planned a birthday party for me with about a dozen girls. What a way to spend one's eighteenth birthday!

I enrolled in the second quarter at the university, more by default than anything else, for my heart was certainly no longer in it. Some classes I just dropped out of, but I did manage to stay long enough to earn a few credits. Early in February, Dad got very sick, pneumonia I believe. Mom and I met him at the depot with a wheel chair, much to his chagrin, and took him home where he would gradually recover. It was nice to have a little time at home before I had to report for active duty. My notice finally came. I reported for active duty on February 29, 1944, and was sworn in the next day.

After a couple of weeks spent getting properly attired and learning the rudiments of military life, I was shipped off with a group bound for Sheppard Field at Wichita Falls, Texas where I would take my basic training. We also took our general classification tests there, or GCTs, which were the military equivalent of an intelligence test. I was fortunate enough to do very well in this test and qualify for just about anything in the military. Next came the "psychomotors," which were designed to test one's balance, equilibrium, coordination, depth perception, and other physical aspects to determine if one was qualified to train as a pilot, navigator or bombardier. Scoring was from 1 to 4, and a score of 3 or 4 was required to qualify to train for any of the positions. I had scores of 4,3,4, which qualified me for any of the three positions. But then we had to take another physical, and once again my nose disqualified me. I have a deviated septum in my nose, which inhibits proper drainage and leads to a more or less permanent sinus infection. Flying with this condition could be dangerous, or at least very painful, so I could not fly. I did have the option of having the septum removed, with the hope that it would allow the sinus to drain, but I had heard horror stories of that surgery and did not want any part of it.

After completing basic training, I endured a seemingly endless period of waiting for orders. Finally I learned that another fellow with a similar name had had that surgery done and had then shipped right out. Meanwhile I was listed as "recovering" from this surgery. In the army this is known as SNAFU (situation normal—all fouled up)! Finally, on the 6th of July, I shipped out to Lowery Field in Denver, where I was enrolled in an armament school to study the remote control gunnery system on the new B-29 bombers. It would last for nineteen weeks and required a GCT score of 120, ten points higher than required for officer's training. I soon learned why. The first two weeks was a quick course in basic electricity. Then we learned the entire system of electronic controls that enabled each of five gunnery stations to control up to three of the five gun turrets simultaneously. Among my classmates were men who had worked as engineers in the development of the B-29 and the Voigt Corsair before they were drafted.

We were on the swing shift, which meant that we went to school from six till midnight six nights a week, and then had a thirty-six-hour pass. It was a tough course, but I enjoyed it, and who could complain about spending the summer in Denver? Sometimes we would rent a car and drive up into the mountains to Grand Lake or Estes Park. The townspeople of Denver were very friendly, the weather was ideal, and the scenery was unmatched. No wonder many of the fellows vowed to return when they got out of the service.

After completing the school, I was sent to McCook, Nebraska, an unlovely spot if ever there was one, especially in the winter. Fortunately I was there only a short while before being reassigned, this time to McDill Air Base in Tampa, Florida. There I would remain for the duration of my service time, with the exception of another three months back in Denver the next summer, where I trained on the computers that controlled the gunnery system.

The weather in Florida was nice enough, although I nearly froze while watching a football game there one night. We spent most of our free time over in St. Petersburg on the beach, but I never did learn to enjoy swimming in the salt water. It burns the eyes, stings the throat, and it smells bad. We had good times too, of course. We met some girls who enjoyed dancing, and there was a huge pavilion that had dances at least every Saturday night, and in between on special occasions. One of the big-name bands would play there about every six weeks. We danced to the Dorsey Brothers and Gene Krupa among others.

St. Petersburg has its "million dollar" pier that extends nearly a quarter of a mile into the gulf. There is a highway that runs out on it and circles the pavilion at its outer end. Green benches dot the perimeter of this circle, for people to sit and watch the waves, the gulls, and the pelicans, which are very tame. One day I happened to be watching a sailor and his girl, as they watched one of the pelicans soaring gracefully in the on-shore breeze. It hardly moved a wing as it glided around the perimeter of the pier, back and forth maintaining an elevation of about forty feet above the pier. It seemed to crane its neck as it watched the couple below. Suddenly it vented its meals of the day before in the form of a long gray streak, which, carried by its forward momentum and the drift of the wind, scored a perfect hit on the poor sailor, whitewashing his blues the full length of his body! I tried not to laugh, but I certainly pitied the fellow as he made a hasty retreat to the pavilion to rid himself of the stench and slime.

I didn't do much traveling around while stationed in Florida, partly because of the pesky biting insects, and partly because every plant that grows there has thorns of some kind on it.

I am used to enjoying nature, but here I found it very unfriendly, and uninviting. A buddy and I did hitch hike up to Winter Haven to see Cypress Gardens. On the road, rides were scarce. After one particularly long wait, we were picked up and after a short distance spotted another G.I. with his thumb out. The driver picked him up too, and quite naturally we got to talking about where we were from and the like. The stranger, whose name was Dave, told us he was from Kansas, which didn't strike me at the time. But when I said that I was from Minnesota, he perked up his ears and said, "We have a summer place up there."

"Where," I asked.

"You have probably never heard of it; it's called Bay Lake."

"My gosh! That's where I live. What did you say your name was?"

"Dave Richie. We have a cabin just a little ways south of Ruttgers."

"Well I'll be darned! My name is Al Knieff. My folks have a summer resort, and I think your parents stayed with us one year."

"Of course, I know the name. I believe that we did stay there before we bought our own cabin."

What were the odds of our paths crossing in this way? And yet everyone has had a similar experience at one time or another. When we got to the Gardens we found them rather run down and unused because of the war. When I told Dave that I had never water skied, he insisted that he find a power boat so that he could give me a lesson. Dave was an excellent skier, and, when we both got out of the service, he had me down to his cabin to give me another lesson and demonstrated going over a big jump. I am sure that he was the first on the lake to do that.

Another interesting trip was to Ocala, where we visited Silver Springs. This was an awesome experience because of the clarity of the water. The springs form a large pond, which gives birth to a good-sized river. When swimming over this pool, one is impelled to keep his feet up to avoid dragging them on the bottom. The sand is right there at your finger tips. Later we discovered that the water is eighty-four feet deep at that point! When we would swim under water and open our eyes, we could easily see another swimmer a hundred yards away. The fish were equally awesome, with sunfish that were literally platter size, and bass that weighed twenty pounds or more.

There were three of us on this trip, and one of the fellows had been a flight instructor for the navy before he was drafted. This seems odd, but he had been banged up a bit when one of his students made an emergency landing in a field, only to find out too late that it had a ditch running across it. While he no longer qualified for military flight, he wanted to do some aerobatics to keep in practice. We found an airfield with an old Steerman biplane for rent, and we were in business. By sharing the one-hour rental fee, he could give us each a half-hour ride. That was really a thrill, sitting in an open cockpit with only a threadbare safety belt to keep us in the plane. Jim started me out with what he called easy maneuvers, like snap rolls. Then we graduated to Immelmann turns, full loops, slow rolls, inverted flying, and finally spins. It didn't help my piece of mind to learn that when the plane was upside down, the carburetor on that model would not work and the engine would stall. The theory was that when the plane was again righted, the windmilling of the propeller would restart the engine. Sure enough, that's how it worked.

After the war in the Far East was over, and we were all just waiting around for discharge, the Air Force gave us a treat. Most of us had never been up in a military plane, so one section at a time, we were taken on a weekend trip to Cuba in B-29s. It was quite a thrill to finally get up in one of those giants that we had worked on for so long. I am sure that some of the boys experienced the seamier side of life that night, but I was well content to go to a jai alai game. I was finally mustered out of the service on May 10, 1946.

Chapter 28

The Big Decision

It was a wonderful feeling to be out of the service and home again at last. I had filled out my frame and put on some weight while I was away. In short, I had gone into the Army a boy and now, though not yet twenty-one, I was coming home a man. It had been an extraordinary experience. "The luck of the draw," as it were, had kept me from seeing combat, although the frustration at not going overseas had once prompted me to try signing up for the Rangers, a special-missions group designed to be dropped behind enemy lines.

It had been an early spring, and the season was already well advanced when I got home. There was plenty of work to be done, and I was ready to dig right in and do it. I designed and drew out a new reservation chart for the cabins, and, as I ponder these words, I look once more with nostalgia at those once-familiar names as they appear on its faded surface. I hauled the garbage, and I mowed the lawns; I wheeled the ice, and I tended to the boats. I went fishing with Dad and sat by the bonfires at night. I was home, and I was happy!

I did want to continue my education, so, in the fall, I enrolled at the Crosby-Ironton Junior College. I was forced to take only electives that first quarter, since the school did not offer any second quarter subjects in the fall. This probably worked to my advantage, as I took courses, like economics, which I am sure have been valuable to me. It was also a chance to get back into the study habit. When winter quarter started, I found how slow I had become with numbers. Math would never again be the cinch course that it had been. That school year passed rather uneventfully.

Our family had lived in Max Ruttgers home that winter as sort of caretakers. Since it was located right on the highway, it was a big advantage for us, as there was no long driveway to keep clear of snow. Also, it had oil heat, so there was no problem of getting up wood for the winter heating season. My folks had also lived here the previous two winters while I was in the service. Spring came extremely early that year, and for the second consecutive year the ice left the lake in March, the only times on record to my knowledge. The following year it would not go out until May 14th, which set a record in the opposite direction.

I managed to talk Dad into making a little maple syrup that spring, although living two miles from there and going to school made everything pretty difficult. It was just fun to do it again after missing three years.

Our major new project that spring was to put refrigerators in the cabins. Through our relatives in Marshall, Minnesota, we contacted a dealer who would sell us ten used machines for $50.00 each and would guarantee them to be in good, working order. So we hooked up the old trailer and headed south for a load of refrigerators. Mr. Carlson, the dealer, loaded what were left in his rig and came back with us to help get them set up and running properly. No more hauling ice to the cabins, or opening the ice house late in the evening while the mosquitos feasted on my blood, to replenish the icebox for someone who had used theirs for making ice cream or cold drinks!

That fall Bill Soshea, a returning veteran like myself, Leonard Treichler, a recent high school graduate, and I enrolled in the Junior College in Duluth. They shared a room in an apartment building, while I had a room in an adjoining apartment. Bill fixed up a little electric hot plate, and we did our cooking in their room. Bill had an old Plymouth, which he could not drive because of an unfortunate license suspension. Len had suffered a severely broken leg that summer in an auto accident and would be on crutches until nearly spring. Automatically I was elected the designated driver.

Schooling was fun that winter. School was quite a ways from our "pad" so we had to depend on the car to get us there. The car's battery was also old and rather unreliable. Consequently we had to park the car heading down hill in the evening, with its wheels turned into the curb. When we were ready to leave in the morning, I would turn away from the curb and rely on gravity to give us a push. We had a good steep two blocks down the hill to get started. If this failed, Bill would jump out of the car, get behind it, and make pushing gestures, which always got us a push and a start. The one time that the car failed to start completely, we had to have it towed into a heated garage overnight, to enable the frozen gas line to thaw out.

We soon developed a schedule that worked very well for us. We were all serious students and worked hard in class. When we were through for the day, we would retire to the student lounge, where we would play ping-pong or just relax for and hour or so, then head for home, stopping for what groceries we needed on the way. This daily stop was required since we had no refrigerator. The milk sat on the window ledge, between the window and the storm sash. There was no room for much more, except maybe some pop. Once home, we hit the books hard. At six o'clock Bill would stop and get dinner ready while Len and I kept at it. After dinner, Len and I would clean up the dishes while Bill caught up with us in the home work. We would finish our studies by nine or nine-thirty; then, if the weather were nice, we would jump into the car and take a ride up the North Shore, often singing the current hit songs of the day like "Beg Your Pardon" or one of the real "oldies" from Steven Foster, or even the military "standards" like "Anchor's Aweigh." It was a great way to relax. If the weather was bad, we would do calisthenics instead.

We located a little tavern just off the highway, where we would occasionally stop for a beer. One night the owner, with many apologies, "carded" us. It seems there was a crack down under way about serving minors. Bill and I were both of legal age, but neither of us had adequate proof, as he could not accept driver's licenses. But Len, who was only nineteen, had a card from a Navy program in which he was enlisted, which made him twenty-one. He could buy a beer, but neither Bill or I could. The owner said, "I cannot legally sell you two a beer, but I am going to give you each one, anyway!"

Len was receiving his schooling and some spending money from the Navy, while Bill and I were both on the GI bill, so money was just a little short. But once a week or so we would splurge and eat out. We found a little cafe back in West Duluth called Tony's Diner that served good food at modest prices, and it soon became our favorite. One evening we had ordered hamburger steak, but when it came we each had a sirloin, with all of the trimmings. It was a gesture that I will never forget. Probably it explains why its name eventually changed to "Antonne's Restaurant."

Len was remarkable in his ability to get around on his crutches. He expected no quarter when he set them in a corner and played ping-pong with us, and he needed none. At school we had wide stairways with a landing and turn in the middle. Len would watch for the chance when a couple of girls were approaching the bottom of the stairs, but not near enough to "help" him. Then he would utter a yelp and fall forward off the landing. The girls would scream, while Len would simply land on his crutches at the foot of the stairs, and with a little smirk on his face, go hopping away! When crossing a street or in a big hurry, he would pick up his crutches and hop on his good leg. Of course he had been a tumbler and cheer leader in high school, and fourteen months on crutches had developed his good leg to where he could do as many deep-knee bends on one leg as I could on two.

During that winter, while they were again staying at Ruttgers, Dad had the old summer kitchen torn off the house and a 20 x 20 foot modern kitchen and bathroom added. It also had a basement under it, so that we could have an oil furnace and hot water heat in the whole house. It was a wonderful improvement, and I would not even miss the trip 'out back', especially in the winter. But I did miss that old kitchen and all the associations it gave me with my youth. I still do in a way.

The same old house with the new kitchen added and a new layer of shakes.

During the spring quarter I tried to come home every weekend. I was doing all of the correspondence for reservations at the resort, and trying to get the yard work done too. It got to be a real drag, and I came to realize that, while my parents could no longer operate the resort by themselves, I could not continue school and run the resort too. So after graduating from the J.C., I decided that I would give up the idea of becoming an engineer and focus on the resort instead. I have never been sorry for that decision.

It seemed strange that fall, not to be going back to school. I would have the opportunity to hunt ducks, partridge, and deer for the first time since high school. But I had to find something else to do, too. I couldn't just lay around all winter. Then we got an invitation from Chester. He and his family were living just outside San Diego, in fact they were building a home there. He was in the school system, driving a mobile shop unit from school to school in the small surrounding towns and teaching shop. They wanted us to come out and spend Christmas with them. My cousin Oscar also lived near there with his family, and Mom had two sisters living in San Mateo. Helen, who had lost her only son while training as a B-24 pilot during the war, and Irene, who had been widowed early and had no children.

So after the deer season was over, we loaded up our Mercury club coup and headed for California. The trip out was harrowing for Mom, who had never seen, or been in the mountains before. As we left Green River, Wyoming, a blizzard set in, and we were forced to turn back to town and spend the night. The next day, the storm had eased up, and we headed out again. Again the weather forced us to "hole up" early at a little town in eastern Nevada. The next day we finally got into Reno, Nevada, where we spent the night listening to trains switching and trucks snorting as they gathered speed for the climb they were about to begin. The next morning Mom broke her mirror, an evil omen, as the stories of bad roads, steep climbs, another approaching storm, and the miseries of the Donner family haunted her imagination. We ate a hurried breakfast and left. We were forced to "chain up" our tires at the foot of the divide, and, even then, we were one of the last cars to be let through that morning as the weather rapidly worsened. But we experienced no further problems.

After spending a pleasant week with Irene and Helen, seeing all the sights and eating at Fisherman's Wharf, we headed down the shore to San Diego. We found Chet and his wife Gladys without trouble, Chet tending his avocados just outside his new home. It wasn't completed yet, and his children, Lelani, Lynn, and Robert were still using a sort of wooden-walled tent as a bedroom. We slept in the as yet unpartitioned kitchen, dining room, living room area with "Queeny," Chet's pit bull dog, who slept on a little square hassock in front of the electric space heater. Mom, ever sensitive to a creature's comfort, covered her with a little rug. The next morning she was still there, with the rug still covering her.

We had a lovely Christmas, sharing it with Oscar and his family just like in the old days back home. Of course Chet had no school that week, so he was able to take us up into the mountains for picnics, and out to see the naval base. One day he took Dad and I out into the Borrego Desert where we spent the night, visited the hot springs and pulled cactus thorns out of Queeny's mouth. I also had a chance to look up an old army buddy, Joseph Reed Scott, or

"Scottie." I spent New Year's Eve with him at a square-dance party, of all things. I had never square danced before, nor have I since, but it was a lot of fun. Our return trip was relatively uneventful. We took the southern route home through Tucson, Arizona, then over to Carlsbad, New Mexico, where we went through the famous caverns. From there we went to Manhattan, Kansas, where we intended to spend one night with the Keiths. We had to spend two extra nights before leaving for home because of a sleet storm that completely closed the roads for a while. The warmth of the hospitality extended to us by the Keiths, and the opportunity it gave us to call on several other friends who had spent their vacations with us, made this little extension of our visit a most pleasant one.

Chapter 29

The Boat Builder

I have always been interested in boats, what made them easy to row, and what made them suitable for use with an outboard motor. After we got back from California, I found a boating magazine in the drugstore with plans in it for building a little plywood boat called the "flying fisherman." It so intrigued me that I decided to build it, with a few minor alterations of my own. It had a "hard" chine, which meant that the sides and bottom met in a well defined sharp line, unlike a round bottom boat where the transition is in a continuous curve. It also had a "planing shelf" with the bottom extending a short way beyond the transom, or rear end.

It looked pretty nice when I got it finished, and I could hardly wait to get it in the water. I had an old 5.4-horsepower, four-cylinder Evenrude outboard at the time, which ran very smooth and nice but was always hard to start. As soon as the lake was free of ice, I mounted the motor on my new boat and started it up. What a revelation. That little boat got right up out of the water and planed! My motor would push one of our regular boats about six or eight miles an hour; now I was going nearly fifteen. I was so thrilled that I couldn't resist telling my friend, Fred Henry, who ran the sporting goods store in Crosby, about it. I also told him about my motor and how hard it was to start. He had the perfect solution. He had just taken on a line of new Mercury motors, and he had a 7.5-h.p. model on hand that he wanted me to bring out and try on my boat. He wanted to see what it would do as badly as I did. That little motor weighed twenty pounds less than mine, but when I turned it loose, it ran up right near twenty-five miles an hour! I was amazed, and I was hooked for good.

That summer they had a centennial celebration in Crosby that featured some boat races. I entered my new outfit in the ten-h.p. class because there was no class for 7.5-h.p. The race started in Crosby and went to Deerwood and back. Mom and Dad were standing on the beach waiting for the finish when the public-address man said, "There's a big white boat in the lead." Even though I was running against several little racing hulls, I won with ease. Then Bob Neel, a friend of mine from the resort, put

Bob Neel and Al standing in Al's boat, displaying their trophies. Ken Wasserzieher stands in his boat with the Elto outboard on the right.

his brand new five-h.p. Mercury on my "big white boat" and won that class. Later, he told me that the motor was so new and tight that at first he had a hard time keeping up, but at the far turn it finally started to loosen up, and he was able to actually throttle-back from then on, to protect his new motor. That's what made the race appear to be close.

In the spring of 1949, we began the final phase of our remodeling project. We chose the Elm cabin to be our first fully modern cabin. Rather than add just enough for a bathroom, we decided to build a large-enough addition for a kitchen and bathroom behind the original living room, and another bedroom behind the old one. All of the shutters were now replaced with sliding glass windows, and the interior of the living room, kitchen, and bath were paneled with knotty pine. The bathroom had to be large enough for the water heater, as well as a shower, stool, and lavatory. Many of the old timers had complained that they did not want us to go modern, but I don't remember of any of them complaining when the "little trail out back" was eliminated. The trend of the future had been defined.

My experience with the little fishing boat had been so rewarding that the following winter my cousin Harlo Wasserzieher and I decided to design and build three new runabout boats. We would sell one of them to pay some of our expenses, and keep one each for our own use. We spent long hours deciding on the dimensions, the trade offs to be made between ultimate speed and handling qualities, and the esthetics of size and shape of the deck and the general above-water appearance. It definitely would incorporate a new transom that I had designed, which would enclose the planing shelf (making it part of the transom), with a cut out area for the motor. We found a white oak tree on Harlo's property ideally suited to our purposes. It had stood out in the open, enduring the full brunt of the wind, which rendered its fibers tougher and less likely to be brash. We were able to get a straight log twelve feet long, which we had sawed into lumber for the ribbing. We ordered brass screws by the gross, and special ordered the marine plywood for the planking.

Finally we were ready to build, and the little garage behind Ruttger's house became our workshop. Our equipment was very meager. Harlo, who had the mechanical instincts of his father, had built a little band saw and a simple sander. He also devised a collar that would go over a wood bit, serving as both a depth gauge and a countersink. When the end of the bit was tapered to fit the tip of the screw, we could drill holes that exactly fit the shape of the screw. This eliminated the possibility that the brass screws would twist off in the white oak.

The first boat was a bit complicated; especially tricky was getting the ribbing to match the contours that we had predicted in our design, which had been arrived at by bending a slender strip of wood between points A and D while also passing through points B and C on our original plan. In a few places the plywood was forced to assume a compound curve, and this was also a problem, until we learned to use a little kerosene on its surface to lubricate the grain. Then we could soften it with hot water without the grain lifting.

We were ready with that first boat the moment there was enough open water between the lake ice and the shore to run it. We must have looked pretty silly, running back and forth in that little strip of water, but the boat performed even better than we had anticipated! We sold our third boat to Dr. Nixon, from Deerwood, and I think that he was as pleased with it as we were with ours. Harlo and his brother Kenny had a 22-horsepower opposed-firing twin Johnson to use on their boat, but I had no motor that would do mine justice. I wound up buying a new 10-h.p. Mercury "Hurricane," which allowed me to run with anything on the lake at that time. It would reach a speed of about thirty-eight miles an hour. It was fast enough to be a thrill, and I used to enjoy taking a pretty young girl for a ride around the lake whenever the opportunity presented itself. The new 35-horsepower Johnson and Evenrude motors had just hit the market,

The new runabout

and invariably some youngster would come out with his to show off. I would let him buzz past me, then open my throttle, and the next thing I knew, he would be heading for shore in disgust.

That summer we also modernized the Linden, Oak, Maple, and Ivy cabins. The Linden and Maple cabins were large enough that this could be done with only a five-by-eight foot bathroom added on. Of course they were paneled, and new windows added where necessary. The Oak and Ivy were our smallest cabins and required more extensive additions. We also added kitchens and bedrooms on them. In 1953, we continued the program with a major renovation of the Lilac into a large two-bedroom cabin. The Willow and Spruce cabins were given an addition across the end, which enlarged the living room and make room for a bathroom. In 1955, the Birch was remodeled in the same way to complete the project.

In 1956, the cabin out near the road became available, and we repurchased it. An extensive addition was added to make it our largest cabin, with three bedrooms. It had been a long and expensive program, but with each remodeling the weekly rate of the cabin was increased by from $10.00 to $20.00 per week.

In the fall of 1950 I needed work for the winter. I learned from "Loki" Lundgren, who was operating the store down near Ruttger's at the time, that he was going to work for Harold Hitchcock that winter. Harold, along with his father and brother, owned and operated a foundry in Minneapolis. Harold had a cabin across the bay from us, so I went over to see him about work, and, as a result, Loki and I both worked for him that winter in Minneapolis, and shared a room as well. I was given a job in the "core" room where the sand cores are molded and baked in preparation for their use in the casting room. It was sometimes heavy work, and always warm. We often had to handle cores fresh out of the oven, which was set at 450 degrees. That heat, plus the oils used to bind the sand, gave me the smoothest and toughest hands that you ever saw. To this day I can handle an egg taken out of boiling water, without having to cool it.

It proved to be a good place to work in several ways. We all got along well together, were paid a good wage for those days, and worked ten-hour days with overtime pay. All fall, we worked on Saturdays as well but stockpiled the time against deer season, which we were allowed to take off without loss of pay. We did the same thing after deer season, in trade for the week off between Christmas and New Years. There were drawbacks, too. It was noisy, and the linseed oil gave off a terrible odor as the cores were baked. But when they were pouring magnesium in the room next door, the fumes were much worse! Sulfur was sifted onto the molten metal to prevent fires, and hydrogen-sulfide gas was produced in the process, as well as sulphur-dioxide, which forms sulphuric acid when it contacts water. Besides stinking, it used to give me severe headaches. In all, I worked at the foundry three winters. A couple of years after I worked there, they built a new foundry further out of town. It has a new ventilation system, which largely eliminates the odor problem.

Chapter 30

Trout Fishing

I never forgot my first trout fishing trip with Bud Rowe; in the summer of 1953, I started to talk to my old friend, Gib (Gilbert Hunt), about trout fishing. We had fished bass together quite often, but we hadn't started on trout yet. Gib loved to camp as much as I did, so I had no trouble convincing him that we needed to explore the North Shore country around Lake Superior. Gib's uncle, Art Hunt, was living up at Sawbill Landing at the time, about half way between Ely and Superior. We knew that he would be more than ready to fish with us and give us some pointers. We decided that we would go the weekend after Labor Day and that Gib would take an extra day or two off from work. By leaving after work on Friday, we would have a full four days of fishing.

Days of planning and packing and digging worms for bait had accelerated our excitement to a fever pitch by the time we headed north that Friday afternoon. We met Art, who suggested that we try the Little Isabella River. He said that, in general, rivers north of the Laurentian Divide do not have trout, but the Little Isabella was unique in this respect. He also told us about Disappointment Creek, which was to become one of our streams of last resort when fishing was poor. It is so small, one would not expect to find trout in it. The trout were small, too, but they seemed always to be hungry, and, oh, were those little fellows good to eat!

This trip set a pattern for Gib and me that would see us heading north at least twice a year, in the spring and in the fall. It became a ritual that would endure for many years and would provide us with memories that we will both cherish throughout our lifetimes. Through the years, the many trips have blended together into a common experience, and only a few of these trips stand out distinctly by themselves. It has become increasingly obvious that those events where everything does not go well imprint themselves most indelibly on the mind. The times that come most readily and clearly to me are those when adversity has had to be overcome. In looking back, I think of these times, not for their discomfort, but for the satisfaction gained in the struggle. We always had fun, but the most fun of all, it seems, was when we met the challenge of wet or cold weather and made ourselves comfortable in spite of the elements!

Our later trips often included others besides Gib and me. Walt Erickson was a frequent companion on these trips, as was Clyde Shaffer. The four of us took many trips together. Walt was a little older, but Clyde was the "old man" of the crew, being in his sixties, and, as such, the butt of many a good-natured jibe. He lived up east of Outing with his mother in a little log cabin stuck back in the woods. He and Walt were both experienced outdoorsmen with much to contribute, from practical knowledge to tales of past experiences. We all shot with the Deerwood Rifle Club, which gave us another common bond.

But in the beginning it was Gib and I. We would go as far as Knife River, where we would invariably buy some smoked ciscos. Then up the shore to the mouth of the Stewart River, where we could pull off the road and sit on the rocks overlooking Lake Superior. There we would eat the first meal of our trip, which always consisted of crackers and smoked fish, with a cold beer to wash them down. Then we would head on down the road until it got late, or we simply got the notion to stop. We would usually get as far as the Caribou River or, in the spring of the year when we had more daylight, to the Cross River at Schroeder. It was a point of honor not to spend the night in a public campground. We much preferred to pull off on some little-used trail that would get us near a river, but would not be frequented by others. A "feel" about being out in the woods and alone is lost if there is any likelihood of strangers coming by. Through the years, we came to know almost every available campsite from Two Harbors to Grand Marais, but our favorites were on the Cross, the Cascade, and the Plouff, which is a small back-country stream that feeds the Temperance River. There were at least two of these favorite spots on each of these rivers, and much of our time was spent at one or the other of them.

Gib fishing a North Shore stream

I particularly remember one of those early trips, when Gib's brother Norm and his wife, Jean, were to join us for a couple of days. Gib and I couldn't wait and went up a couple of days early. Darkness caught us part way up the North Shore, so we pulled off the highway at Palisade Head. There was a little trail that wound its way up to the top of this headland. We had nearly reached the top, when we found a wide spot where we could get our vehicle off the trail. Making a camp under these conditions was to become routine for us, and could usually be accomplished in ten minutes or less. We always started with a waterproof ground cloth that was about eight by fourteen feet. We would blow up our air mattresses and lay them within a foot of the top of the cloth. Next came the sleeping bags. Then we pulled the bottom end of the ground cloth up over and past the bags to make a sort of tent. If the weather were clear, we would fold the cloth down, then back up to where we could reach it, if it should rain. By tucking the sides under, we could sleep quite warm and dry if it didn't rain too hard. But this night we had been tired and in a bit of a hurry, and it did rain! I woke up the next morning with my feet in a puddle of water and my bag wet halfway up.

We mostly explored that day, and evening found us back inland on the Brule River, or Arrowhead as it is now called, where we made camp. The weather was pretty wet and cold, so we erected our tent that night. The next morning the clouds appeared to be breaking up, so we spread our bags out and left the tent flaps wide open so things would dry out a little while we fished. Wouldn't you know, we got about a quarter of a mile downstream when the clouds suddenly closed up, and it began to rain hard. We were more than a little damp by the time we got back, and so were our beds.

That evening we were supposed to meet Norm and Jean at the Ox Bow campgrounds on the Temperance River, about three or four miles above Tofte. We had to choose a spot that they could find. We were already asleep when they got in, but, in the morning, there they were, sleeping in their van. We had a quarter of an inch of ice in our water bucket that morning. Our bags hadn't quite dried out from the day before, but by leaving our socks on we were reasonably comfortable. In no time, the coffee was boiling, the bacon sizzling, and the pancake batter ready to fry. As we ate, we regaled Norm with tales of the dangers to be avoided in "these parts" and cautioned him to be particularly alert for "side hill swamps." We had talked of these before, and of course he wasn't buying any of it.

After breakfast, our first order of business was to replenish our water supply. We knew of a spring nearby, although it did entail climbing a hill a short distance from the road. We found the spring with no trouble, and, while Gib was filling the water container, I led Norm just over the top of the hill, and started down the other side to show him something. I guess he didn't realize that I was carefully stepping on rocks, and, in no time, he was well over his boot tops in mire. Norm let out a yelp and scrambled to safety, while Gib and I roared with laughter. "We told you to be careful around these sidehill swamps," I said, still smirking. I don't believe Norm quite appreciated the humor in the situation, but he did learn to believe us!

The fish just wouldn't cooperate that trip, but we still had fun showing off the country and trying to fish a bit here and there. After Norm and Jean left, Gib and I headed for the Disappointment, where we caught twenty-three small trout. That evening, while we cleaned our trout on the edge of a little lake, a mink came along and tried to take some of them from us. We said no to that and ate the whole bunch of them ourselves.

One of our most favored camps was a short way inland on the Cascade. The drive to it was rather round-about and ended at an old abandoned home-site high above the river. We would drive down across the field where the old house stood and camp in a scattered grove of young pine and balsam some hundred feet or more above the river. Just upstream from there, the river went over a forty-foot waterfalls into a deep pool. The not-too-distant roar of a waterfall makes beautiful music in the otherwise silent wilderness, while the scent of the pines on the soft spring air mingles with the smoke from the camp fire to create an aura that lives forever in my memory.

One such night I was camped among those pines with Chet Powers in his camper. We had had a successful evening fishing in the pool below, and had enjoyed our meal of fresh trout. Chet did not have hip boots, so he did his fishing in old tennis shoes, wading only when necessary. He left his shoes on the bumper of the truck to dry out overnight, and I left my smelly creel on a nearby bush. The next morning, as we were preparing to head for the river, Chet said, "Al, what did you do with my shoes?"

I said, "I haven't seen your old shoes. Where did you leave them?"

"Right here on the bumper. Come on now, quit kidding around."

"No, really, I haven't seen them. I think my creel is missing too. I wonder if a bear or something got them. Let's take a look around."

A careful scan of the area showed me the trace of a trail left in the heavy dew. In a short distance I found one of my trout lures, then a shoe, somewhat worse for wear with teeth marks, then finally the other shoe in even worse shape, and finally my creel in total shambles! Another lesson learned; had we been sleeping outdoors, that she bear and her cubs would probably not have been so brave.

One late fall trip we got to that same field well after dark threw our bed rolls out on the grass and went to sleep. At about five the next morning, we were jolted to awareness by a frightening blast of sound that came from nearly on top of us. We both chuckled when we realized that it was an old buck that had nearly stumbled over us. I'll bet he was more scared than we were when those two apparitions reared up out of the grass in front of him!

Speaking of animals, I recall another night in the same area. I had taken Jim Fagan, a boy who was helping me that summer, on a camping and fishing trip as a reward for his good work. We could no longer drive to the field, so we parked a ways back and backpacked down to the river a half mile or so below where we normally camped. I had a particular spot in mind, one with a spring nearby and a nice flat area near the river for our camp. When we reached the general area, we threw off our packs and went along the river to find "just the right spot." Of course, Jim was excited and jumping from rock to rock along the rivers edge, while I kept looking for a good campsite. We had gone only a hundred yards or so when I heard something in the brush. There stood a big black bear on her hind legs with her hair all on end no more than fifty feet from me! I stood very still and watched until she moved off a ways and "woofed" to her cub to follow. Only then did I take my eyes off her long enough to get my camera ready and take her picture. That night we hung our grub high from a tree and kept our fire going a little later than usual.

Another favorite "campground" was on the Plouff. Farther back from Lake Superior, it wound its relatively leisure course through a wide valley and provided an entirely different ambience than the rushing rivers we usually fished. We would drive in on an old logging trail that more or less followed the river through cutover and brushy areas, until we came to a nice level open spot only a few feet from the stream. It was particularly good in the spring when the larger streams were too high for good fishing. I still remember at least one very wet camp that the four of us made there, when the tent and the extra tarp were put to good use.

The Cross River enters Lake Superior at the little town of Schroeder. Upstream, no more than a mile or two from there, is another of our favorite campsites. Here, at the head of a series of falls and rapids, we could fish downstream in the white water and pools, or upstream in a quieter section that was easier to fish. When the old road was dry and passable, we would drive further up stream another mile or so and get above the last high falls, onto a stretch of seldom-fished water. Some of our largest trout came from the Cross, along with memories of otter playing in the river beside a log jam, and the still wet footprints of a moose wandering down the trail ahead of us.

The single, most impressive event that we experienced while fishing along the North Shore happened on one of our earliest trips. We were camped on the lower Cross River and had doubled back to explore the Manitou River. Art had told us of a beautiful "hole" under the high falls above the road. It was well hidden in a deep canyon. He said that he had first reached it by climbing into the top of a tree, and then climbing down the tree to the river. We found the spot easily enough, and slowly worked our way down the precipitous slope, going from tree to tree and using whatever handholds and footholds nature had seen fit to provide.

At the bottom, we found a pretty little ledge about thirty feet long, six feet wide, and perhaps two feet above a large pool formed by the waterfall, partially hidden by a point of rock that jutted out to our right. To the left was a reach of moderately fast, deep water, confined by the near vertical walls of the canyon we had entered. Hurriedly we baited up and began casting into the foam below the falls. The action was fast under the falls, and we soon had several nice trout, including one brown trout that was nearly fourteen inches long—one of the largest we ever caught on the North Shore. We could also drift our bait downstream for the length of our lines, and caught several more there. Even the best of holes play out after a while, but we resolved to return the next day and try it again.

We came back once or twice each of the next two or three days and always caught nice trout. The trip into and out of the hole, once so precarious, became routine with experience and practice. The third day was dark and cloudy with a little mist falling, but we just had to go down into the hole one more time. By now, the fish had been pretty well worked over on that little stretch, and fishing was slow. There was some beautiful water downstream a couple of hundred feet, however, where a sand bar extended over half way across the river and guarded a deep hole where the river had cut under the abutting rock wall. Carefully I worked my way along the ledge we were on as it gradually receded out of sight under the water. To my delight the ledge continued to be about eighteen inches wide and only knee deep as I worked my way toward the sandbar with Gib close behind.

We had been floating our baits ahead of us as we went, and our objective was nearly at hand when my hook fouled on a rock or log and I could only brake the leader and retie. I suggested that we just go on to the sand bar so that Gib could be fishing while I retied, but Gib said no, do it now so we can both fish when we get there. I had just finished my job and was about to proceed when we heard a roar from above. We looked up in time to see what appeared to be about a truck load of rock, loosened by the rain of the night before, come tumbling down and land on the sand bar where we were headed!

We debated for a bit—we had come this far, and since no more rock had fallen, we decided to go on and give that good spot a try. We reached the sand bar safely and began fishing, but always with one eye watching for more rock. After a few casts, I looked at Gib, caught his eye and said, "Do we really want to fish here?" He said, "No, let's get the hell out of here."

We fished that good hole on several subsequent trips, with varying degrees of success. The last time we tried it, we had a number of little bites without catching anything until Gib finally hooked—a tiny sunfish! We never bothered to try fishing there again.

Chapter 31

Montana Revisited

During the 1950s, as we completed our modernization program, our little resort continued to prosper. Our average number of weeks of rental per cabin grew from eight to nearly ten, and with the increased rates warranted by the improvements, our income increased correspondingly. The biggest share of our guests returned year after year, and indeed many reserved a year in advance. It gives me pleasure and satisfaction to recall, as I go back over the old reservation charts, not only the names but the friendships we developed with so many wonderful people. This has been the nature of our business, to bring happiness to people and to establish lasting friendships with them. The sprinkling of lights across the bay became a solid line of lights that Mom often referred to as her "passenger train"—as the cabins all lit up on a warm summer evening. Many of these cabins were built by people who had first come to Bay Lake as our guests.

We still look across the bay to Steve Souder's lights. He first came with his parents in the 1950s, and his dad's "Pink Lady" was a regular sight, as it towed water skiers across the bay. The Kinneys and the O'Briens spent a number of summers with us, and their lively, fun-loving families were a constant pleasure. Well, almost. Mrs. O'Brien would spend a month at the lake with her five children. This proved to be a real problem in logistics for her, in order for her to get them all here at the same time, with all the clothes and paraphernalia for a month's stay. One year she brought a load of things a week early and stored them in our garage. These stored items included a surf board that one of her boys had built himself, but had not had a chance to try out. He pleaded with me to give it a try for him, and I reluctantly agreed.

That week included in our guest list was a young man in his early twenties, who, through courtesy, shall remain nameless. As a boy, he had spent time here with his uncle. Now he had just finished college and had a week off before reporting to his new job. To celebrate, he and his new wife were spending the week at the lake. He was an athletic type and an ideal candidate for the surfboard test. I, of course, could not try it because I had to drive the boat. He agreed, so, on Monday afternoon, I hooked the surf board behind my boat, he climbed aboard, and we started off across the lake. Granted, he was not experienced in this sport, but he was an excellent swimmer, and I expected no problem. He started out kneeling on the board and then, as we gathered speed, he stood up. Immediately, the board began to swerve violently from side to side, and off he went. Being a good sport, he climbed right back on, and we tried again. Again the fishtailing of the board threw him. We tried several times, and always with the same result. He could get up on his knees and go along quite well, but when he tried to stand, off he went. By now we were well down the bay and in deep water. I said, "This simply isn't working. Just lay on the board, and I'll pull you back."

There was only a moderate chop on the water, and as everything appeared to be going nicely, I gradually increased the speed, until we were skipping right along, with my friend laying flat on the board. Suddenly the front of the board caught in a wave and began to dig in. That board went straight to the bottom of the lake with my poor guest too startled to let go. I could only kill the motor and wait for the board and its one-time occupant to reappear. He came up first, looking for all the world like a whale as he spouted a gigantic plume of water from his mouth. I immediately circled back to him, and, as I drew alongside, he grasped the gunnel with one hand and literally vaulted into the boat.

"Shun o'va bich," he gasped. "I loft my teef"!

Now I'm not one to laugh at another's misery, especially when he is considerably larger that I am, but it really was one of the funniest sights I have ever seen. The poor guy had just been fitted with new dentures, both top and bottom, and, when he spouted all that water, he spouted his teeth right with it. His teeth now lay in twenty feet of water. Fortunately he was able to call his dentist and explain the problem. He went back to town the next day, and by evening he was back with his new teeth.

Sometime in the winter of 1954/1955, Gib and I got to talking about Montana and the possibility of traveling out there to see the country we had both heard about so much from my Dad. Gib had purchased a new 1955 Chevy station wagon that would be ideal for the trip. We began checking on food that could be packed in, clothing that would be required, and the type and amount of fishing gear we would need. Our trip up the North Shore that spring became a trial run for the big adventure.

By Labor Day we were all set to go the following week, but I had come down with a bad cold that would not let up. The day after Labor Day, I talked my doctor into giving me a penicillin shot so that I would be fit to go. Thursday evening I didn't feel too well and had a headache, so I retired early. Friday morning it was still dark when I woke up and stumbled down to the bathroom. I turned on the light, but all I could see was a faint red glow. Painfully I pulled my eyelids back with my fingers, to be greeted by the horrible apparition that was my face. It was swollen beyond recognition. My throat was sore, and my eyes, when I could find them, were red and weepy. All my joints were swollen to twice their normal size, and large raised blotches covered the remainder of my body.

I could hardly wait for the doctor's office to open, and, when it did, I was there. I had to wait over an hour while other patients came and went, as I had no appointment. All the while my back ached fiercely, and I was totally miserable. Finally I was let in, and, when the nurse saw my condition, she said, "Why didn't you tell me it was an emergency?" I had, but it hadn't registered. When my doctor saw me, he called for the other doctors to come in and see the fix I was in, and they all had a good laugh. I was given a shot of adrenalin, which made my heart pound like crazy, but it didn't really help that much. The next morning I went back in and had a shot of cortisone, which did the trick. I had had a reaction to the penicillin, and the results were actually life-threatening. I was told that I was okay to travel but to continue with the cortisone pills.

Tuesday morning we got up early and were on our way. I felt pretty good, just a little tired and achy. We drove straight through until about four A.M., taking turns driving for about two hours at a stretch each, while the other slept. We dared not try to go further, because we were running short of gas, and the station at Browning, the next town, would not be open. So we slept for a couple of hours, then drove on in and got there just as the station was opening. The drive over Marias Pass and around the southern tip of Glacier Park was beautiful, but we could hardly wait to get to the little town of Coram where we would buy what fresh supplies we would need and get our fishing licenses. The season license was expensive, so we opted to get two three-day licenses that would run consecutively, and not start for two days. It was by far the cheaper way out, who knows if it was legal?!

We began our trip up the Southfork of the Flathead by crossing the Hungry Horse dam. Imagine looking out over a vast expanse of water on one side of the car, and straight down five hundred feet to the river below on the other. We had the misfortune to be traveling behind a grader that left a high windrow of gravel in the center of the road. When we caught up with him, we had no choice but to attempt to jump the windrow or follow along behind at ten miles an hour. As soon as we had a reasonably straight stretch ahead, Gib made the jump. Alas, we cleared the gravel but could not stop in time to stay on the road. We finally stopped, off the road, and about twenty feet down the mountainside. Fortunately it was not terribly steep right there. The grader came back and got behind us. With the end of his blade under our rear bumper on the lower side, he pushed us back up on the road. It was an exemplary piece of maneuvering on his part.

The trip around Hungry Horse Reservoir was tedious, but extremely beautiful. We were particularly excited to come upon a sign proclaiming Knieff Creek, which had been named after my dad. We finally pulled in to Spotted

Al and daughter Erin standing by the Knieff Creek sign in Montana in 1994.

Bear Ranger Station in mid afternoon, where we set up a temporary camp and made ready for the following day. We had planned to use Duluth packs to carry our gear, but at the last minute Gib had borrowed a couple of light, exterior frame packs, which were far easier on our backs. We took a little hike up along the river before making our supper (dinner was the noon meal in those days) and going to bed early.

When we got those packs on our backs the next morning, I wondered if I would be able to make it at all. I was still sore and stiff from my penicillin reaction. Once on the trail, my aches and pains seemed to let up, and we were able to go right along. There were mile markers along the trail, and in one hour we would make three of them and then take a rest. The trail was wide and well worn, as packers used it regularly to take hunters up to the high country where the elk season was already open. But it was constantly going up hill and then down again, and the bright sun was actually hot. As the day progressed, the effort began to take its toll. The first spot that we could recognize for sure was the Meadow Creek Ranger Station, located at the foot of a box canyon. Above the canyon, we should find the camping spot, with its little spring nearby, that Dad had described so vividly. We passed a packer's lay-out camp where the hunting parties would stop for the night, and shortly thereafter came upon a foot bridge over the main river, just ahead of its entry into the canyon. Upstream we could just see where Bunker Creek entered the river.

We found the campsite with no problem, but we were so sweaty and tired that we dropped our packs where we stood, slid down to the ground with trees at our backs and promptly went sound asleep. I'm not sure how long we slept, but, when we awoke, the shadows were long, the air was cool, and I was so stiff that I could hardly move. I tried to help Gib gather boughs for our beds but soon had to give that up in favor of doing the thatching, while he did the gathering. We ate a good supper and were ready for bed by dark. We did not pack in air mattress, just a ground cloth, but those three tiers of boughs, thatched to a springy depth of six or eight inches, felt mighty good just as they were. During the night some little critter scampered across my shoulders, waking me briefly, but I was really too tired to care.

The next morning we awoke to bright sunshine on the trees across the river, while the river itself was still in deep shadow. It was downright chilly, and we were glad for the extra clothing we had brought. We mixed up our pancakes, and I looked for the sugar we had brought to make syrup. I found the brown sugar all right, but the white sugar, which was to furnish most of the sweetening, proved to be nothing more than powdered sugar and totally useless for making syrup. What a horrible disappointment! As we contemplated our dilemma, I glanced up, and there, wedged between two trees, was a nearly full can of Log Cabin Maple Syrup, left there by some previous camper! From then on our trip went exceedingly well.

Campsite overlooking the junction of Bunker Creek with the South Fork used by Gib and Al in 1958

After breakfast, we donned our hip boots, and Gib took off down the two hundred feet of steep embankment to the river. I did not dare to try it, as my hips and back were so sore that I could scarcely walk. I just ambled slowly down the trail until it came close to the river farther on, and gave me easier access to the water. I had only fished a short while when Gib came up to me. About that time I had a strike out in the swift water, and the battle was joined. I waded out into the stream as far as I could in that swift water and worked the fish in to where I could net it. It was a Dolly Varden or bull trout and just barely eighteen inches long, which was the minimum size limit for that species. Then Gib showed me his prize, a big "bull" that was a full twenty-four inches long! We staked our fish out on a piece of heavy line and continued our fishing. From that moment on, my recovery was swift and sure.

At a point just above where Gib had caught his fish, there was a shallow riffle where I decided to wade across. At that point the river was nearly a hundred feet wide, quite swift, and came nearly to the top of my hip boots. In the future, I went upstream to the foot log that lay across the river about ten feet above the water. It had a hand rail, which made it easier going. From there on upstream, the river was relatively narrow and deep. There were quiet stretches where the water was only ten or twelve feet wide, with little or no visible current, but nearly black in color and with no sign of bottom. In other areas where the river was twenty feet or more wide with a modest current showing, we could see the bottom plainly and measure the depth at twenty feet or more. Cut-throats, the most common native trout in the area, could be seen in schools of twenty or more, just idling along near the bottom, totally uninterested in anything we had to offer them. We found that if we just worked our way along the river, keeping back from the shore so as not to disturb anything, we would occasionally see a trout surface, which meant that it was feeding. We would then put a grasshopper on our hooks and flip them out to fall in the current. This usually meant another nice cut-throat, about fourteen inches long, to clean for our evening meal.

We worked up stream in this way for several hundred yards until we came to a spot where the river was so narrow that we could have easily jumped across, had there not been a sheer rock wall on the far side. The whole river was flowing through this narrow gate. Just below the gate, the river widened some from the far side, forming an eddy. It was in this eddy that I first spotted **The Trout**. We could see it plainly as it appeared to just sit and wait. Suddenly, it would dart out and strike at a white fish as it went by and presented the trout with a meal. The white fish it was eating were about twelve inches long. What a prize this would be for us! I started fishing for it immediately, offering it everything that I could think of, but to no avail. After an hour or so I gave up, and it was Gib's turn to try. His luck was no better than mine. As the shadows began to lengthen, we headed back to camp, a nice mess of trout in our creels and great expectations for the next day.

The next morning we made straight for that gate with our fingers secretly crossed that **The Trout** would still be there. Sure enough, it was. Now it was Gib's turn to lead off, but once again that trout wanted nothing that he offered. Meanwhile, I fished downstream, but close enough to keep an eye on Gib and his progress. Finally he backed off again and motioned for me to take over. I had been watching that trout, and the only time that it would look at our bait was when it flashed by too close. I got the idea that the flash would scare the whitefish, and that the trout darted at the bait only to make it go away. So I put on a little number eight Colorado spinner, a ridiculously small bait for so large a fish, but flashy and likely to disturb the white fish. It worked! Several times the big trout made a pass at the spinner as if to hit it rather than eat it. Finally, it got too close, and I had it hooked. Now what to do? I had only a six-pound tip on my leader and could in no way horse that big trout. It just sat there in the eddy, and I couldn't budge it. Finally it moved out into the main current, and away we went downstream. I couldn't think of turning it, or even slowing it down much. Suddenly I felt a ledge of limestone at my back. I could no longer follow the trout, and the ledge was too high for me to get over. Then I heard Gib say, "Here." He had seen what was happening and had gotten up on the ledge. Quickly I handed the rod up to him, as the backing line on the reel was nearly gone. While he followed the trout downstream, I found my way up onto the ledge and gave chase. When I caught up, the trout was just going into a large, deep pool that afforded me a chance to turn it. We fought in this pool for a while, then it was off downstream again. The next big pool that he came to had a bunch of logs lodged at its lower end, and I knew that this was it. Turn him now or lose him. So I dug in my heels and hauled on the line. It held, and the trout turned. We had been fighting for a long time. Slowly the trout came to the surface and I eased him to shore, belly up, where Gib waited to net him. It was soon apparent that the net was too small, so Gib came and got mine also, and between the two of them he brought the fish up onto the rocks. It was only then that I discovered that he had been hooked with only one of those little number eight hooks, and then not in the mouth, but underneath, between the pectoral fins. No wonder he had fought so hard! Now we each had a big "bull" to take home.

The Trout measured over twenty-nine inches long, and when I got him home (after being gutted and gilled, salted, and packed out), then kept only cool for a day before being deep frozen for over a week, he still weighed seven and a half pounds. He must have weighed twelve pounds when fresh out of the water.

We had met a woman who was taking care of the line camp at Meadow Creek while her husband cooked for a party of hunters up in the high country. She offered to give us the salt laced with streptomycin to put on our fish for the trip out and to put them down in her "cool well" on the night before we left to get them thoroughly chilled. They both kept perfectly.

Al posing with a nice string, including The Trout

The last day of our stay on the South Fork, we devoted mostly to exploring, going up stream for a couple of miles and also up Bunker Creek a ways. We also managed to catch enough trout for one more good meal. The trip out was uneventful—we left quite early in the morning and got out just after noon. It was remarkable how much our conditioning had improved in such a short time. When we reached the ranger station, we hauled our packs down to the basement and weighed them, out of curiosity. One was fifty-three pounds, and the other fifty-five!

We drove out around the east shore of the reservoir on our way out, past the little Trout

Lake to which Dad had so often referred, and then headed north to Eureka, Montana, where my uncle, Larry Reiley, had a cabin on Glen Lake. The lake was located several miles from town, and was still largely undeveloped. Its shore was lined with balsam, larch, and stately pine, and its water was crystal clear. Larry's cabin was made of logs and had a huge stone fireplace in which he could easily burn four-foot lengths of wood. My cousin, Lorrie, was working locally and living at home. It took little persuasion to get him to accompany us on another little pack trip, this time into the Blue Bird basin country, where Larry had helped to build, and was part owner of, a little cabin on one of the several lakes in the area.

Gib and I spent the next day fishing up in the area of the Yaak River. The little stream that we fished was full of a little native trout they called "Spec's," which never get very large and have no limit on them. Later we came upon an old road that was no longer used and found it to be loaded with shaggy-mane mushrooms. That evening we all enjoyed a meal of fresh trout and fried mushrooms.

The following morning, Larry drove the three of us up into the mountains to a trailhead. From there, Lorrie led us up along an ill-defined trail into the basin country. At one point we appeared to have lost the trail, but we soon came upon a little lake, where Lorrie again got his bearings. It was not long before the cabin came into view. It was as rustic and natural a setting as could possibly be imagined, with the little clearing among the huge trees, on the shore of a little lake, with a big, bald, rocky mountain for a backdrop. The logs with which the cabin was built had been cut right on the spot, as it was located over five miles from the nearest road and up a steep grade the whole way. A log lay ready on the saw buck for those who needed fuel.

Inside, the bunks and table had been made from smaller poles, while the benches were simply half-logs with pole legs under them. There were also two chairs, each hewn from a length of log about three feet in diameter. Each log stood on end, with a portion cut away to form the seat and the backrest. The two stoves and the cupboard deserve special mention. Each had been packed in on the back of a mule. The cookstove was small but made of heavy cast iron. The heating stove was made from the largest barrel I had ever seen. How they had managed to pack them in, I will never know. Windows and a door had also been packed in, but the item that had given the most trouble had been the shakes covering the roof, or at least were supposed to have. But they made an awkward bundle that finally loosened up on the pack saddle, shingling the whole mountainside as they fell. In the end, they split new shakes by hand on the site.

Fly fishing from shore was a pleasant change from wading the streams, and we had no problem catching all the trout we wanted to eat. It was also an ideal way to get to know a cousin I had never met. Of course, we had packed in all of our food, but I will never forget my amusement when I opened the cupboard door and found no less than nine containers of salt and seven of pepper!

We took a different route out of the basin, which led us first up a very steep mountainside to the top of a sharp ridge that connected two peaks. We detoured to one of the peaks with an abandoned look-out station on it. The view was spectacular. To the north, and only a mile or two away, was the Canadian border. The mountains that way were extremely rugged and lacked any timber. To the south the terrain was more gentle, and only the peaks were above the timber line. Below us, the little lakes sparkled like blue gems set in a sea of green.

Larry met us at a different trailhead at the appointed time for our return trip. The switchbacks on this road were so sharp that on two occasions we had to back up the truck to negotiate the turns! Back at the cabin that evening, we had another long chat with Larry, as he told us more of his experiences in the mountains. He told of his elk hunting trips with his friend "Pard," how they back packed deep into the mountains. One time one of the horses had slipped while they were crossing a dangerous slide area. The horse had been saved, but all of their "snake bite medicine" was lost!

Now Larry was an honest man, but there were times when temptation had led him to bend the game laws a bit. He told of how the Montana big game tags were simple cardboard "tie-ons," which, in his words, "One could wear one of them suckers out in a season if he was a mind to." Doubtless the wardens were aware of this failing, and eagerly awaited a chance to "get him." One fall he started out up the mountain in search of grouse, all legal and above board.

Larry and his dog hadn't gone far, when the dog scented a bear and started out in hot pursuit. Unfortunately, the bear soon realized that he was much bigger than the dog and should be the chaser rather than the chased. This sudden turn of events left the dog with only one recourse. He came to Larry for protection, and stood behind him, barking furiously. The bear, fully incensed by now, kept right on coming. He would take the man, too, if he had to, to get at the dog. Larry was in a real fix. All he had to defend himself with was his shotgun with fine shot. He didn't want to wound the bear, then it would really be dangerous. So he let it charge right up to within thirty feet, then shot it in its face, blinding it. The bear stopped and put its front paws to its face, exposing the soft throat area, where Larry was able to shoot it again and kill it.

Larry owned the little hotel in Eureka and ran the town's favorite pub. What a story to regale his patrons with! The news spread like fire in a broom factory, and soon the whole town was talking about Larry and his bear. Of course the game warden heard the story, too, and, while Larry was well within his rights to defend himself, he had neglected to report it to the warden. He was, therefore, found guilty of killing a bear out of season, and made to pay a fine. Larry didn't complain very loudly. He just figured he probably had one coming, and besides, it sure was good story for the bar business.

And so our vacation in Montana came to a close. We came home with wonderful memories and the vow that we must return. Then Gib made a truely prophetic observation, "Even if we can not come back, no one can ever take this trip from us." We almost went back one time, but that is another story. Then Gib's health failed him, and he is no longer physically able to do that sort of thing. I have been more fortunate, and have been back three times. But I have also learned that, in a very real sense, we can never "go back." Situations change, and we change. That is what life is all about. I have enjoyed my return trips immensely, but I will never again make that first back-packing trip with Gib.

Chapter 32

New Obligations

By 1960 our little campground had grown into a trailer park of sorts. The tent trailers were beginning to give way to the "solid body" travel trailers of today. Electric lines had long since been run overhead to provide power, and now we extended our water lines from the cabins to include several taps in the camping area, as the new trailers had provisions for hooking up to water. Most did not yet have toilets, but sinks with drains meant that provisions had to be made for the disposal of "gray" water. This we accomplished by using fifty-five-gallon drums as we had for the cabins. As the cabins had been modernized to include complete baths, we had installed septic systems to serve one or two cabins each. We would soon be faced with the same problem in the trailer park.

In the spring of 1960, I began making plans to upgrade the trailer park in accordance with the new regulations being instituted by the Minnesota Department of Health. I would begin by getting running water to every designated site and later provide sewer outlets for each. This entailed putting in four septic tanks of over one-thousand-gallon-capacity each and manifolding them together in series. The last tank needed a section divided off to form a pumping station for the effluent, which would be pumped to a drainfield located in our open field, far from the lake or any residence. I would then be one of the first in our area to comply with the new laws. This, however, was still several years down the road.

I sent notice to the state of my intentions, and on July 14, I received acknowledgment from the state. On July 30, the hotel inspector came in and informed me that I must remove every trailer in the park by August 1, as I was not yet licensed as a trailer park. I asked him specifically who enforced this order, and, when he could only say that he supposed that the county would have to do it, I said, "Thank you, goodbye." I then left him to spot a trailer that had been pulled in as I was talking to him. I never heard from that inspector again. That fall I began the long and arduous task of turning the old campground into a trailer park.

The western edge of the old campground sloped down into a swampy area behind a sandy ridge that followed along the lakeshore. Much of this area was too low to be used as it was, but could be easily made usable by adding a little fill without actually infringing upon the swamp itself. The sandy ridge was set back from the current pressure ridge by perhaps twenty feet, leaving a low area there, which would trap water in the spring but was not actually a swamp. Here too, a little fill and a little leveling would add another two hundred feet of usable shoreline to the future trailer park. All of this took place before there were any restrictions on filling in near the lake. Today this sort of project would require special permits. The fill all came from a sandy hill on the back part of our property.

After the rough work was done, I spent most of one fall hand raking and smoothing the area to prepare it for trailer sites. By 1963 I had taken the power down out of the trees and run it underground to the various sites, and had run in a separate electric service to the area. The advent of plastic pipes made running water lines to the individual sites much easier. Still, it was quite a project, as I put them all in by hand digging. The sewer lines, when we finally put them in, were also dug by hand.

All of this work updating our property did not prevent Gib and me from taking our usual trips up to the North Shore. Nor did it prevent us from thinking about a return visit to Montana. In fact, our plans were beginning to gel for the fall of 1964, when fate interceded. That June Chester, always the avid airman, flew a light plane back here from California. After a short visit, he would pick up his brother-in-law in St. Cloud and they would fly up north for several days of fishing. Chet's younger daughter, Lynn, accompanied him on the flight East and planned, I believe, to spend much of the time in St. Cloud. She changed her mind, however, and spent most of it here at Bay Lake.

Lynn was a beautiful young woman, and I enjoyed reacquainting her with the area. As a teenager she had spent one summer here, working for the Fullers at their resort. Since then she had been married and had a three-year-old son, Jay. But her marriage was an unhappy one, and she was in the process of obtaining a divorce. Those few days sped by, and, when she left, I realized that there was a huge empty spot in my life. We began writing frequently, then calling back and forth. Finally, I persuaded Gib that we should alter our Montana plans and go to California instead, where he could be my best man when I married Lynn. He could then drive her little car back here for her, while she and Jay and I took a more leisurely route home.

When we returned we lived in one of the cabins for a short while, as we had to make ready a spot just west of the house for the new mobile home we planned to buy. Everything went pretty much according to plan, but as soon as we could get settled in the new home, I would have to go back to work. I had always worked in the winter, sometimes traveling, but preferably working as close to home as I could.

I got a job with the new "Trail-a-Sled" company that had recently started up in Crosby, building snowmobiles. I started out blowing fiberglass into the molds to make the hoods and bodies of the sleds. It was not a very nice job, as the fumes were horrible, and the ventilation poor at best. I stuck it out as long as I could, but

Al and Lynn with Lynn's sister, Lonnie, and her husband, John

finally the headaches became too much for me, and I had to quit. I am sure that the transition was difficult for Lynn. The way of life here in Minnesota was vastly different from that of southern California. Lynn was an active person who was always in need of challenges. She took up painting and did quite well with it.

That January Lynn announced that she was pregnant without any great degree of enthusiasm, I thought. I guess it happened before we had really given it much thought. The pregnancy went well, although it did worry me when Lynn went horseback riding that spring. Then there was the time I talked her into driving the boat for me while I water skied. It was a new boat I wanted to try out, and, wouldn't you know, I pulled out too hard on a corner, and one of the back panels of the transom pulled right off! Lynn swung around to pick me up, and I had to yell at her to get to shore—fast! If I had let her stop for me, the boat would have taken on a ton of water, and probably sunk in the bargain. In spite of all this, our daughter was born on August 29, 1965, none the worse for our escapades. My chief memory of the event was being made to feel unwelcome around the hospital by the staff and, to a lesser degree, by Lynn herself. I had taken her in to the hospital early in the afternoon and was quickly asked to leave while they put her to bed. I was then allowed to see her again for a brief moment, then told that I would have to go to the waiting room. There was no further word until the doctor came out and told me, "I couldn't have any more children—for at least nine months!" He then let me go in to see Lynn and our new baby daughter, whom we named Kirsten Louise. I was promptly asked to leave again, as Lynn would have to feed the baby! That did it—I went home and drank most of the case of beer I had bought for Chet and Gladys, who were due to arrive the next day.

Horses were Lynn's first love. She had acquired her first horse, a part Arab, as a young teenager by working long hours for a boarding stable and baby sitting. How it must have hurt her to give it up when she married the first time. Now she was living out in the country with plenty of room for a nice pasture, a little barn, and a corral. While I didn't share her great enthusiasm for horses, I was amenable to learning, and Lynn got her horse, another half Arab mare. The pasture fence, the little barn and the corral were built, and we were in the "horse business." Those were relatively good times. Lynn rode in endurance races, both locally and in Wisconsin. I even rode one fifty-mile race myself. The culmination of Lynn's riding achievements was the summer that we traveled to California with Dr. Nixon and his wife. Lynn would ride his horse in the Tevis Cup race; a race of a hundred miles. It was run in the High Sierras, and the contestant had to finish the race in under twenty-four hours to qualify for a beautiful silver commemorative belt buckle. Lynn completed the ride in the allotted time and was awarded her buckle.

During this period of time, my father's health was gradually declining. While his mind remained remarkably clear, the heart condition that had plagued him for so many years continued to take its toll. He still enjoyed taking his little granddaughter for a walk, and talking with the "old timers" when they stopped by in the evening. He had celebrated his eighty-sixth birthday on July 6, 1967, and had told me that he had lived his life, a full and happy one, and that he was ready to go.

Bud Rowe and his family stopped in unexpectedly that summer, to spend a few days with us. He came up to the house that evening and chatted with Dad until nearly ten o'clock, getting him to recall once again, the stories he had told Bud of his adventures in the West. Shortly after ten o'clock I heard Mother calling to me. Dad was gone. Though I continue to miss him, I feel closer to him as the years go by.

By 1971, the work of modernizing the trailer park had been completed. We now had twenty-two licensed and approved sites for seasonal campers or small mobile homes, all rented on an annual basis. I was again working for "Scorpion," the new name for Trail-a-Sled. In 1968, I had begun working in the parts department, and that winter I was given the responsibility for all of the warranty work done by the company. While I didn't have to work in the summer, I did work later into the spring than I had been, and Lynn had to take responsibility for much of the spring cleaning. The following fall the company moved the Minnesota distributorship to Brainerd, where I was put in charge of the parts room and the warranty department. I worked there for the following two years.

Lynn had decided to complete her education by enrolling in the University Without Walls, through the University of Minnesota. She majored in psychology, and spent quite a bit of time at the Brainerd State Hospital as a volunteer. I don't believe that Lynn ever cared for the resort work, and we had talked of renting only by the season. By the early spring of 1973, three of our cabins were taken on this basis. We had been drifting ever farther apart, and when Lynn applied for and got a job with a state institution at Fergus Falls, I knew our marriage was in deep trouble. I was heartbroken, but in retrospect it was Kirsten, and Jay, too, who would suffer the most.

Chapter 33

The Storm

This was my situation in the spring of 1973. My wife was living and working in Fergus Falls. Jay and Kirsten were home with me, after spending part of the winter with their mother. I had changed jobs the fall before, and was now working for Ray Madison as a snowmobile and small implement salesman out of Brainerd. I had Ruth Nystrom working full time for me. She had been coming to the resort with her parents for many years. Now, having finished high school, she was working for the summer before entering college in the fall.

*Monday, June 25th, was a typically beautiful Minnesota spring day. The air was warm, without the hint of a thunderstorm in the offing. The resort seemed strangely deserted for that late in the season. There had been a full house the day before, with people everywhere. Six of the eleven cabins were still rented, although one of the parties had gone to town and another was away for the day. Over half the residents from the twenty-two trailers in the trailer park had gone back to town for the week and would return again the following Friday night. There were still about forty people at the resort, down from well over a hundred the day before.

In the late afternoon, black clouds appeared in the west, and soon it began to sprinkle. Taking refuge in our mobile home, I turned on the radio in time to hear a tornado warning, which extended fifty miles on either side of a line from Redwood Falls to Hibbing. Curious, I checked on a state map and found that we were situated in the geographic center of this huge area. My immediate reaction was one of mild concern. Tornados actually cover such a very small area, and the warning was for over twenty thousand square miles. Further, we hear tornado alerts so frequently when none actually occur that we become desensitized to their meaning. I did, however, try to tune in our local radio station, which prides itself on giving local weather warnings and minute-by-minute information when storms are in the area. Static from the local storm cut out any chance of reception.

It was with some sense of relief that I looked out and saw that the storm was passing well to the north of us. Heavy black clouds and roaring thunder and lightning were clearly visible, but were already apparently receding to the northeast of us. Meanwhile, it had started to hail—huge stones the size of golf balls or larger—but falling straight down with practicality no wind. They made a spectacular sight as they fell into the lake, each stone sending a miniature geyser three to four feet into the air. The sky to the south was a clear blue, which shaded into a light overcast gray overhead. There was certainly nothing in this to alarm us; we watched with fascination as the hail continued to fall for perhaps fifteen minutes, and the ground grew white with its accumulation.

At approximately 5:22, our telephone rang. It was a friend of mine who lived about five miles west and a little south of us, at the south

*This account was written in the winter of 1973 as part of my U.W.W. experience.

end of Nokey Lake. He had been out in his yard and had seen a funnel cloud form. He watched it dip into the lake and continue on eastward. When he realized that it appeared headed in our direction, he ran into the house to call and give me warning. The tone of his voice convinced me that his warning was real, even though the sky was still only very slightly overcast, and patches of blue remained clearly visible in the south. The storm to the north of us had moved on, and the rushing sound of the hail drowned out all other sound. As I hung up the phone, I saw a car tearing madly down our driveway and wondered if its driver was bereft of his senses. I remember wondering at that instant, why the hail striking his windshield, at the speed he was going, didn't shatter it.

I quickly called to Ruth to get Jay and Kirsten and take them over to Mom's big house next door, and I followed right behind. As we entered the back door of the house I paused to tell Ruth of the warning I had just received. I didn't want to alarm the children or Mom needlessly, as I still doubted that we were in any real danger. After all, how could my friend pinpoint the hundred-yard-wide path of a tornado so exactly from that distance, even assuming the funnel didn't lift long before it got this far?

I walked hurriedly through the length of the house and opened the kitchen door, which faces west. It was then that I first heard that unique roar that accompanies all tornados, and saw the white sheet of water that was thrown up ahead of the eye of the storm as it crossed the bay of the lake. It appeared to be no more than two or three hundred yards away from us at that moment. As calmly as possible I told Mom and the others that it looked as though we could be in for a severe storm, and that we must take refuge in our storm cellar. This was a cave dug into the hill behind the house and lined with reinforced concrete. Its entrance was no more than fifteen feet from our kitchen door. My mother, usually very frightened by the prospect of a severe wind, was very calm as she looked for her sweater and appeared undisturbed. I had to yell at her that we were going into the cellar "right now!" As we left the house, I could see the trees across the bay whipping violently, and sheets of water racing madly ahead of the peripheral winds that hid the funnel from view. I literally forced them all into the cellar, deliberately leaving the back door of the house open, as I had with the mobile home when I left. I immediately closed the cellar door behind us, but as soon as I did so, I realized how frightening the complete blackness would be for the children. Furthermore, I had an irresistible urge to watch what was happening outside. I stood in the doorway of the cellar with the door opened against my chest and watched as the storm hit, scarcely seconds after we had left the house.

My field of vision was restricted as I stood back in the doorway of the cellar, the house screening the view to the east. In those few moments I witnessed and felt the ultimate release of natural energy. My vision could penetrate perhaps two hundred feet into the eye of the disturbance. Water and debris whirled in a pagan dance of violence. Trees did not fall, but were slammed violently in one direction, and then another. A young birch tree, perhaps thirty feet high, bent until its uppermost branches touched the ground. It did not break! Tops of other trees whipped violently past as they headed toward the eye of the storm. The roaring, hissing, whining sound was overpowering. Such sound had often been described as that of a thousand runaway locomotives. I will concede this to be as accurate a description as any, yet truly, it is a sound unique to this particular form of violence and cannot be properly equated with any other that I have ever heard.

Scarcely thirty seconds from the time we had entered the cellar, the violence abated and we stepped out into a new world of devastation. I recall saying, as I was watching the devastation, "My God, there won't be a tree left standing." Fortunately, this was not true, but why and how will forever mystify me, for in many areas of the path of this storm, this statement was literally true. Downed trees, piled one on top of another, blocked all vision to the right or to the left. In front, the lake was full of debris of all kinds; half-sunk and overturned boats, parts of docks, tree tops and drifting boards. Looking up over the end of the house we could still see the funnel, nearly white, disappearing into the light overcast as it raised. There were still patches of blue sky to the south. Only then did I become aware of Kirsten screaming hysterically, overcome with emotion by the devastation she beheld. I tried to give her a word of reassurance, then left her with my mother and hurried off toward the trailer park where most of the guests were. My first concern was to cut off the electricity, and to find out if there were any injuries or deaths.

I had to climb over a barricade of fallen trees before I could even see in that direction. Six giant basswoods had fallen in a tangled heap, blocking the way and tearing off a corner of the garage roof. It was with intense relief that I discovered that the damage was less severe as I moved toward the park, after first cutting off the power where it came from underground. There were trees down on three of the four cabins, but the damage appeared to be minor. As I approached, people came from the cabins and reassured me that no one had been hurt. I returned to the house and met Ruth who had voluntarily gone down the shore in the other direction. She was white and shaken as she reported that "all of the cabins are gone!" I could not fully comprehend her meaning, until I started in that direction myself. Six cabins in a row had been totally destroyed. Parts of walls and roofs floated in the lake. The rest was piled in broken heaps among the fallen trees. Interestingly, there was practically no debris left on the actual sites where the cabins had stood; only their concrete support piers remained. Bedding, furniture, and personal effects hung from the crumpled limbs of the few trees that were left standing. From a distance I saw a form draped over a fallen tree, and had to force myself to take a closer look. It was only a bedspread rolled up and blown there by the wind, and not a body. But it hung in the area of one of the cabins that had been occupied. There was no sign of life, nor could I see a car, although one could easily have been hidden under the rubbish. I did see a motorcycle near where a cabin had stood but did not recognize it.

This picture, the one on the right, and the one on the next page show the damage done by the tornado and taken during the clean-up

It was impossible to follow the driveway because of the maze of fallen trees, so I worked my way to the beach, and along it to the seventh cabin, which stands out near the county road. It was still there but largely obscured by trees that had fallen across it. I did catch a glimpse of a man going around the cabin and thought that it was one of the occupants. Later I learned that all three of them had gone out to dinner before the storm and that the motorcycle, which did belong to a guest, had been stripped of its accessories. When I reached the highway, I could hear the whine of sirens and the roar of chainsaws starting up. The highway itself was blocked, and powerlines were hanging down across it.

I made my way along the road away from the storm area, until I met a car trying to come through. I stopped them and told them that the road was blocked, then rode with them to the White Hawk where I called Lynn to let her know what had happened, and that we were all safe and unharmed. I then immediately returned home to find one of our neighbors, Bob Ruth, already there to help. He had noticed the smell of propane gas and had turned off the supply at the main tank, a task that, in my confusion, I had neglected to do.

As I stopped to talk with Bob, I saw the man from one of the destroyed cabins approaching. I told him how glad I was to see him, as we were not sure if there had been anyone in his cabin or not. He said, "My God—where is my

family?" Again I felt the oppressive fear of having to look through the rubble for mangled bodies. Fortunately, it turned out that his wife had heard a warning of the approaching storm and had driven off with the rest of the family in their second car before the storm hit. I later learned that they had broadcast very detailed accounts of the storm's progress, which would have given us ten to fifteen minutes warning of the impending disaster, had I had the local radio station tuned in.

Kirsten had given my mother and Ruth quite a scare by disappearing shortly after I had left. They finally found her up in the field, checking on the wellbeing of her horse. After checking on the children and making sure that my mother had someone to stay with her, I got out my chainsaw and started down our west driveway, to help a crew of neighbors who were already clearing the road from that direction.

The power line that served the trailer park had been stretched to within a few feet of the ground by a falling tree. In a remarkably short time the power company truck was there to clear the line and restore power there. The main line to the rest of the resort was also down, but it took nearly two hours for a bulldozer and several chainsaws to open a lane for the power truck to reach this outage. With this repaired, we still had to wait for the morning light to examine the remaining lines before we dared restore power to the buildings that were left. It also meant that we must all go without water, as both of wells operated on that circuit.

At 10:00 P.M., I called a halt to any further work for the night, as I knew that it would require many days to clear all of the rubble from the road and remaining cabins, and working under the handicap of darkness would only increase the inherent risk from falling debris, boards with exposed nails, and broken glass.

With the children in bed, and comparative calm restored, I still was not ready for sleep, but sat long into the night, drinking coffee and pondering the enormity of the problems that lay ahead. The clean-up job would be long, and

hard, and heartbreaking, as each broken tree and pile of debris would bring nostalgic memories of happier times.

The first priority, after restoring the utilities, would have to be devoted to the remaining cabins, as they were all occupied and would remain so for the remainder of the summer. Three of them had trees down on them and all had broken windows and other minor damages. With the occupied portion of the resort restored to at least a semblance of normality, I could devote the rest of the summer to removing the wreckage from the area of total destruction.

The following morning dawned bright and clear and warm. It was as though Nature, ashamed of the havoc she had wrought, was trying to make amends, for the weather remained exceptionally nice for the remainder of the summer. Friends and neighbors started arriving by 7:30, all eager to help with the clean-up. For the next two weeks I found myself kept busy directing my volunteer crews, which often numbered from ten to twenty men, women, and teenagers, some with trucks and many with chainsaws. The Salvation Army and the Red Cross each came in several times a day with coffee, pop, and sandwiches for the workers, and an almost festive air prevailed.

Much of my time, that first day, was taken by the news media seeking interviews and pictures. Planes and helicopters were constantly overhead, and the lake was alive with boats of all sizes and shapes with their crews of interested sightseers, most armed with cameras to record the havoc. I never did take pictures myself, for I was too busy and preoccupied with trying to clear away all but the memory of what had been.

On land, the sightseers were more of a problem, as they continually tried to drive through, causing minor traffic jams and interfering with the workers. Most were merely curious, but unfortunately, there are always a few who seek to profit from the confusion of such a situation. The sheriff's office maintained road blocks for several days, but even this was not always effective, while many who honestly came to offer assistance were turned away.

Deciding what to do with the rubble was one of my main problems. Fortunately, I have a field where we could pile all of the branches and brush from the fallen trees to await burning in the winter. Anything large enough to make a saw log was saved to be sold for lumber. Much of the remainder was taken by neighbors to be used for firewood. Debris from the cabins was more of a problem. Sections of walls and roofs remained in tact, and presented the possibility of salvage lumber. On the spot burning would have been the easiest way, but the risk of fire spreading or someone getting burned would have been ever-present, and the separation of valuable salvage lumber would have been difficult, if not impossible, to control. So I determined to tear apart the remaining sections and to haul anything that reasonably resembled useful lumber to a back lot for possible future salvage.

I will never cease being grateful to the many friends and neighbors, and, indeed, the many whom I scarcely knew, who helped me to restore order after the storm. While these volunteer groups were busy cutting, hauling, and sorting, I found myself literally running from one group to the next, directing the flow of the clean-up, setting priorities on the various jobs, and lending a hand wherever one was needed.

I hired a carpenter, who thoughtfully stopped by to let me know that he was available, to do the major repair on the remaining cabins. Rafters and roof boards had to be replaced where trees had fallen on them, and one large cabin had to be jacked up and moved back onto its foundation. This, of course, required the services of a house mover as well. Temporary gas, water, and electric lines had to be installed and docks rebuilt. One of my guests from the trailer park volunteered to replace broken window panes and damaged screens. A friend from town lent me two additional chainsaws, and the Department of Natural Resources assisted in removing large sections of cabins from the lake.

During this time I was continually asked if I planned to rebuild the cabins. I realized that this could not be done. In the first place, the new zoning laws forbid any building within one hundred feet of the lake. Our cabins had all been within fifty feet of the water or less, and while the "grandfather" clause allowed the restoration of damaged cabins in the area, those that had been totally destroyed could not be rebuilt without observing the new set-back restrictions. Further, the resort industry had undergone a dramatic change in the twenty previous years. Increased population, high-speed roads and automobiles, increased leisure time, and a higher standard of living had shifted the demands of the traveling public away from short term rental units. Many bought travel-trailers or campers, and spent their vacations touring. Many others, with more leisure time, were seeking permanent lake homes of their own. Lakeshore property values had already shot up from the $10.00 per front foot for desirable lakeshore to $100.00 per foot and more for choice lots. Property taxes had increased accordingly. The cabins that we lost had each occupied about one hundred feet of choice shoreline. By 1973 I could have sold it for $150.00 per foot or more. The cost of building comparable cabins had also increased several fold. Furthermore, new cabins would have had to be built with more luxury in mind, and would probably have to be insulated and winterized. I simply did not have the money to invest in such a large venture.

Lynn came back for a few days that summer. I would see her walking along the lakeshore, doubtless seeing it as it had once been, as well as the mess that was left. She finally came to me and announced that she couldn't face it, and wanted out of our marriage. If I would let her have the children, she would not ask for any of the property. I had no choice but to agree, I would not risk having my daughter lose this part of her heritage, as she surely would have if the property had been split.

When we are young, we almost knowingly cast our lot, not so much for a particular line of work, but for the position in society that we will one day achieve. After completing two years of college, I had decided that my field, engineering, would not bring me to the style of life that I would find most rewarding. So I discontinued school in favor of taking over the operation of the family resort. While I have never regretted this decision, I have always wondered if there wasn't another field of endeavor that I could pursue along with the resort operation that would help me to fulfill a basic need for creative achievement. Conservation and natural science have always appealed to me, satisfying my great love for nature. Perhaps these factors formed a subconscious reason for my not wanting to pursue an even more commercialized development here on the lake. I enjoy sharing our native environment with people, yet concentrations of "people developments" always diminish the more rewarding aspects of nature.

The trailer park that we had operated for many years had always been rewarding, in that the guests return year after year and there is always a waiting list for any vacated spot. Because of this, a sense of mutual ownership has developed, together with a community spirit. With this experience to draw from, I could now visualize a new community in the area where the cabins had been destroyed. I rationalized that since good lakeshore had become so very scarce, and the demand so great, surely I would be able to find fifteen families who would be willing to join with me in developing a community of lake homes. The Winston College Dictionary defines community as, "a body of persons having common interests and privileges, living in the same locality," also "joint participation, sharing or ownership." My community, then, would be more than just a location; it would involve the sharing of the beauties of nature that surround us here and, to some degree at least, a way of life.

As the summer passed and the major part of the debris was cleared away, my concept took more definite form. I realized that the storm, terrible as it was, had presented me with an opportunity that had once seemed entirely out of reach. I would build my community of mobile home sites, and lease them on a long term basis. I decided to return to school to study ecology. This would give me a solid foundation for developing my community with a minimum of disturbance to the nature that I loved and wished to preserve, and at the same time develop the land for its best and highest use. The University Without Walls concept of completing an education off campus through an unstructured course of study, reinforced with the assistance and guidance of the university staff, was ideally suited to my needs. My concept for a course of study was approved by the University of Minnesota as a valid learning experience and I was enrolled for the winter quarter.

Chapter 34

Rebuilding

The winter of 1973/1974 was the worst period emotionally through which I have ever had to live. I had moved into the old home with my mother, since the kids were no longer with me, and, with Dad gone, there was no reason for us both to be living alone. I spent the days cutting and burning the tops of the hundreds of trees that had fallen in the storm. I would open a little area near the fallen tops and start a fire, then cut and throw the brush on the fire till only the trunks remained. It was hard work, and dangerous too, as often the trees would be hung up with each other, and one never knew when the saw would be pinched, or what direction the trees would fall. It did serve to keep my mind from dwelling on the loss of my family and the physical problems I faced.

Nights were another matter. I would be dead tired and ready to go to bed early, but, by two or three in the morning I would wake up, and the "might have beens" of my life would rise up to haunt me. Further sleep was then impossible. I will be forever grateful to the University Without Walls program, which provided me with the incentive to shift my thoughts into a more positive and productive vein. I would study for a few hours, then perhaps catch another little nap before it was time to return to the cutting and burning.

By spring the devastated woods had taken on quite a different character. There were still a few large trees standing, and many of the little maple saplings, which I had left when I brushed out the sugar bush, had come through the storm unscathed and were now flourishing. But my "woods" had more the aspect of a field with a few scattered trees on it, and the lakeshore where the cabins had been was even more forlorn.

The piles of logs I had amassed over the winter were sold to a local sawmill for what I considered to be a pittance, considering the time and work they had cost me. But the mill had to consider the additional risk they ran to their equipment when sawing logs taken from an area so close to dwellings, where the chance of hitting nails imbedded in the trunks in years past was greatly increased. And if the mill had not taken them, I would have had to hire someone to haul them out, so I really couldn't complain.

Now I could begin the actual laying out of my mobile home "community." Fortunately, my cousin Henry, who was a county engineer living at Litchfield, was able to come up and help me establish a few lines and elevations from where I could start. My friend Louie Smilich was al-

Louie Smilich burning the debris hauled into the field during clean-up

ways on hand to help me, whenever I needed it the most. His heavy equipment did all of the necessary leveling and grading, his back hoe dug the trenches for the water and sewer lines, and his wholesale buying connections allowed me to buy the thousands of feet of plastic pipe that I needed at rates that I could afford to pay.

Laying out the actual sites was a time-consuming project in itself. To begin with, I wanted my sites to be much larger than the five thousand square feet then required by the state. The setback from the lake would be no problem, as the driveway was over a hundred feet back from the lake and the area between the road and the lake would be a "commons" area with no development on it, except for the one remaining cabin located out near the road. I settled on a width of sixty feet per site, which allowed me to place the homes on each site without cutting trees. After having lost so many, I could not bear to cut another tree simply to make room for a mobile home. The lengths of the sites would vary from one hundred twenty to one hundred eighty feet, as this was the distance from the road to a steep little embankment in the rear. The two shallower lots actually became eighty feet wide. This arrangement gave me room for seven sites along the lake. Later I would add another row of sites up on the embankment, which would look out over the lower sites and onto the lake.

The exact location for the future mobile home within the site had to be figured very carefully to keep them somewhere near the center of the site, and to allow for mobile home widths of either twelve or fourteen feet. I would allow nothing narrower than twelve feet and nothing shorter than fifty feet, as in this way I was also restricting the age of the home to some extent. The front, or hitch end of the home, would be facing the lake, but angled slightly to the left so that the large windows on the right side of the home would have some view of the lake also.

When this was finalized, I had Louie dig a trench for my water lines. It had to be at least six feet deep for the pipe to be frostproof, and extend from our well house to the new park area and along near the rear of the sites. The heavy-duty plastic water line was two inches in diameter. At each site there was an insulated riser that brought the water to the surface for the home attachment, with a shut-off plug at the bottom reached by a long rod that could be lowered through the center of the riser. The later models have a shut-off valve that can be turned from the surface, thus able to be closed without shutting off the main water supply. When these were all in place, I had Louie partially fill the trench, then I had Don Carlson, our local electrician, run power lines in the same trench. This works out fine, except when a riser goes bad and has to be dug up. Then invariably I have to call Don to splice a wire that gets cut off when we dig!

The sewer lines had to be twenty feet from where the water lines were buried. They were dug much shallower, as there had to be a steady, gradual slope down to the top of the battery of four septic tanks, which would receive the sewage. From there it was pumped far up into our field, where it entered a large drain field. While these lines are subject to freezing in the winter if there are leaky faucets to inject a slow trickle of water into the lines, they have worked out extremely well over all, with only minor problems.

I choose to run liquefied petroleum gas to each site, where it was metered to the individual homes. This saves a great deal of confusion, as well as a lot of money for the homeowners, and a modest mark-up allows me to recoup the cost of installation as well. This involved the use of extruded steel pipe coated with plastic both inside and out to eliminate the chance for electrolysis, which, under certain conditions, can cause leaks.

Instead of a full concrete pad, I ran two ribbons of reinforced concrete on which the wheels of the mobile home rest. They would also afford a suitable place for blocking the home. This worked out fairly well, except that, while the wheel width was generally the same, the frame width varied enough to make blocking on the concrete difficult or impractical. In the later sites, I discontinued the use of cement runners entirely. The new, larger homes are often sixteen by eighty feet, and require individual cement footings for the blocking.

All of this took a great deal of time, especially since I was doing nearly all of the manual work myself, but, by the fall of 1975, I had seven sites nearly ready for use. I also received my degree from the University of Minnesota that fall. My problem was, how could I find the people to fill this new "niche" in the tourism industry? I was looking for families who wanted a home on the lake, either for summer use only or for the entire year. They would have to be willing to buy their own mobile home, which necessarily meant that it would be a relatively long-term commitment. I knew there was a demand for just this sort of operation, but how was I to fill it with a minimum of advertising and still retain some measure of control over the potential clientele? Of course discrimination was illegal, but I wanted to be sure that the class of people we had always had would not suffer. Over eighty percent of our business had always been comprised of people who came back year after year. Now we would have to build up an entirely new cliental.

At that time, Don Renquist and his wife, Connie, had one of the remaining cabins rented by the season. Connie's parents, the Trevetts, also had the large cabin that remained out by the road, booked by the season. Mr. Trevett and his wife had been living in the Log cabin at the time of the tornado and had taken great interest in watching the development of the mobile home park. The next spring, when he saw that I was having some problem getting started with the renting, he came to me and said, "You need to get the first home moved in, that will break the ice and more will soon follow. What will you charge me to move a home in on the lot out by the road, where it can easily be seen? I will put in a nice yard and see that it is well kept up to create a good image for you."

As I thought it over, it made a lot of sense to me. I had planned to charge $70.00 per month for the new sites, although I had been advised that I could get as much as $100.00 per month for them. But since my rates were already low for what I was providing, I hated to make any further cuts. Finally, I went to Mr. Trevett and told him that I could not cut the monthly rate, but if he wanted to move in a nice trailer and help me develop that site, I would cut $10.00 per month off the rent if a year's rent were paid in advance. By doing this, I would generate the ready cash that I needed to pay off some of the debts I had assumed, and save myself some interest.

Mr. Trevett was agreeable and began looking for a suitable mobile home. On August 15, 1976, he had a mobile home moved in on the first lot. He worked hard getting a nice lawn started, watering the spruce trees that I had moved in to create the required "screen" from the highway, and generally helping me in every way he could to promote my new venture. The response was dramatic. By the end of October, five of the seven sites had been rented. The other two would rent within a year, and I could concentrate on the second phase of my program.

The upper tier of sites would be easier, in that I already had the general layout in mind, but there would be more trees that would have to come out, and I would have to lay out a road along the edge of the little swamp behind the new sites. The frontage of the sites would have to curve gently, as the sites followed the configuration of the hill and gradually blended in with the alignment of the highway to the east. This would make for somewhat wedge-shaped lots on the curve—very wide in the front but somewhat narrower than sixty feet in the rear.

The first eight lots on the upper level were ready for use in the spring of 1979, and, by 1982, an additional seven sites had been added, including my original mobile home and the site it occupied prior to the tornado. Eventually two more sites would be added up on the hill, but west of our home. Our little community had grown to a total of fifty-one units, including the five remaining cabins and the twenty-two seasonal sites west of the cabins.

Mobile home sites completed and occupied

Chapter 35

Judy

In 1976 my life finally began to turn around. I no longer had the type of home life I had been accustomed to because, while I lived with my mother, I no longer had a wife and my daughter lived with her mother. Nor did I have any real income, with only five cabins and the little "recreational vehicle park" to supply not only my daily needs, but to finance building the new park as well. But I was making a fresh start. I had completed my education and the first phase of the construction of my new mobile home park was nearing completion. My confidence in the future was returning.

A good friend from Crosby, Bob Ray, and his wife Sally had moved their travel trailer out to the park and were now spending much of the summer there. Bob was not only my barber, he was also a lodge brother and a member of the rifle club with which I had shot for many years. More than mere friends, they were the type of people who show up from time to time in our lives when we need them most and give us that little boost in morale that keeps us going.

Late in the afternoon Bob would often ask me to come in and help him "drown a couple of ice cubes." Scotch never tasted so good as it did on those occasions. One such time, as we sat enjoying our drinks, I saw an unfamiliar head go bouncing around the end of the trailer. What would an attractive young gal whom I hadn't met be doing running around Bob's trailer? "Oh, that's my niece, Judy," Sally explained. "We told her about the little trailer that's for sale over on the back row, and I think she is interested." Sally called her in and introduced her as Judy Meuwissen. It turned out that I had met her before. When Bob had his installation as Master of the lodge he had asked Judy, who was a commercial artist and photographer, to take some pictures. How could we forget that? When the pictures came back, we found that the studio had ruined the lot of them. So we had to go through the whole process of posing all over again. This time Judy had used the wrong film or left the film out or something! On the third try, she did get a couple of decent pictures.

Judy did buy the little trailer, which surprised me. Single girls in their thirties with good jobs in the cities just didn't do that. Of course her job did allow her to take three-day weekends quite often. She started right out fixing up the trailer, putting skirting around it and making a sort of wooden patio floor in front. All this without asking for help from anyone. I couldn't help but be impressed! I later learned that her father was a master carpenter, which obviously had contributed to her skills. Of course I saw her quite often when I went down to Bob and Sally's, but in all fairness they didn't try to push us together. I later learned that Judy is not one that you "push"!

Before the tornado, we had had our furnace for boiling maple syrup out in the woods behind the cabins on the east end of the resort. The tin-roofed shelter (that had been Bill Hagen's "kitchen") had been moved out there to protect the sap pans while we were boiling. The shelter had come through the storm with only minimal damage, but was in the way when I started putting in the mobile home sites. So I had moved it back to the west end, next to the swamp, and just let it sit. Now it was close to Judy's trailer and also to her neighbors, the Ennises. One day Judy came to me and asked me what it was for. This led to a long discourse on syrup making, with the upshot being that Judy wanted to know when I would start making syrup again and where I would put the furnace. I couldn't believe the interest she showed. She even wanted to help me get things ready. How could I resist such an offer?

That fall, after Labor Day, when my other duties had eased up, we got to work on our new project. Years before, when we had filled in along the lake to make more room for trailers on the west end, we had taken the fill from a sandy hill up behind where the old barn had stood. After the storm, all the debris from the cabins had been piled in this area with the idea that what could not be salvaged could be used for sap wood. This would be the logical spot for the furnace. By moving some of the scrap boards and doing a little shoveling, we soon had a suitable site prepared. The vertical poles that supported the shelter had been shortened to make it easier to move. Now, by nailing planks along the sides and across each end, we were able to get the shelter to balance on the rear of my pickup. Off we went, up the little trail that led to the future sugar bush, with Judy and Glen Ennis holding onto the rear end to maintain its delicate balance. What a comical procession we must have been.

Once the shelter was in place, we had to block it up and level it on concrete footings salvaged from the old cabin sites. Even then there were horizontal beams across that forced one to duck his head every time he walked under them. Through the years I have gotten so I remember them—most of the time! Others are often not so fortunate. With scavenged bricks, more concrete footings, and a little new concrete we managed to shape up an "arch" to support the two sap pans. My friend, Orv Rubow, who now lives on the approximate site of Kehwassie's old home site, welded up a smoke stack from two discarded hot-water tanks, and, with these wired in place, we were ready for business.

Having Judy help me had been fun and had given me the impetus to get going on the syrup again. That winter she continued to come up for an occasional long weekend. Boy that little trailer must have been cold, but she never seemed to mind. And sure enough, toward spring, she was there to help me make final preparations for the syrup season. A friend, Don Bamford, who lived nearby on Hamlet Lake, volunteered to help also. Judy took some vacation time during the syrup run that year and became a regular part of the operation. Don would come over whenever there was sap to gather or syrup to take off. In the evenings Judy and I would sit up there by the pan and drink hot toddies made from boiling sap with a little rum and nutmeg for flavoring. It was important that we keep the fire going strong until at least ten or eleven o'clock before we put in the final firing for the night. It was the only way we could keep up with the flow of sap and not overtax our storage capacity. By morning only a few coals would be left, and the sap in the pans would have evaporated down by over half.

The "sap gang," showing off the operation to a couple of guests

These evenings were the time when Judy and I got to really know each other. Her mother, Signe, had been born and raised a few miles north of Crosby near Perry Lake. I knew her uncles, Bill and Elmer Olander, very well, as they had also shot with the rifle team. While Judy was from Minneapolis, she had spent much of her summer vacation time either at the Olander farm or with Bob and Sally Ray. We talked of our mutual friends and our past experiences, but seldom, if ever, of the future. We were just good friends enjoying what we were doing.

The following summer I suffered a severe setback, though it could have been much worse.

Late one afternoon, while water skiing, I felt a strange sensation in my chest and signaled to go in. I felt all right except for a strange weak feeling in my stomach. It persisted into the evening, and, when my cousin Ken Wasserzieher came for a visit, I could hardly sit still to talk with him. I knew something was wrong and I should not go to bed. I kept monitoring my pulse, and when, about 2:00 A.M. it reached forty beats a minute, I decided that it was time to drive in to the hospital and see just what was going on. When I got there, the nurse read only thirty beats per minute; I was put right to bed and given a potent shot of some sort. The next morning the doctor told me that I had had a heart attack.

I don't remember much about the next few days, except that Judy scolded me vigorously for not getting her up to drive me in to the hospital. I got along fine after spending two weeks in the hospital, except that I remained sort of weak for a while and would sometimes experience, or think that I was experiencing, that same weak feeling in my stomach. Surprising what nerves and the power of suggestion will do to you, isn't it? They never did discover any real damage, and I have often thought that nerves were the primary cause of my problems.

The following spring Albert K. Miller, a friend from across the bay, stopped by while we were working out near the road and asked if we needed some help. Of course an extra hand was always welcome, and we would miss Don who was no longer available to help. Al was an older man, retired from the military, who seemed to need something to keep him busy until he could get back to work in his beloved garden. His enthusiasm and quiet good nature added greatly to the comradery we enjoyed as we spent those long days in the woods.

There was always something happening to add spice to what we were doing. Even before we tapped, there was wood to get ready, since we wouldn't have time once the run started. One day I cut down the stump left when a huge white pine had blown over, leaving a snag over twenty feet high. It came down with a mighty crash, and out of the top of it came a big fat momma raccoon and her four babies from the year before, looking very bewildered at their rude awakening. Fortunately they didn't seem to be injured, but they did give us an angry scowl as they plodded off through the deep snow!

We would generally stop for a break and coffee, both in the morning and in the afternoon. Al's wife, Goldie, would send over the best homemade cookies or rolls that you ever tasted, and, if we hadn't been working as hard as we were, we would have all gained a whole bunch of weight. As it was, I think that I managed to add a couple of pounds. After the experience with my heart, I seemed to tire a little more easily, and after lunch I would sit back in my big chair and relax for a few minutes before heading out again. Okay, I napped a little! I probably needed it. At any rate I was soon ready to go again.

During this period, we were tapping the trees on the property that adjoins ours on the west. It was a relatively dense woods that included some beautiful big maples, but, in order to gather the sap without an unreasonably long hand carry, we had to drive in on a little trail that was modest under the best of conditions but downright mean when the melting snow left puddles of mud and goo to navigate, as well as the tight and narrow turns. Fortunately the four-wheel-drive pickup was well suited for this task, though the others were happy to leave the driving to me. But I suffered an infection that kept me out of the woods for a few days that spring, and Judy was forced to take over the responsibility of driving for me. With some trepidation she drove to the back of this woods, where she and Al loaded the tank with sap. Al, considering discretion to be the better part of valor, opted to walk out and check the condition of the frost in the road, as the frost was rapidly going out of the ground, making the road worse with each passing moment. He finally yelled back for her to come on out, but to "Hit it hard when you get to the mud hole and don't stop for anything!" Judy's faithful dog, Mandy, took her usual stance in the back of the truck as Judy started out. All went well for the first few yards, until the truck approached a sharp turn with a nasty patch of mud square in the middle of it. Judy knew that she would need momentum to carry her through the morass. Following Al's directions, she engaged the four-wheel drive, and, with the engine racing in low gear, she hit the muck with reckless abandon. Suddenly a tree appeared directly in her path. She dared not stop in the middle of the mud, so she frantically hauled on the wheel. Alas, the slippery conditions held the truck on its line of flight, and Judy froze at the wheel as the truck hit the tree dead center! With scarcely a thud, the dead snag went flying up over the hood and over the rear of the truck as well, to splash harmlessly in the mud behind, while the truck finally came to a stop well beyond the mud hole. With a mighty leap, Mandy left the truck and headed for home as fast as her legs could carry her, never bothering to look back, while Al bent double in a paroxysm of laughter. Sheepishly, Judy crawled from the truck to find that no real damage had been done, except to her ego, so she, too, could join in the laughter. The remainder of her trip to the sap shack was uneventful.

Many are the syrup seasons that have passed, with many a fond memory of the odd little incidents which continually added spice to our chores. Al continued to play an active roll in our syrup making activities until June of 1991, when he was called to join the ranks of those who tend their gardens and tap their trees in the Celestial Realm. He will always be missed, as will all of those who have shared the comradery of the maple syrup season with us down through the years, and have now gone on.

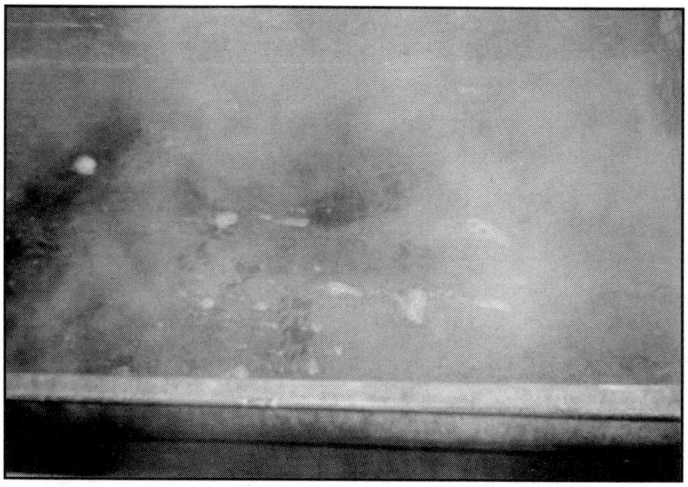

A late-night visiting raccon left his footprints in the rear sap pan

Chapter 36

A Whole New Life

During the rebuilding of the sugar bush, and its first years in operation, Judy and I had continually grown closer and closer together. I remember so vividly one day in late April of 1977. The syrup season was just over, and Judy had helped me to bring in the buckets and spiles for washing before returning to Minneapolis and her job. We had spent the last afternoon sitting down by the lake, enjoying the soft warmth of the beautiful spring day, and dreaming of who knows what. Then she was gone, and I realized how much I missed her. Of course, we had written to each other from time to time, but now I felt impelled to write another kind of letter, one that would perhaps reveal my inner self to her in a way that I had not previously explored, even to myself. So I wrote:

"A light breeze tickles the surface of the water and sets it laughing against the side of the boat. It is a pleasantly cool breeze, but it has the hint of spring in its breath—not yet the sweet pungency of a full-blown spring, perspiring in the labor throes of the rebirth of a world lain dormant by winter's icy blasts—but only that trace of newly exposed earth and swelling buds that alert us to its coming.

The clouds, what there are, are white and fleecy, skimming lazily overhead as though enjoying their first spring outing.

The water is still cold and clear from its long winter's confinement, when no waves could break its serenity. Soon the sun will stir this very still world and generate a great surge of revitalization to its very depths—but for now, the weeds are down, and the water's pristine clearness reveals the deepest secrets of this frozen world. I see no fish, for they are still in awe of the brilliance of the high sun and will postpone their explorations until the friendly cloak of darkness descends.

A last fragile patch of drift ice is tentatively exploring the shoreline for a convenient mooring.

Our resident loons are back, and in their exuberance they are practicing touch-and-go landings as they walk the water with their wingtips, and laugh from the sheer pleasure of it. High above, a great hawk pirouettes on motionless wings, as he cries to his mate and stakes his claim to that particular bit of airspace. On the shore, the red-winged blackbirds are noisily disputing their territorial claims in the marsh grass, while the robins do the same in the tree tops. A pair of mallard ducks are arguing over their future nesting site down in the shallow bay, where an occasional black stump gives promise of the forest of lily pads that will soon emerge. A great blue heron stalks with stately strides as he scans his favorite stretch of beach for an early-rising frog or an overly venturesome minnow on which to dine.

It is a day for drifting and dreaming—for pondering the promises of great wisdom written so lavishly on every hand—for assimilating truth. Unfortunately, you are not here to share this experience with me, so I will turn again to washing my sap pails and let my imagination do the drifting for us both."

Over four years later Kirsten would read this letter to those assembled on the joyous occasion of our marriage, held in the living room of Grandfather Knieff's original home here at Bay Lake.

That letter ushered in the beginning of a whole new life for me. Until then I had considered the difference in our ages to be an insurmountable barrier to anything other than a platonic relationship. Judy's reply did much to disencumber me of that notion, although I still had occasional misgivings.

In August of that year, Judy quit her job in Minneapolis and bought a cute little house in Crosby. I knew that she had been looking for one, but I didn't even know that she had bought one until after she had already moved in. I guess I am just naturally slow at catching on! Even then it was over two years before we were married. I will not offer any form of reason or excuse for this. I know that one of the reasons I used was the fact that I was living with my mother, who was now over ninety years old. She remained quite sharp and active, but Mother had had a couple of little "mini" strokes. They lead me to feel the need to have an older woman live with us and care for her, as I had to be free to take care of my work. I did not feel that I should ask Judy to move into a situation like that.

In the spring of 1981, Mom suffered another and more severe stroke. She fell, broke her arm, and had to be moved into the nursing home in Crosby. I knew then that the time was drawing near for her to leave me, and my heart ached for the kindest, dearest person that I will ever know. Each time that I went in to see her, the decline was evident, and her prayers for release from her troubled existence were almost more than I could bear. On Labor Day evening I went in to see her, then stopped over at Judy's for a few minutes before going home. As I headed south from Deerwood, I saw a brilliant meteor streak across the sky in blazing glory, an omen that I could not disregard. Minutes after I drove into the yard, I was followed by Judy, with the message that the hospital had called, and that Mom was gone. Thank God for Judy, and the help she gave me during these most troubled times.

I went deer hunting that fall, as usual, and stayed in the little homemade trailer that had been the "camp" for so many years. But now our numbers had dwindled until, after the first weekend, I was the only one left to enjoy it. Of course, I had stayed and hunted alone before, but this year was different, and I was ill at ease. Monday evening I could stand it no longer, so I drove down to Crosby to see Judy. We talked for a few minutes, then I blurted out, "I don't want to go on living alone. Let's get married."

She said, "You haven't asked me yet."

"Will you?"

"I'll have to think about it for a while. When do you want to do it?"

"Well, deer season lasts through next Sunday, then Thanksgiving will be the following Thursday. How about the Saturday after Thanksgiving?"

"But it's so soon. How can we possibly get ready? I haven't even said I'll marry you yet!"

"Oh, come on, Jude, I'll stay down tonight, and tomorrow morning we'll go into Aitkin and get our license. Then I'll go back to camp until Sunday or Monday. You can send out some invitations, and we'll have the following week to get ready."

So that was the way our wedding was planned. I returned to deer camp on Tuesday afternoon, alone, but knowing my days of being alone would soon be over. I hunted the final five days of the season, but for the life of me I can't remember if I even saw a deer that year. Still, the time was not wasted, for I had a lot of thinking to do and plans to make. We scrambled pretty hard when I got back from camp, and on the Saturday afternoon following Thanksgiving, we were married. Not only did we have house guests, we served twenty-one people a sit down dinner that we had prepared ourselves!

We didn't go on a honeymoon right away

Al, Kirsten, and Judy on Judy and Al's wedding day

but opted instead to wait until after the holidays. When we left home, it was snowing heavily, and, when we reached Minneapolis, where we planned to spend the night with Judy's parents, there was already a foot of new snow on the ground. The snow was still coming down when we left the next morning, and we raced the weather all the way through Iowa. We later learned that over eighteen more inches of snow had fallen in Minneapolis before that storm let up. But even the snow could not dampen our spirits as we headed south in Judy's little Ford Courier. We first visited her brother Bill, his wife, Carol, and son Mike in Waco, Texas, then on down to San Antonio to visit the Ennises, whom we had become very close to. Leaving there, we headed west to Arizona to see Bob and Sally, and then on to California where Chester and Gladys Powers and my cousin Oscar live near San Diego. It was a fun trip, doing all the things that tourists do, seeing all the things that tourists see, but in truth I believe we were both happy to get home again and to settle into our regular routine of daily life.

Naturally, we had to get home in time to tap our maple trees, and scarcely was that season over when the annual spring clean-up had to be gotten under way. It was fun to be working and planning with someone again, and the summer sped swiftly by. So I was taken completely by surprise when Judy said to me one morning, "I have called and made an appointment with my gynecologist in Minneapolis." I was immediately concerned that she was not well, but she reassured me that she was fine, saying, "It's just what often happens after people have been married for as long as we have." I was flabbergasted! Not that I should have been, of course, it was just that we hadn't really planned it this way. Sure enough, the doctor told us that our family would increase in size early the following April. Naturally we were both somewhat shocked at first, but this sensation soon wore off, and was replaced with the thrill and joy of the realization that we would soon be parents.

Pregnancy at Judy's age is always somewhat risky, not only for the mother but because of the added risk of Downs Syndrome. But Judy was fine. She went deer hunting with me that year, and early in March we even tapped a few trees. After the first batch of syrup was off, Judy started getting restless and wanted to be closer to her doctor. With the help of a young woman staying in one of the trailers, Al Miller said that he could keep things going. With that settled, we went down to Minneapolis and moved in with Judy's parents until the baby was born.

It was with some trepidation that I faced this event, as memories of Kirsten's birth were still strong in my mind. I could not have been more wrong! We had taken the birthing classes that winter, with me as the coach. Now I discovered that they really weren't kidding. I was with Judy that whole day, from her early morning warning that things were about to happen, through the day-long wait, observing her contractions for her, and, most wonderful of all, I was at her side through out the delivery. I was immediately given our new daughter to hold for a few moments, then laid her gently on her mother's breast. What a beautiful, perfect little girl Judy had given us! And what a proud and happy procession we made as we returned to Judy's room where her parents waited for us. I'm sure tears of joy dimmed my eyes as I handed our little girl over to her Grandma Signe. Judy had come through the ordeal with flying colors and with never a request for chemical relief of any kind. We had decided to call our little girl Erin, after my mother's wonderful Irish

Baby Erin with her faithful friend, Mandy

nature, and Evaleena after Signe, whose middle name is Evaleena. In three days Judy and Erin were back at Grandma and Grandpa's, and in five days we were on our way home.

Erin's arrival meant quite a reorganization of our daily life style, but we adjusted without problem or complaint. Our pets, Mandy, the dog, and, Tigger, the cat, were both compliant if not down right solicitous of the baby's welfare. Mandy would allow any amount of prodding and poking without complaint, while Tigger took to catching an extra mouse and leaving it on the doorstep every day or two, no doubt to insure that Erin would receive an adequate diet.

As our guests returned for the summer, they all made a fuss over our little girl and helped us to spoil her pretty badly. That's what is supposed to happen isn't it?

Chapter 37

Retrospect

Over a century has passed since my Grandfather came to Bay Lake to find a quiet place to finish rearing his family and to live out his years in peace. I have often wondered what he would think of his little homestead, if only he could see it as it is now. It is nearly impossible for me to comprehend the changes that have come about during this relatively short span. I am sure that Grandpa Knieff was familiar with the telegraph, which came into use in 1844, but the telephone did not begin to realize its commercial potential until the late 1870s. Since then have come the development of electric power, the age of the automobile, and the myriad other inventions that have so vastly changed our way of life. I am "penning" these words, not with quill and ink, but with a word-processing computer, whose capacity to convey knowledge stuns the imagination of even those who work with it on a daily basis.

Yes, Grandpa, from where you now reside, I am sure you are aware of these developments. The evolution of life itself is but a part of that Grand Scheme of which you and I are but minute parts. Yet it is not the evolution of life that occupies my mind as I type these words. It is the preservation of this small tract of land that has passed from your stewardship to that of my father, and now to me. Have I succeeded in preserving its integrity while bending it to my will and wresting my living from it? Certainly, it has changed greatly since you first saw it, as has the whole of the nation and the greater part of the world itself.

Most of the giant pines are gone now, many of them felled by you and your sons to provide the lumber from which you built this house in which I still live. But a few of the originals that you knew so well are still left to remind us of that era of long ago. And the field, which was so laboriously cleared to provide land for your crops and livestock, is now being replanted to pine and spruce to furnish a safe haven for the wild creatures that remain in abundance, as well as for the esthetic beauty they will once again lend to the landscape.

Most of those ugly wires, that once served to convey the electricity on which we so strongly depend, have been buried and are no longer eyesores. We no longer have a "dump" out back to collect the unused remains from our daily living. Instead they are carefully sorted, with the recyclables being returned to industry for future use, and only the totally unusable being hauled to the county land fill. We retain a little garden which we till every spring, in the hope that some of our guests will take up the challenge along with us. We deem it a success although the gophers, woodchucks, raccoons, and even an occasional deer reap the greater share of its bounty.

The road through the eastern part of the property has once again been widened and changed, much to our discomfiture at the wanton loss of so many beautiful trees. By way of compensation, we have been left with an open "duck pond" beyond the road in the old meadow. The beaver, which have increased in numbers to the point of becoming a nuisance, have enjoyed it. I even saw some ducks in it once this spring!

Gone are the bullrushes that once guarded these shores from the thrust of the prevailing south wind and the surge of the winter ice. In their place has risen a profusion of docks, capable of mooring more than fifty boats of all sizes and shapes. There is an ugliness about them it is true, one of the inevitable concessions we must make if we are to share the bounty of this glorious heritage with fifty other families. From the youngsters, and indeed the oldsters too, who cast their worms in search of sunfish from these docks, to the deadly serious bass boats of the young adults that set out for an evening quest for bigger game, to the ponderous poontoon boats from which our senior citizens may enjoy a leisurely cruise on a quiet summer evening, comes the justification for this mar on the otherwise bucolic scene.

But it is the community of people who share this haven with us, of whom we are most proud. Some of the families have been represented here for over sixty years. There are couples who met here and fell in love, who now bring their children. The west end is populated primarily with younger families, though not entirely. They have no winter water available, and must confine their use to the summer months, from May through October. The east end has larger sites for larger homes. The facilities are usable all year around, and many are occupied by retired people, some of whom also have homes in the south, where they fly when the weather turns cold here. Others live here all year. A trend has developed whereby the older residents from the west end gravitate to the east end as sites become available there, often leaving their former sites to their children. Originally the two ends remained separate and distinct from each other. Each group had their own parties and get togethers with little intermingling. Now, more and more, this separation is dissipating, and the community spirit is encompassing the entire park as one unit.

The east end of KSA before any development had been made

We have deliberately made the maintenance of the individual sites the responsibility of the individual lessee, in part to keep our rates as low as possible, but also to increase the sense of pride that each feels, not only for his or her own site, but also for the park as a whole. This concept has worked remarkably well. Naturally, we are responsible for the entire commons area, and if someone is physically unable to mow their lawn, or is away for an extended time, we see that the yard is kept up. This is rarely necessary, as their neighbors usually do the job before we have the chance.

In short, everyone here works together not only as neighbors but as friends. As the

The east end of KSA as it appears today

owners, we must at times make the final call. But generally we participate as regular members of the community. This, I believe, is the highest compliment that can be paid to a landlord. Many of the private cabin owners around the lake came to know Bay Lake first as guests at Knieff's Shore Acres. That they remain friends, after these many years, attests to relationships developed by my parents and the way that they conducted their little business. What a pleasure it is when friends from long ago, finding themselves in the area, drop in to chat a bit and renew memories of the past!

What of the future? I plan to live out my life span right here, doing the things that I love best, among the people who have made this opportunity a reality. I am sure that Judy feels the same way. But what of our girls? Kirsten now teaches school in the Phoenix area, where she recently bought a house. Will she ever be ready to trade the sunny sands of Arizona for the lusty winter winds of Minnesota? I have no idea, nor would it be either wise or proper for me to attempt to influence her in this decision. Erin is still in school where she is doing very well. But what future will she choose for herself? Again, only the passage of time can answer these questions.

The heritage of Bay Lake has been forged by the good people who have trod its shores in ages past, beginning with the American Indians who were its first proprietors. We can only trust in God that His work will be carried on.

Kirsten, Erin, and Al camping on the upper Cross River

My story would not be complete without including the following lines:

MEMORIES
of a departed friend, Gilbert Arthur Hunt,
December 13, 1925—June 23, 1995

Today is filled with beautiful memories, yet I am sad. I feel a loss that will never be replaced, and I am impelled to mourn. Yet I know I must rejoice, for these memories are the very essence of my existence.

I remember two four-year-old boys meeting for the first time on a tiny island, where their fathers were building a log cabin. They watched the mother loon on her nest and the baby ducklings as they swam by, shepherded by their mother. They played in the clear waters of the sandy beach, dressed only in their birthday suits and rejoiced in the freedom. They shared their lunches, eaten from their tin pails, as they watched the fluffy spring clouds drifting by. They dreamed of the future, and they developed a friendship that would never waver.

As children their time together was limited, four miles was a long way in those days. But high school brought them to shared classrooms and a shared social life. They double dated on their first junior-senior prom, and watched the sunrise as they escorted their dates home. Before they could participate in the second, the wings of war had interceded, and they were both in the military.

I remember how, after the war, their mutual love of nature and the lure of the wilderness led them to the North Shore of Lake Superior and the wild streams that feed it. Oh, how I remember those nights spent far from any permanent abode, with bedrolls spread under the twinkling stars. How we listened to the nightsounds as we watched the embers of our campfire slowly fade and die. How we relived the tug of the stream on our boots and the thrill of a heavy strike by an unwary trout.

How could one forget a trip to Montana with its miles of back packing, where we relived the tales my father had so often told of the wilderness, while it still existed in its purest form? Or the planned second trip, which was diverted to California where one friend stood up for the other in marriage?

I remember those many deer hunting trips with the little home made trailer, where as many as six of us lived for over a week of adventure in the woods, enjoying the comradery we shared with our mutual cousins.

But most important of all are all those little memories of daily living; when one had a need, the other was there to share. There was never a need to keep the score, and that is the most precious memory of all!

Yes, I am sad, for I have lost not only a Masonic brother but the closest that I could ever have to a real brother. And for having had that privilege, I will forever rejoice!

Gib, as I will always remember him

Epilogue

Dad, once again I have traveled to Montana, to walk again those trails you so loved to tell me about. Judy, Erin, and I spent two nights at the campground at Spotted Bear near the old ranger station that you knew so well. As we walked the trails, even some of the old original ones, and swam in the chilly water of the river, I had a feeling of being nearer to you than I had been since you left us. Later we spent a couple of nights at a campground near Swan Lake. Now its waters are alive with jet skis and water skiers. But its pristine beauty remains, and, as we drove far up the Lost River in search of huckleberries, we re-entered the land you knew so well. The beauty and sheer majesty of the surroundings engulfed me, as I came to understand how much you gave up when you returned to Minnesota. I will always be drawn back to those mountains and will forever cherish the memory of you telling those stories of your experiences in them.

But I love our old homestead too, as I am sure you did, and will do my best to preserve its integrity, as you did while you had it in your care. I will do what I can to instill that same reverence for the land in my two daughters. We can not prevent change, nor should we even try, as change is as inevitable for the land, as it is for those who inhabit it.

Yet I resent change, in that I can never go back to the way that I was yesterday. As I live each day, I change with the events that I experience. Reliving or changing the past is impossible, except in the hidden recesses of the mind. Our living biosphere experiences the same unalterable change. Is this the ultimate meaning of life, as it flows on in its inexorable journey? Yet, in all, we do have it in our power, in some measure, to influence the course of events that inevitably contribute to the very changes we so often resent. It is this influence that represents the measure of our advancement toward that state of civilization to which mankind has for so long been striving. And it is the subjugation of our personal pride and desires to the common good that allows us to make a worthy contribution toward that ultimate goal.

I have been extremely happy to have been spiritually reunited with you and those I have written about, as I have striven to untangle the twisted web of our heritage, and to display it here, for those who would delve into it. I hope that I have done justice to those whose lives I have touched.

Meet the Author

Albert L. Knieff has spent his entire life, except for two years of military service, living on the old family homestead on Bay Lake in north-central Minnesota. An only child, he grew up listening to the tales his father told of moving into what was then a wilderness area. He also told of his travels to Oregon, Alaska, and his years as a forest ranger in Montana, before moving back to take over the old family farm at the beginning of the first world war.

Al was born in 1926, about the time his parents began converting their half-mile of lake shore into a campground and resort with housekeeping cabins. He grew up playing with the children of the guests and serving their parents in any way he could. As he grew older, he played an ever more active role in the operation of the resort and its eventual modernization. After completing his stint in the Air Force in 1946, he took over the active management of the family business.

In 1973 Al saw a tornado destroy six of their eleven cabins. This led him to finish his college degree in ecology and to the development of the modern fifty-one-unit mobile-home park that he and his wife, Judy, and daughter, Erin, run today.